Single in New York

Victoria Sandvik & Michael Ian Bergman

BOB ADAMS, INC.
PUBLISHERS
Holbrook, Massachusetts

Published by Bob Adams, Inc.
260 Center Street, Holbrook, MA 02343

ISBN: 1-55850-172-X

Printed in the United States of America

J I H G F E D C B A

ACKNOWLEDGMENTS

We'd like to thank the many people who made the publication of this book possible: our publisher and editor at Bob Adams, Inc.; the owners and managers of the organizations who took the time out to respond to our questions in such detail; and the singles who opened up to us and shared information about their personal experiences to give us insight into their lifestyles.

Special thanks to Suzanne Ajzenburg, Gregory Cole, Shoshanna Malett, and Patrick Tyson: your contributions are much-appreciated—without you it would have been hard to get the job done.

— *V.S.*

To the East 82nd Street crowd: All of you Upper East Side singles inspired this concept. The machine lives! Special thanks to Bob, Debbie, Rich, Mike, and Pete—my New York friends who showed me what being single is all about. This book would have never been possible without you.

To my loving family and friends. Thanks for believing in my crazy ideas.

— *M.B.*

DEDICATION

Dedicated to my loving family for their ongoing support
of my writing endeavors—and to John, whose love has enriched my life
more than I could ever have imagined and whose belief in me
has propelled me to follow my dreams.

— *Vicki*

To Pappa, the greatest man I ever knew.

— *Michael*

TABLE OF CONTENTS

PREFACE

Being single in New York—and trying to hook up with someone special—can be a frustrating experience. But it can also be wonderfully exciting, when you take full advantage of what New York has to offer. Where else can you go to a different bar or dance club every night for the rest of your life and still not have tried them all? Where else can you satisfy a craving for Thai food at one o'clock in the morning, and then go for a romantic horse-and-buggy ride in the moonlight? And where else but New York can you hear fifty different kinds of music on any given night, from classical to reggae?

Our wild and crazy city may get a bad rap sometimes, but those of us who live here can't imagine living anywhere else. Okay, New York does have its drawbacks, as even the most loyal New Yorkers can admit. Maybe we even find ourselves occasionally fantasizing about getting away from it all—retreating to an oversized house in the country, complete with backyard and two-car garage.

So let's talk about New York's flaws first and get them out of the way. New York can be an unfriendly, hostile city. If you accidentally make eye contact with someone on the subway, you might be the next victim of a psychopathic serial killer on the loose. You can't walk around the city for more than ten minutes without passing a homeless person huddled by the side of a building or rummaging through a garbage can. And if you're driving through New York on a typical afternoon, it may take you half an hour to get through three traffic lights—and another hour to find a parking spot.

But let's face it: You can't beat New York when it comes to restaurants, bars, clubs, museums, art galleries, and theaters. Nightlife in this never-sleeping city is as varied and exciting as you could possibly want. You can dance till dawn, ice-skate to the stunning backdrop of the glittering city skyline, go bowling at midnight, work out at a health club that has a swimming pool, racquet courts, a bar and a disco—all under the same roof, and take a class in anything you ever wanted to learn.

The pessimist in you may be asking, *What good is this wealth of culture and entertainment when I have no one to share it with?* Maybe you look back wistfully to your good ol' college days, when all you had to do to meet someone was strike up a conversation on campus or hang out on the library steps—whereas now you only go on dates the third Friday of every month. Maybe you work in an office where there are only two employees who are of the opposite sex—one married, the other six months away from retirement. Or maybe you've been concentrating so hard on your career that the only socializing you do is at the laundromat on Sunday afternoons. Or could it be that your friends have fixed you up on so many "dates from Hell" that you've thrown in the towel and decided to become a monk?

Everyone has gone through it at one time or another. the nightmarish dates, the lonely nights that stretch on for weeks or months with no relief in sight, the unfulfilled craving for hugs and kisses, the despair over not being able to connect with anyone on a meaningful level.

We've all sat in front of the VCR on a Friday night, drowning our sorrows in a pint of Haagen Dazs and secretly resenting our friends for being either married or attached—or at least dating. You ask yourself: *What's wrong with me? Why can't I meet anyone? Why don't my relationships work out?* By the end of the evening you're so entrenched in self-pity you can barely get up to insert the next videocassette.

But when you're finished crying in your beer or whining to all your friends that you're destined to be alone for the rest of your life, take a good look at what's really going on. Re-evaluate your lifestyle. Have you really been open to meeting people, or have you been building a protective wall around yourself—daring someone to break through it? Do you keep setting your standards higher and higher so that no one but a demigod or goddess will be able to meet them?

If you think long and hard about it, you will realize that you actually have limitless opportunities to meet people if you take an active approach to being a New York single! There's an amazing wealth of opportunities at your fingertips, and all you have to do is reach out and seize these opportunities. We've already done the research for you! Just set aside a few hours to read this book (even the busiest, most career-minded of you can spare a couple of hours), and you'll discover hundreds of opportunities to hook up with friends and lovers—not only in New York City but throughout the tri-state region. Then make a list of ways you'd feel most comfortable meeting new people: places you've read about that you'd like to try, clubs you'd like to join, charities you could volunteer for.

Forget about the fact that you can be surrounded by millions of people and still feel lonely. Forget about all those boring, endless dates you've had with people your well-meaning but meddling friends have fixed you up with. Forget about the guy who dumped you for a younger woman, or the girl who was using you for your Gold Card.

Suspend your cynicism, discard your emotional baggage, and start over!

Try something you've never done before. You might be surprised to find out, after hitting a few of the dance clubs and bars, that you're really a party animal! Maybe you love the outdoors but never had anyone to go hiking or biking with before. Maybe you just think you don't like health clubs because you've never gone to one. You may find a great companion through a dating service (no, people who sign up with dating services are *not* desperate—they're nice, normal people just like you). And you'll probably make some great friends along the way as you become more involved with a variety of activities. The point is it won't help just to read this book; you have to *use* this book. Join some of these singles' clubs or special-interest organizations, enroll in a dating service, or hit the New York bar scene one night. But remember: meeting someone is not a life-or-death mission. It is fun. Lighten up, go out, and take a friend with you. Do whatever it takes to make you comfortable.

Going out in New York doesn't mean renting three videos and getting pizza on a Friday night. People aren't going to beat down your door and pull you away from your VCR—they're not even going to know you're there. The only way to meet people is to go out. If it's your budget you're worried about, worry no more. We've given you lots of places to hang out that can cost you even less than the three videos and pizza. So retire your video membership card and get out there!

SOCIAL & CULTURAL CLUBS

Social clubs are sort of like extended families. They give you a sense of camaraderie and guaranteed companionship on a regular basis, and many of them cater to people who are interested in a specific activity. Let's say you're someone who has a passion for the theater, or an interest in classical music, or an appreciation of gourmet food and fine wines. You might have a hard time finding people to share your passions with. Your friends may humor you occasionally, but they're sometimes put off by your deep involvement with a particular pursuit.

You "cultured" singles will be happy to know that there are many people who share your appreciation for art or music or literature—and there are organizations that bring you together with people who have similar tastes.

If you're looking for a social club with a more general focus, one that organizes all sorts of activities, you can join one of the community centers, like the Y or a neighborhood association.

Or maybe you're second-generation Greek or Irish or Italian and you're interested in exploring your heritage. There are plenty of social clubs whose members all belong to a particular ethnic group or a particular religion. There are even some clubs limited to people of the same profession, or to people who are going through similar circumstances (e.g., single parents, or widows and widowers).

Read through our listings and see which ones interest you. If you want to seek out others beyond the ones we've described, check the Yellow Pages under "Social Clubs" or check classified ads and directory listings in various local newspapers and regional magazines.

SOCIAL CLUBS

BRONX SINGLES ASSOCIATION

WHERE: Depends on the event. Call Donald at 212-518-8231 for a schedule.

WHAT: Activities include discussion groups, dances, bowling nights at Fiesta Lanes, coffee breaks at the Pelham Diner, Atlantic City Junkets, Octoberfests (featuring food, open bar, and dancing to DJ music), and holiday parties like the Halloween Costume Ball.

HOW MUCH: Atlantic City Junkets and the Octoberfest are $25.00 per person. The Halloween Costume Ball is $7.00 for members, $10.00 for nonmembers. Sunday Bowling is $10.00 a person, and dances are $7.00 for members, $10.00 for nonmembers.

CLUB FIT

WHERE: North State Road
Briarcliff, NY 10510
(914) 762-3444

Lee Boulevard
Jefferson Valley, NY 10535
(914) 245-4040

1 North Broadway
White Plains, NY 10601
(914) 946-0404

WHAT: This health club sponsors "mingles" with refreshments, music, dancing, and cash bar at multi-sports clubs—but you don't have to be a Club Fit member to attend the mingles. These social events are totally separate from the health club's workout activities, and they're held once a month at various locations.

WHO: You have to be 28 or older to attend. The ratio of men to women varies for each mingles event—so don't let first impressions prevent you from going to a few of them.

HOW MUCH: Mingles cost $15.00 to attend; $10.00 if you're a member of the health club.

KINGS BAY YMHA

WHERE: 3495 Nostrand Avenue
Brooklyn, NY 11229
(718) 648-7703

WHAT: As at any of the "Y" associations, this one offers numerous activities and events, including some geared specifically to singles. There are weekly Sunday brunches at the Kings Bay YMHA for different age groups, featuring various speakers. A support group for single parents also meets twice a month, led by a social worker with a master's degree in that field. The support group gets together for various outings (such as trips to museums), dances, dance classes, and discussions. Participation in the support group is open to Kings Bay Y members.

WHO: The members are usually 30 and up. In the single-parent support group, the majority are custodial mothers.

HOW MUCH: Annual Y membership for a single-parent family is $225.00, individual membership through age 64 is $205.00 a year, and individual membership for those 65 and up is $110.00. If you pay in advance, brunch is $4.00 for members and $5.00 for non-members; if you pay at the door, it's $5.00 for members and $6.00 for non-members. Participation at support group events is free for members, $5.00 for non-members.

LENOX HILL NEIGHBORHOOD ASSOCIATION

WHERE: 331 East 70th Street
New York, NY 10021
(212) 744-5022

WHAT: This is a non-profit organization offering programs and services to more than twenty thousand Upper East Side residents. It's been around since 1894! Activities include: swimming (in a sixty-by-twenty-foot heated pool, which is divided into slow, medium and fast lanes), a gym program that offers organized volleyball, basketball, and paddleball games; game-room activities such as billiards, Ping-Pong, air hockey and backgammon; fitness center workouts on Universal equipment, stationary bicycles, and weights; exercise classes that teach body shaping and toning, yoga, and weight training; jogging in Central Park with an intermediate runners' group; summer Saturday get-togethers on the sundeck belonging to LHNA; trips like tubing on the Esopus River in the Catskills; and workshops.

There's a membership application to fill out, which you can find on the last page of their program catalog.

WHO: To be a member you have to live, work, or attend school in Lenox Hill, between East Fifty-ninth Street and East Ninety-sixth Street in Manhattan. All ages are welcome, but the majority of the two thousand members are in the 25 to 35 age group. About 60 percent of the members are single, and the mix of men and women is about fifty-fifty. Non-members can be invited as guests, but those who aren't guests of members won't be allowed to use the recreational facilities.

HOW MUCH: Membership is $250.00 a year. Look in local papers for special first-time rates.

LORRAINE'S HIGH SOCIETY SINGLES, LTD.

WHERE: P.O. Box 211
Seaford, NY 11783
(516) 795-6203

WHAT: Conversation, dancing, and dining are the main activities of this nine-year-old organization, which has a mailing list of over 5,000 singles. A breakdown of this mailing list shows that one-third are from Queens, one-third from Manhattan, and the remaining third are from New Jersey, Connecticut, and Westchester. Events are scheduled for four to six times per month.

To become a member, just call for a brochure and then attend one of the parties. If the party is to your liking, you can put your name on the mailing list.

WHO: Upscale professional singles in their thirties, forties, and fifties.

HOW MUCH: There is no membership fee, but participation at each event will cost you about $12.00 which includes gourmet buffet, DJ entertainment, and dancing.

MARION SMITH SINGLES/MARION SMITH TRAVEL

WHERE: 611 Prescott Place
North Woodmere, NY 11581
(516) 791-4852
Marion Smith Travel: (800) 698-TRIP

WHAT: Get-togethers at this social club include tennis parties, dances, moonlight sails, summer barbecues, whitewater rafting trips, and New Year's Eve parties. If you put your name on the mailing list, you'll get information about all the upcoming events—and if you become a member, you'll be admitted to the events at a discount.

Every week about nine activities are scheduled. Party buses are arranged to transport everyone to the events.

Marion Smith Travel offers discounts on all travel. It's one of Club Med's four largest agents in the United States, and if you book a Club Med vacation through Marion Smith Travel, you can save $150.00 off regular prices.

WHO: Members are singles aged twenty-eight to forty-eight with men and women equally represented. In its fifteen years of operation Marion Smith Singles has attracted about forty-four thousand active clients throughout the tri-state area.

HOW MUCH: A one-year membership costs $60.00. Admission to dances ranges from $8.00 to $20.00; tennis parties are $20.00 to $29.00.

PARENTS WITHOUT PARTNERS

This is a national organization with hundreds of chapters. To find out about the chapter nearest you, contact the organization's headquarters, located at 8807 Colesville Road, Silver Spring, MD 20910; tel. 301-588-9354. Some local groups go under the name Parents Without Partners but are not officially chartered by PWP, Inc. Here's the rundown on one of the chapters we contacted:

WHERE: 3400 Irwin Avenue
Bronx, NY 10463
(212) 884-5584

WHAT: The focus is on activities for single parents with their children, such as picnics, parties, trips to the zoo, dances, and "meet-to-eat" get-togethers. To become a member you must attend an orientation session, which is held two or three times a month in a member's home. At the orientation you'll be asked to talk about yourself and your life as a single parent. You'll also be asked to supply a professional reference verifying that you're a single parent. Members get together for about ten events a month—you'll usually have to make your own transportation arrangements. You don't have to be a member to participate in the dances and picnics.

WHO: Members range in age from 20 to 70. There are more women than men in this chapter.

HOW MUCH: The first year of membership costs $30.00; to renew for a year costs $27.00. Attendance at the dances is $6.00 for members and $8.00 for non-members; the cost to attend a picnic is $3.00 per family.

PHYSICALLY DISABLED SINGLES GROUP

(Greater Five Towns YM/YWHA)

WHERE: 207 Grove Avenue
Cedarhurst, Long Island, NY 11516
(516) 569-6733

WHAT: This social organization provides social, recreational, and cultural programs for singles with significant physical disabilities. For the past seven years it has sponsored activities such as dinner parties, theater parties, concerts, guest lectures, rap sessions, and group celebrations of Jewish holidays. Members get together three times a month.

The organization provides wheelchair-accessible van transportation for most excursions that take place outside of the "Y" building.

An example of a recent excursion was a field trip to the American Museum of Folk Art, which forty group members attended.

WHO: There are eighty members, most in their thirties and forties. The minimum age is 25. There's an even mix of men and women.

HOW MUCH: There's no membership fee, but members pay $2.00 to $4.00 to attend each event.

PROFESSIONAL SINGLES ASSOCIATION

WHERE: P.O. Box 1228
Groton, CT 06340
(203) 449-0004

WHAT: This organization gets together for rap sessions, concerts, plays, monthly dances, house parties, weekly volleyball, weekly happy hours at TGI Friday's, brunches, hiking and biking trips, and tennis in the warmer months (April to November). On holidays they serve potluck dinners for those members who don't have other companions to celebrate with. There are also three day-trips sponsored each year (the destinations vary) and a week-long ski trip. You can join a car-pool for most of the events.

Call Jan Miller at Professional Singles to find out when you can attend a new members' orientation session. You'll also be asked to fill out an application.

WHO: There are about 550 members. Membership is about 40 percent male, 60 percent female, and ages range from 30 to 60.

HOW MUCH: $20.00 includes annual membership and a subscription to PSA's newsletter. Admission to parties is $1.00 if you're a member, $3.00 if you're not. Admission to dances is $5.00 for members, $7.00 for non-members.

ROLYNN'S SOCIALS

WHERE: 838 McLean Avenue
Yonkers, NY
(914) 963-7720

WHAT: Holiday parties and socials are sponsored several times a year. Coffee and cake are served, and guests can bring their own liquor if they want to.

HOW MUCH: Socials cost $7.50 per person to attend.

SHORE SIDE SINGLES

WHERE: Connecticut Yankee Motor Lodge
Exit 74, Route 195
Niantic, CT 06357
(203) 669-6560

WHAT: This singles' group meets at Barnaby's (The Crystal Room), the restaurant at Connecticut Yankee Motor Lodge, for Sunday night singles' dances. Get there between 7:00 and 8:00 p.m. if you want to take advantage of the free buffet. Dancing starts at 8:00 p.m. and goes on till 11:30 p.m.

WHO: The group is open to singles aged 20 to 60. The ratio of men to women varies from week to week.

HOW MUCH: Members pay $5.00, non-members, $8.00.

SINGLES ALTERNATIVE

WHERE: 206 New London Turnpike
Glastonbury, CT 06033
(203) 633-0600

WHAT: This organization is not a singles' club per se but a promoter of social events. It sponsors five dances a week, six Saturday-night specialty formal dances a year, theater excursions, and a variety of day trips.

Singles Alternative also publishes a quarterly newspaper that lists the array of activities and other items of interest to singles.

WHO: Events are open to 30- to 60-year-olds.

HOW MUCH: Annual membership is $20.00. Dances are $7.00 for members, $9.00 for non-members.

SINGLES CONNECTION OF RIVERDALE

WHERE: P.O. Box 1203
Riverdale, NY 10471
(212) 796-1227

WHAT: The basic premise of this club is to meet new friends and engage in activities with them—house parties, rap sessions, lectures, local trips, and dinner gatherings. To join, just write to their P.O. box number.

Members meet twice a month. If you don't have your own car to get to the events, don't worry about it—you can carpool with the others.

This non-profit organization was started pretty recently, and the first meeting was held at a local restaurant. Forty people showed up. According to the president and founder, they're dedicated to launching a fun-filled calendar of events.

WHO: This club is for singles in their thirties and forties. Men are outnumbered by women by a one-to-six ratio. Guys: Go change that ratio!

HOW MUCH: Annual membership is $20.00, and the price of events ranges from $10.00 to $50.00.

SINGLES GROUP/NEW OUTLOOK GROUP

WHERE: 67-09 108th Street
Forest Hills, NY 11375
(718) 268-5011

WHAT: These are two separate singles groups formed by the Central Queens YM-YWHA. The Singles Group gets together for brunch, organized discussions, and lectures. The New Outlook Group also attends discussions and lectures, but instead of brunch they have coffee and cake. Both groups meet every Sunday at the Y.

WHO: The Singles Group members are between the ages of 28 and 50, and the New Outlook Group is open only to singles who are at least 55 years old. Women attend in slightly larger numbers than men do (about a three-to-two ratio).

HOW MUCH: The cost of the Singles Group is $5.00 for members and $7.00 for non-members. The New Outlook Group is $1.00 for members and $3.00 for non-members.

SINGLES SERVICES OF THE SAMUEL FIELD Y

WHERE: 58-20 Little Neck Parkway
Little Neck, NY 11362
(718) 225-6750, Ext. 243

WHAT: The Single Parent Family Center consists of the following rap groups and support services: divorce support groups, parenting workshops, groups of children from separated and divorced families, personal growth workshops, assertiveness training, empty nest syndrome support groups, young widows/widowers bereavement and support groups, mature singles group for 45- to 59-year-olds (this one is for all singles in that age group—not just single parents), relationship groups, and Wednesday night rap groups.

There's also a monthly dine-out group and monthly socials for all singles aged 30 and over.

All groups are led by certified social workers.

WHO: "Who" depends on the group. The singles and single parents groups are attended by 30- to 49-year-olds, and the mature singles groups are for 45- to 59-year-olds. There are usually six women for every four men, but there's an even mix at the parties, dances, and socials.

HOW MUCH: $65.00 annual membership fee entitles you to a discounted admission on Wednesday nights as well as discounts on the various other support groups and workshops. The cost of attending parties and dances is $10.00 for members, $12.00 for non-members; the Wednesday night group members pay $3.00 and non-members pay $7.00. Individual and family therapy, crisis counseling, information and referral services, and a subscription to the Samuel Field YM-YWHA newsletter are available to members at no charge.

THE SOCIAL CONNECTION, LTD.

WHERE: R.R. 4 Lakewood Drive
Katonah, NY 10536
(914) 232-4291

WHAT: Get-togethers include parties, ballroom and Latin dancing, Wednesday-night dance lessons, and travel weekends. This nineteen-year-old organization also publishes a newsletter that details its activity schedule.

WHO: There are about 300 members, but since you don't have to be a member to attend the parties or dances, attendance is usually greater than the membership. The average party attracts anywhere between 250 and 500 people, and the weekday dances are attended by about 250 to 300 people. For the most part, everyone falls in the 35 to 65 age group.

HOW MUCH: A one-year membership costs $45.00; members get discounts at parties. A one-year subscription to the newsletter costs $9.00.

TALL CLUB OF LONG ISLAND

WHERE: P.O. Box 8013
Garden City, NY 11530
(516) 694-5345

WHAT: The first chapter of the Tall Club was established in 1939 (yes, half a century ago!) in California. There was a need for such a club, especially for tall women, because they found it difficult to meet men that matched their height or that were willing to "look up to them."

Club members get together for meeting on the first and third Monday of every month. In addition, they participate in a variety of activities, such as picnics, beach parties, house parties, fundraising, traveling, and attending movies together.

WHO: The Tall Club of Long Island has seventy to eighty members. The majority are in the twenties to forties age group; members are required to be at least 21 years old.

How tall do you have to be, you might be wondering? Women must be at least 5′ 10", and men must tower at 6′ 2" or above in order to be a member.

HOW
MUCH: Annual membership fee is $25.00.

CULTURAL CLUBS

CLASSICAL MUSIC LOVERS' EXCHANGE

WHERE: P.O. Box 31
Pelham, NY 10803-0031
(800) 233-CMLS

WHAT: This service, now in its eleventh year, brings together unattached classical music lovers. To become a member you must fill out a biographical profile that poses questions as specific as what your vocal range is, who your favorite composers are, whether you attend opera, and what your favorite magazines and books are. You'll also be asked to write your own two-line profile, which will be sent monthly to members. Based on the short profile, members can decide whether they'd like to receive a copy of someone's longer profile. After receiving the profile, a member can call or write to that person; the organization doesn't get involved in the communication after that point.

WHO: Between a thousand and twelve hundred members belong to this service nationwide, ranging in age from mid-twenties to fifties. Each month about two hundred new members sign up. Most of them are professionals—lawyers, engineers, physicians, psychologists, scientists, architects, writers—and many are professional musicians. One-third of the marriages reported were between members who lived three hundred to a thousand miles apart. Who says you have to be in the right place at the right time?!

HOW
MUCH: A six-month membership costs $65.00. Profiles are $2.00 each.

LEWIS HARRISON INSTITUTE

(a.k.a. Great Conversations/Dinner Parties)

WHERE: 40 West 72nd Street
New York, NY 10023
(212) 724-8783

WHAT: This five-year old organization sponsors dinner parties, brunches, and lectures for singles. Dinner parties are held on Friday and Saturday evenings; brunches are on Sundays. Dinner usually includes wine, salad, bread, a pasta dish, main course, and non-alcoholic beverages—in a non-smoking environment. Members get together seven times a month.

WHO: Most members are in the 33 to 40 age bracket.

HOW MUCH: Each dinner party or brunch costs $20.00.

MUSIC & ART LOVERS' CLUB FOR SINGLES

WHERE: 3739 Nostrand Avenue, Suite 333
Brooklyn, NY 11235
(718) 252-LOVE (5683)

WHAT: This is a social introduction service for lovers of the arts. Members contact other music and art lovers for the purpose of socializing, making new friends, attending activities together, and dating. To become a member, a client must fill out a two-page personal profile detailing such information as religion, educational status, profession or occupation, physical characteristics, interest in marriage, musical interests, art interests, cultural interests, and hobbies. Club members engage in a variety of activities: cruises with dancing, dining and music; operas; dinners; concerts; shows; musical get-togethers; and workshops. All events are open to non-members as well, but are discounted for members. Events are held every few months, but there are psychic workshops offered monthly (to members only) where they explore psychic phenomena, learn to develop their psychic powers, engage in group meditation, and explore individual healing.

Club members meet through the monthly newsletter, *The Museletter*, which provides an updated listing of members along with the four- or five-line descriptions they have written about themselves. If one member's interest is piqued by a particular description, he or she can send $2.50 to the service to obtain that person's personal profile.

A bimonthly newsletter called *The Clubletter* is also distributed to all members. It announces club-sponsored events and highlights special activities going on around the tri-state area. A special section, which contains advertisements, announces new members.

WHO: The club has about a hundred members ranging in age from 21 to 60. Most are in the 35 to 45 age group and live in Brooklyn, Manhattan, and Queens, but there are members residing throughout the greater New York and tri-state area.

HOW MUCH: A one-year membership costs $54.00.

THE SINGLE GOURMET

WHERE: 133 East 58th Street
New York, NY 10022
(212) 980-8788

WHAT: In its eleventh year, this social organization brings singles together for dining and conversation at restaurants selected to provide diversity of cuisine and decor. A variety of ethnic restaurants and haute cuisine is offered. Usually, a four-course meal is served (all included in one flat fee paid in advance). At some ethnic restaurants a banquet menu offers multiple dishes in each course to give people a proper introduction to that cuisine.

Participants generally have forty-five minutes to mingle before sitting down to eat. The group is divided into tables of eight to ten people. The Single Gourmet arranges seating so that people will sit with others of their own age group. Several dinners are held each month, both on weekends and during the week.

Besides dining events, members attend Broadway and off-Broadway shows, tennis matches, horse shows and other sporting events, whitewater rafting, whale watching, and domestic and overseas trips.

Members of New York's Single Gourmet automatically have reciprocal membership in other Single Gourmet groups in eighteen cities throughout the United States and Canada. Members receive a monthly newsletter that describes upcoming events in detail.

WHO: People who appreciate a good meal accompanied by stimulating conversation will enjoy this organization.

HOW MUCH: The first year's membership costs $75.00; the price drops $40.00 for each year's renewal. Dinners are priced in the $25.00 to $50.00 range. Non-members may only attend as the guest of a member; they pay an additional $5.00 over the cost of the event.

SYMPHONY SINGLES

(New Orchestra of Westchester)

WHERE: 111 North Central Avenue
Hartsdale, NY 10530
(914) 682-3707

WHAT: The focus of this group is to bring together singles who have an interest in classical music. You can attend the monthly dessert fests—events that have attracted as many as 250 people—featuring sit-down chamber music concerts, desserts, and wine. Every Thursday evening there's a singles drop-in that serves a dual purpose: socializing and volunteer work. About twenty members show up after work to help the non-profit New Orchestra of Westchester stuff envelopes for promotional mailings. Since that doesn't take too much brain-work, it's a good opportunity for people to get to know each other—and coffee and cake are served. This setting provides you with an opportunity to meet a select group of people you wouldn't ordinarily meet.

To join Symphony Singles, just call the number above and ask to be put on the mailing list.

WHO: Members are mostly upscale professionals and corporate types, ages 30 and up. Women tend to outnumber the men, but not by much.

HOW MUCH: There is no membership fee, but the monthly dessert fests cost $15.00 to attend. This covers the concert, food and wine.

THEATRE THREE

WHERE: 412 Main Street
Port Jefferson, NY 11777
(516) 928-9100

WHAT: Hosts "Single Thursdays," an evening of theatre entertainment with wine and hors d'oeuvres.

OUTDOOR/RECREATIONAL ORGANIZATIONS

After a grueling week at work of racing the clock to meet those deadlines, you realize that the only time you saw the light of day was when you ran over to the deli to get a sandwich. And that was the only exercise you got, too. Now the weekend is here—and the weather forecasters have promised two days of bright blue skies! You were supposed to do your laundry—which has been piling up ominously—and you'd also vowed to replenish your empty refrigerator. But you can't ignore the dazzling sunshine and balmy temperatures. The great outdoors is beckoning you!

You may be content to just pick up the Sunday *Times* and a few goodies at Zabar's and have a picnic lunch on the Great Lawn in Central Park, or to head out to Jones Beach early in the morning. But you should also know about the many outdoor clubs and recreational organizations out there. These offer a wide variety of group outings, such as biking, hiking, rafting, canoeing, sailing, and skiing, to name just a few.

Don't worry if you don't have a car. Transportation is usually provided in the form of car pools, mini vans, or buses. If it's not, you'll be given detailed directions on how to get there by train or bus.

Another concern you might have is whether you're in good enough physical condition to go on certain excursions. Not to worry. The recreational clubs have already thought of that, offering activities that require varying degrees of physical exertion. You can go on a bicycle tour that covers fifty miles of rough terrain, or you can take a leisurely ten-mile bike ride with frequent rests.

You'll also have to decide how much time you want to devote to your outing: one day, a weekend, or even a week-long trip. If your goal is to meet someone, you might be better off with a longer excursion so you'll have a chance to really get to know your fellow group members. Even on the one-day trips, however, there's plenty of time to get acquainted: on the bus, during the recreational activity, and at mealtimes. At the end of the day you can exchange phone numbers with anyone who struck a chord in you. At the very least you'll expand your circle of friends. And if romance happens to blossom, too—that's an extra bonus!

We've also included some suggestions for tempting getaways that are sure to lure you away from the city. Some are day trips, some are stayovers—all in the tri-state area. You've probably never realized how many beautiful retreats there are in the surrounding regions, and how easy it is to get to them. Just call up a couple of friends, throw on a pair of walking shoes, and head out to the

Jersey Shore or City Island or Bear Mountain.

Leave your car at home, hop aboard the Long Island Railroad, which will take you to the ferry that carts you over to Fire Island—and enjoy an afternoon of sunshine, swimming, and seafood. Or, if you're in the mood to mix nature with culture, take the M4 bus way uptown to the Cloisters in Fort Tryon Park—where you'll see breathtaking views of the Hudson River and a superb collection of medieval art. And when's the last time you went to the Bronx Zoo? Have you forgotten how much fun that was? Do you remember the tropical rain forests of Jungle World and the World of Birds? You could easily spend the entire day at this mammoth zoo and still not get a chance to see all the varieties of animals housed here.

Another great place to indulge the child in you is Coney Island's Astroland Amusement Park, whose famous Cyclone ride has been eliciting shrieks and squeals for over half a century. When you've had your fill of the rides, you can stretch out on the white-sand beach or take a dip in the Atlantic Ocean.

If you're used to spending your weekends and vacations hanging out at home, it may be a little difficult at first for you to coordinate the little details that go into these excursions—details like figuring out how to get there, what to bring, what to wear, and what to do once you get there. Our advice: just concentrate on getting there, and then let your instincts take over once you've reached your destination. Get the feel of the place, explore it on foot, and don't be shy about asking the people around you for specific recommendations.

You'll be amazed what a difference a change of scenery can make, even if it's just for a day, for your state of mind. You'll leave the day-to-day anxieties behind as you watch the city skyline recede until it's just a small, insignificant speck. Who knows? You may return to work on Monday morning with a whole new lease on life—or you may just be counting the days till you can embark on your next adventure!

So don't wait for the summer share in the Hamptons or the occasional ski weekend to commune with nature. There are so many recreational activities going on every day of the year, and so many interesting places you can get to within an hour or two. Go with friends, or go alone if you can't recruit anyone. Because no matter what you're into—hiking, bike-riding, kayaking, mountain climbing, swimming, or playing tennis—you're sure to find a group that shares your athletic interests and your passion for the outdoors!

APPALACHIAN MOUNTAIN CLUB

(New York/North Jersey Chapter)

WHERE: 202 East 39th Street
New York, NY 10016
Headquarters: 5 Joy Street, Boston, MA 02108
(617) 523-0636

WHAT: This is an environmentally conscious, back-to-nature organization that's been around for over a century. Offers a wide range of outdoor programs, activities, and educational opportunities in and outside of New York City, including lectures and leadership training. Activities include trail work, hiking, biking, canoeing, skiing, mountaineering, windsurfing, and sailing. Transportation is sometimes provided to excursions by way of car pools, but detailed instructions on how to reach destinations via public transportation are written up in the catalog of events. Activities are scheduled for practically every day of the year. Members also receive ten issues a year of the *Appalachia Bulletin*, which lists hundreds of activity and workshop offerings, Club and conservation news, and information about educational programs.

Members get special discount rates at AMC huts and lodges, discounts on AMC books and maps (call for a catalog of offerings), and discounts on AMC workshops and guided hikes.

Your membership contributions are funneled into support for AMC's research and conservation projects—such as ozone research, river protection, solar energy use, air quality and visibility studies, and rare flora and habitat protection efforts.

WHO: There are thirty-seven thousand members nationwide, from youths to the elderly.

HOW MUCH: Cost is $40.00 for a one-year membership, $1,000.00 to become a lifetime member.

COUNTRY CYCLING TOURS

WHERE: 140 West 83rd Street
New York, NY 10024
(212) 874-5151

WHAT: This sixteen-year-old biking club offers a wide variety of bicycling and walking tours for people aged 7 to 78. Tours are led by expert guides; groups are small; participants are given detailed maps and directions. Twelve-speed bikes can be rented and a support vehicle accompanies all tours to provide assistance and to transport participants' luggage.

Cycling tours are designed for all levels of fitness. Walking tours, although leisurely, require that participants be in good physical condition and are able to walk an average of seven to ten miles a day.

Tours offered range from one-day excursions to the countryside just beyond New York City to winter vacations exploring the Caribbean islands of Guadeloupe and St. Croix. Three-day holiday weekend tours include "Chesapeake Cycle & Sail," "Vermont Valley," "Cape Cod," and "Pennsylvania Dutch" bike tours. "The Great River Road and New Orleans Vacation" is a six-day tour that features cycling, sightseeing, a paddlewheel boat trip, dining, and jazz entertainment.

Van transportation is provided for those who need it (bikes can be boarded on vans), departing from 140 West Eighty-third Street between Columbus and Amsterdam Avenues.

WHO: There's no formal membership; people just register for whichever tours they're interested in attending. So the kinds of people you'll meet on any given tour depends on who signed up for that one.

HOW MUCH: There is no membership cost; prices of tours vary widely. A three-day Vermont Valleys cycling trip costs $339.00 per person; the "France: Brittany and Normandy" cycling tour costs $1,445.00, excluding airfare.

OUTDOOR BOUND

WHERE: 18 Stuyvesant Oval, Suite 1A
New York, NY 10009
(212) 505-1020

WHAT: It's what the name suggests: an outdoors club. It's also a travel club. Outdoor Bound has been organizing trips since 1982 to places like upstate New York, South Jersey, the Catskills, Adirondacks and Berkshires, New Hampshire, Maine, Vermont, eastern Long Island, the Shenandoah Valley (Virginia), and Pennsylvania. There's also a week-long trip to England.

Choose from a variety of activities: hiking, canoeing, rafting, kayaking, cross-country and downhill skiing, snowshoeing, and camping. Most overnight trips have lodging at charming country inns. Trips range in length from one to eight days. Transportation is by passenger vans, which depart from Twenty-third Street and First Avenue in Manhattan.

A catalog is distributed to members each season with one-paragraph descriptions of each trip. It also rates certain activities, such as hikes, according to level of difficulty (easy, moderate, challenging, very challenging).

WHO: There are about ten thousand people on the mailing list. Ninety-eight percent of those who go on Outdoor Bound excursions are single—mostly in their twenties, thirties, and forties. The balance between men and women shifts depending on the kind of trip you choose.

HOW MUCH: A one-year membership costs $30.00, but you don't have to be a member to attend any of the events. Members get $10.00 to $75.00 discounts on trips, and price reductions are often available if you provide your own car.

As a reader of this book, you're entitled to a special deal. The founder and director of Outdoor Bound, Seth Steiner, has extended an offer of free membership and all member discounts to anyone who reads about the organization in this book. So photocopy this page and send it in with a request for free membership!

OUTDOOR SINGLES

WHERE· P.O. Box 6674
Queens, NY 11365
(718) 353-5506

WHAT: Similar in focus to Outdoor Bound. Activities include day hikes, ranging from leisurely five-mile walks through state parks and nature preserves to more strenuous mountain and wilderness hikes; canoeing; tubing; rafting the rapids; beach picnics; swimming in mountain lakes; mountain horseback riding; bicycling; and, in the winter, cross-country skiing.

Outdoor Singles also leads two- to seven-day trips to the Catskills, the Adirondacks, and New England, as well as winter weekend trips to the ski slopes in Killington, Stowe, and Sugarbush. Transportation is always organized from mid-Manhattan.

Outdoor Singles also has a travel hotline, through which you can book any air, rail, cruise, tour, Club Med trip, or singles' weekend at discounted rates.

WHO: This is for active people who love the great outdoors—mostly between the ages of 25 and 50. Men and women are evenly mixed.

HOW MUCH: Membership costs $50.00 for the first year; $70.00 for two years. Prices of trips vary, but members get discounts on all-day and most weekend trips, and priority reservations. For $6.00 you can be put on the mailing list to receive a calendar of upcoming events.

POCONO WHITEWATER ADVENTURES

WHERE: Route 903
Jim Thorpe, PA 18229
(717) 325-3655

WHAT: Organizes daytrips and weekend getaways like rafting down the Lehigh River, mountain bike trips, inn-to-inn bike tours, turbo-canoeing (which combines the best features of a kayak, canoe, and raft into one), and playing SKIRMISH in the Poconos.

One excursion is called the "Ribbon of History Floatrip," which starts out with a four-hour rafting trip from Jim Thorpe (the rafting capital of the world) downstream to Bowmanstown, where you'll stop for swimming, sun-bathing, and a riverside luncheon or barbecue.

Another offering is Capt. Jack's Dinner Cruise: a guide paddles you downstream from Jim Thorpe to Lehighton, where a barbecue awaits you in a hemlock-lined picnic grove.

HOW MUCH: Costs for the adventures are as follows: $29.00 per adult for the Summer Floatrip, $37.00 for the Spring/Fall Floatrip, $37.00 for the Capt. Jack's Dinner Cruise, $32.00 for turbo-canoeing, $43.00 for whitewater rafting excursion, $39.00 for mountain biking trip, $27.00 for SKIRMISH.

SOUND SAILING CLUB

WHERE: 32 Lenape Trail
Denville, NJ 07834-2018
(203) 977-2422

WHAT: A club for singles who are interested in sailing. (You'd never have guessed from the name, right?) If you join this club, you'll participate in raft-ups, races, and other on-the-water activities; they also host cocktail parties and house parties. During the winter there are skiing and sailing trips. Members get together at least once a month.

To become a member, get one of the current members to sponsor you and introduce you to the board. The board will take a vote about bringing you in as a member, and if you're accepted, your name will be published in the club's newsletter.

WHO: The club welcomes all single sailing enthusiasts ages 30 to 60 from New York, New Jersey, and Connecticut. The club has an even mix of men and women. Ninety percent of the members are single. Most have their own boats.

HOW MUCH: There's a $50.00 initiation fee, and then $35.00 annual dues.

TRAVEL CLUBS

If you've ever traveled alone, you know what the drawbacks are. Aside from the loneliness and boredom, solo travel is more expensive than traveling with companions. Hotels, airlines, cruiselines, and other travel operators almost always tack on a surcharge for single travelers—giving you the feeling you're being punished for not having a companion.

Well, did you know that there are travel clubs out there that organize trips for groups of singles so they don't have to travel alone? Some even match you up with one travel companion—either of the same or opposite sex, your choice—and some of these organizations sponsor major events exclusively for singles at various resorts.

So the next time you're planning a vacation, don't get discouraged if your friends can't go with you. Just call one of the travel clubs listed below and ask them to send you a brochure of their upcoming itineraries.

Bon voyage!

AMERICAN JEWISH CONGRESS INTERNATIONAL TRAVEL PROGRAM

WHERE: 15 East 84th Street
New York, NY 10028
(212) 879-4588

WHAT: The AJC has been operating its travel program since 1958. All tours offer opportunities for sightseeing with a special emphasis on Jewish sites and the history of the region being visited. All participants *must* be members of the American Jewish Congress.

Call the AJC to receive a catalog of their complete offerings (over forty tours to six continents), but take note of their special tours for singles:

"Israel for Singles" is a fifteen-day tour for singles under age forty, sponsored once a year. The cities included in the tour are Tel Aviv, Haifa, Galilee, and Jerusalem.

If you're a very active traveler who loves the outdoors, you might want to opt for the "Israel Adventure"—although that one's for singles and couples. On this tour you'll see Israel from many perspectives as you participate in hiking, mountain climbing, jeep driving, and a desert safari. Accommodations are in comfortable hotels, inns, and kibbutzim, but because of the amount of exercise the sightseeing portions of the tour demand, you must be in excellent physical condition to attend. Highlights of the tour include an archaeological dig in central Israel, hiking the Jerusalem Hills, and a visit to the Red Sea resort of Eilat—featuring a disco cruise on the Red Sea. Cost: $2,595.00 for the fifteen-day/thirteen-night tour, plus $390.00 for a single room.

"Holiday in Budapest and Prague" is an eight-day tour with two departures a year—one in winter, one in the spring—and offers general and Jewish-oriented touring in these two ancient cities. You'll also get to attend cultural performances in each city. A separate tour manager will be assigned to the single travelers on this tour—ages 30 to 50.

"Costa Rica Adventure" is designed for singles and adventurous couples under age 45. Accommodations are at the Cariari Hotel and Country Club in San Jose; highlights include a two-day jungle tour, a cruise on the Rio Colorado, an expedition into the Tortuguero National Park's rain forest, a cruise-picnic in the Pacific Gulf of Nicoya, visits to volcanoes and plantations, a bullfight, and white water rafting. Cost: $2,195.00 from New York, plus $400.00 for a single room.

ARROW TRAVEL—SINGLEWORLD CRUISES & TOURS

WHERE: 311 Main Street
Ansonia, CT 06401
(203) 734-7272

WHAT: Anyone who is single or traveling alone is eligible for membership in Singleworld—now in its thirty-fifth year as an operator of cruises and land tours. Contact David Conti at Arrow Travel to receive a catalog describing the Singleworld tour offerings in detail, but first read on to find out what a Singleworld vacation is all about.

Singleworld groups are booked as part of a larger tour—so you can either hang out exclusively with other Singleworld members or roam freely and mingle with everyone on the tour. The way to identify fellow Singleworld members: everyone gets an identifying T-shirt along with their final travel documents. There are two kinds of departures: one open to passengers of all ages and the other for travelers aged thirty-five and under. (The age restriction applies only to the Singleworld group—not to all tour participants). Members dine together and participate in members-only land excursions.) Singleworld tours are available on twenty-two different cruise ships, to destinations such as the Bahamas, the East Caribbean, West Caribbean, Bermuda, Alaska, the Mexican Riviera, Tahiti, the Mediterranean Coast, and Scandinavia/Russia.

The land tours, ranging in length from ten to fourteen days, include "Europe Leisurely" (England, France, Switzerland, and Italy);

"Alpine Holiday" (Switzerland, Austria, Germany); and "Berlin Moscow, Leningrad."

Prices vary, so consult the catalog—but to give you a general idea: a three-day cruise to the Bahamas would cost you $450.00 (that includes the flight); seven-day Caribbean/Mexican cruises are priced from $650.00 for the cruise portion only; the "Europe Leisurely" tour costs $1,418.00 plus air fare.

You can request to be matched up with a roommate for shared accommodations: your roommate will be a member of the same sex as you, and sometimes the tour operator can arrange to match you up with someone in your age range.

Singleworld Members are eligible for double, triple, or quad share accommodations. Group sizes vary and can't be guaranteed. As a member you pay a fee of $25.00 a year, which entitles you to a complimentary subscription to the quarterly *Singlesworld Newsletter.*

CLUB MED

WHERE: 40 West 57th Street
New York, NY 10019
(800) CLUB-MED

WHAT: A vacation concept for those who want to get pampered. Club Med has been a household word for decades now (they started running tours in 1950), and for some of us conjures up images of wild, uninhibited pleasure-seekers who want nothing but sun and fun. Maybe that perception is partly due to Club Med's ad campaign; for ten years, they claimed to be the "Antidote for Civilization." Well, there's more to the Club Med vacation concept than pure, unadulterated pleasure—although, when you think about it, who could ask for anything more?

Club Med Worldwide owns, operates, or manages 110 vacation villages in 33 countries, and many of these destinations are off the beaten tourist path—French Polynesia, the Ivory Coast, Malaysia, the Maldive Islands. Club Med also operates its own cruise ship, *Club Med I,* which offers a variety of Caribbean itineraries.

Sixty percent of the travelers who are booked on Club Med are single, divorced, or widowed, and the median age is 35. Another notable statistic to give you an idea of who you'll encounter: 68 percent of Club Med vacationers hold professional, executive, or managerial positions.*

A wide variety of sports and recreational activities are offered at all Club Med vacations: scuba diving, horseback riding, tennis, swimming, and much more. Specialized sports vacations have been

---

* These statistics are based on research conducted by a professional marketing organization on behalf of Club Med.

designed to accommodate those travelers who wish to perfect their skills in a particular sport while on vacation.

Club Med recommends its Playa Blanca, Buccaneer's Creek, and Turkoise vacation packages as especially appropriate for singles. Club Med's Mexican village in Playa Blanca offers an active vacation in beautiful tropical surroundings. By day, you can engage in a variety of sports (rock climbing, horseback riding, scuba diving, and fitness and circus workshops), and if you still have the energy when the sun goes down, there's nightly entertainment and dancing. New to this Club Med village are a variety of workshops designed to enhance personal skills: workshops for would-be comedians, musicians, magicians, and computer art specialists. In the Comedy Workshop, the art of improvisation is taught by guest performers from the cast of *Chicago City Limits*.

Buccaneer's Creek is on the island of Martinique. Relax on the beach or participate in any number of watersports and land-based activities. The restaurant turns into a nightclub after hours, so you don't have to turn in early.

Turkoise is situated on the island of Providenciales in the Turks & Caicos, and features a swimming pool with water polo area, restaurant and cocktail lounge, dance floor, theater, and a brand new disco.

Club Med has made a commitment to providing single rooms at many of its villages: there is no extra charge for single accommodations at Caravelle on Guadeloupe (Caribbean), or at Huatulco, Playa Blanca, and Sonora Bay (Mexico). At other Club Med resorts there is a 20-percent surcharge for those who request single accommodations (at Buccaneer's Creek in Martinique, Paradise Island in the Bahamas, and Turkoise in the Turks & Caicos Islands).

For singles (and couples) who want to travel with their children but also want some time to themselves, there's Kid Med. This program was established over twenty years ago in Club Med's European villages, and today there are thirteen Baby Clubs for infants between four and twenty-three months, and thirty-eight Mini Clubs for children aged two to eleven. The Baby Clubs have professionally supervised nurseries that are open from 8:00 a.m. till 6:00 p.m. every day, and babysitters are available after hours as well. Mini Clubs offer staff-coordinated meals and services like circuses, "Pony Clubs," and other recreational activities.

Club Med vacations can be booked directly through Club Med, or through tour operators such as Richnik's (212-807-0500), Weekends Unlimited (212-779-7728), and Ultimate Travel (914-237-1913).

HOW MUCH: Here are some examples of cost, not including airfare: the weekly rate to stay at Club Med's Mexican Village in Playa Blanca ranges from $600.00 to $1,000.00, depending on what time of year you go. The weekly rate at Turkoise ranges from $950.00 to $1,600.00, and at Buccaneer's Creek, from $770.00 to $1,570.00.

HUDSON RIVER CRUISES

WHERE: P.O. Box 333
Rifton, NY 12471
(914) 255-6515

WHAT: If you like water travel but can't afford a cruise to faraway destinations, how about taking the *Rip Van Winkle* up the Hudson River for a narrated cruise of the Catskill, Mid-Hudson, and Highland regions? If you haven't been up in those parts, you may be surprised by how picturesque the scenery is, and it could turn out to feel like a real vacation!

You can choose from a variety of trips: a full-day excursion to West Point and the U.S. Military Academy; the Great Estates Cruise (which sails to Hyde Park and back, past Hudson River mansions); the Lighthouse Cruise (which visits three lighthouses); and the Esopus Island Cruise (this takes you to the Vanderbilt Mansion and back).

Okay, now for the evening cruises: you can enjoy a three-hour dinner cruise with buffet-style dinner and a romantic sunset; or a three-hour music cruise that features dancing to the sounds of a live band. Suggestion: get advance tickets for the dinner and music cruises. They're very popular.

The *Rip Van Winkle* can be rented out for private parties, club outings, cocktail cruises, and the like. Maybe you can even pull together a singles outing on one of these cruises. Call for details on how to coordinate this with Hudson River Cruises.

HOW MUCH: Here are the most current prices available: $15.00 round trip for the West Point excursion; $10.00 round trip for the Great Estates and Lighthouse cruises; $8.00 for the Esopus Island cruise; $20.00 for a dinner cruise; and $12.00 for a music cruise.

RICHNIK'S/PERKS

WHERE: 362 West 23rd Street
New York, NY 10011
(212) 807-0500

WHAT: Richnik's/Perks is a travel/social/recreational club that specializes in discount travel. It's the number-one sales agent for Club Med vacations. Richnik's is for singles aged 33 to 55, and Perks is for the younger set: 21 to 35. They sponsor tennis parties, socials, weekend trips (bus transportation is provided), volleyball, and lectures.

One of Richnik's/Perks' popular winter getaways is the ski resort at Copper Mountain, Colorado (seventy-five miles west of Denver). The instructors there offer skiing lessons for eight different levels of expertise, snowboarding courses, and racing instruction. You can also get videotaped footage of your progress.

If you want to book a Club Med vacation through Richnik's, all you have to do is pick the village you're interested in and let Richnik's and Club Med take care of the rest of the details. You'll pay one all-inclusive price for airfare, baggage handling, transfers at your destination, meals, activities, and entertainment. The only extra cost would be for special excursions, such as a two-day tour of ancient ruins in Mexico.

During their sixteen years of operation, they've attracted about twenty-thousand members. Richnik's president Richard Wernick feels that people who attend their events have good potential for meeting someone, but stresses that "We believe in the concept of doing some activity and meeting someone by chance. . . . Love just falls into place naturally."

HOW MUCH: Costs are $35.00 for annual membership, $25.00 to attend tennis parties, and $10.00 to attend socials.

TRAVEL COMPANION EXCHANGE (TCE)

WHERE: P.O. Box 833
Amityville, NY 11701
(516) 454-0880

WHAT: This organization, now in its eleventh year, does not sell travel or arrange tours—it publishes a bimonthly newsletter for single travelers throughout North America, filled with travel tips, travel news, information about travel discounts, and suggestions for singles about what destinations to visit. The remainder of the newsletter is devoted to listings from singles seeking travel companions or dating companions.

TCE has over five thousand members nationwide, from age 20 to 70-plus. The organization's motto is: Why Travel Alone?™, and it refers to itself as the place Where 'Singles' Become "Doubles"™. It is not strictly a matchmaking service, because applicants can request a travel companion of the same sex, but it does provide excellent opportunities to develop romances as well as friendships.

Applicants fill out a "Personal Profile Page," which, in addition to standard questions about physical traits, educational background, occupation, and religion, asks about habits and travel preferences to ensure traveling compatibility—such as language abilities, preferred accommodations (i.e., sharing same room or cabin, connecting rooms, or separate rooms), destinations you've already visited, available means of travel (i.e., your own car, boat/yacht, motorhome, etc.), and the budget you're willing to travel on.

In addition to the profile, members submit an anonymous "Mini Listing," which is circulated to all other members as part of TCE's newsletter. Members can request a copy of a particular person's profile from TCE's office. (Contact Jens Jurgen, founder and president.)

Members usually develop a friendship before they actually travel together, so that the trip is more comfortable for both companions. There have been cases where members have traveled for free because other TCE members have picked up some or all of the travel costs in exchange for companionship. (For some, money is no object.)

HOW MUCH: You can receive a sample issue of the newsletter for $4.00, postage paid. Introductory membership dues range from $6.00 to $11.00 per month, with a six-month minimum. Rates are higher for those who want to be matched up with a travel companion of the opposite sex. Newsletter subscriptions cost $36.00 a year (no match-up involved). TCE also offers a Quest hotel discount card for $19.95 a year, which enables the card-holder to stay at over 1,300 hotels and inns throughout the United States at a 50-percent discount.

TRAVEL IN TWOS

WHERE: 239 N. Broadway, Suite 3
N. Tarrytown, NY 10591
(914) 631-8409

WHAT: Travel in Twos matches singles with compatible travel partners of the same sex and books them on whatever kind of vacation appeals to them. Among the offerings are an escorted package tour to Europe or to the Orient, an independent itinerary to a European or United States destination, a vacation package to the Caribbean, and a ski package to a western United States destination.

The organization also publishes a quarterly travel newsletter, which lists numerous tour offerings run by a variety of singles groups and general tour operators.

To become a member, call the company to request a brochure; then fill out the questionnaire and mail it back with your registration fee. This organization tends to appeal to the middle-aged and older crowd.

HOW MUCH: One-time registration fee is $10.00. The brochure will detail the tour prices for you.

ULTIMATE TRAVEL

WHERE: P.O. Box 679 Centuck Station
Yonkers, NY 10710
(914) 237-1913
(212) 978-8513

WHAT: This company arranges travel discounts for singles or offers the lowest price available on one-day or weekend excursions and on longer trips that cater exclusively to singles.

Ultimate Travel will also help you lay out your vacation plans and recommend destinations that are commonly frequented by singles.

Among the singles' vacations promoted by Ultimate Travel are Club Med, Club Getaway, Super Clubs, singles weekends at The Concord (an upstate New York resort), ski trips to Stowe, Hunter Mountain, Killington, Vail, Austria, and Canada, and a variety of cruises.

The annual Concord Singles Weekend usually attracts a turnout of about five hundred singles in their twenties, thirties, forties, and fifties. There are cocktail parties and round-robin seating, designed to expose you to a lot of different people, and you can use the recreational facilities at the resort—indoor tennis courts and swimming pool, as well as horseback riding. You also can get hooked up with a roommate to reduce your occupancy rate.

HOW MUCH: Weekend trip prices range from $150.00 to $400.00; for longer trips, expect to pay anywhere between $399.00 and $2,500.00, depending on what's included in the package and how long you'll be staying. Day trips are priced at $35.00 and up.

UMBRELLA SINGLES

WHERE: Church Street, P.O. Box 157
Woodbourne, NY 12788
(914) 434-6871
(800) 537-2797

WHAT: This twelve-year-old organization is aimed at providing unique resort vacations: domestic and international travel designed specifically for singles in separate age categories—22 to 39, 35 to 49, or 40-plus. Each program incorporates the setting, menu, guest speakers, entertainment, and activities most appropriate to a particular age group.

Every year, holiday programs include New Years, Washington's Birthday, Memorial Day, Fourth of July, Labor Day, Halloween, Thanksgiving, and Christmas getaways to top resorts.

Summer promotions offer two- to seven-night stays at various Catskill and Pocono resorts. And 1992 marks the twelfth year that Kutsher's Country Club (upstate New York) has hosted the Annual Singles Celebration—an Umbrella Singles reunion weekend that attracts almost a thousand singles.

Weekend or week-long rates include deluxe accommodations, three gourmet meals a day, private cocktail parties nightly, guest speakers and rap sessions, organized sports activities and tournaments, and use of all health and fitness facilities. Plus, there's round-robin seating in the dining room and nightclub, nightly entertainment, dancing to DJ music during lunch and dinner gatherings, and dance contests until the wee hours of the morning.

Four times a year, Umbrella Singles hosts a Stardust dance weekend. Geared to beginner, intermediate, and advanced dancers, each program, hosted at a different luxury hotel, offers workshops in ten to twelve dances and round-the-clock dance music provided by three DJs and by top Latin orchestras. The dance instructors give private lessons and coordinate the nightly dancing entertainment. The sites of the Stardust dance weekends for 1992: the Villa Roma Country Club, the Concord Hotel, Pines Hotel, and Nevele Country Club.

HOW MUCH: There is no charge to be on the Umbrella Singles mailing list. Brochures about upcoming events are mailed every six to eight weeks. To receive literature and additional information, call the Umbrella Singles office between 9:00 a.m. and 6:00 p.m., Monday through Friday, or Saturday from 10:00 a.m. to 1:00 p.m. Prices of events vary: Examples—$165.00 to $220.00 per person for the Stardust Dance Weekend, and $125.00 to $175.00 for the Singles' Halloween Weekend at Brown's Resort Hotel.

WORLD YACHT CRUISES

WHERE: Pier 62
West 23rd Street at the Hudson River
New York, NY 10011
(212) 929-7090

WHAT: Sail around Manhattan on the Royal Charter with World Yacht Cruises every day of the year, and choose from a variety of options: Sunset Dinner Cruise with Dancing; Liberty Luncheon Cruise; Sunday Brunch Cruise; or Midnight Dance Cruise. A word of advice: Don't show up without a jacket and tie on the dinner, brunch, and dance cruises if you're a guy—and ladies, look "proper." In other words, leave your jeans and sneakers at home.

You can also charter a yacht for private and group events; call the charter specialists at (212) 627-2775 for assistance with the arrangements.

HOW MUCH: Costs are as follows: Sunset Dinner/Dancing Cruise: $45.00 Sunday through Thursday; $50.00 on Friday and Saturday. Liberty Luncheon Cruise: $22.00 with buffet, $12.50 without. Sunday Brunch Cruise: $29.50.

BARS & DANCE CLUBS

Some of you are workaholics. You're driven to succeed (and get rich), and your social life has become a low priority on your "to-do" list. Often, deadlines or closing that major deal you've been negotiating for six weeks determines when your weekend starts.

Maybe you're happy with the way things are, and the only relationship you're looking for is the love affair you have going with your career. But our guess is that some of you are putting in longer hours than you need to so you don't have to deal with the singles scene, or to avoid going home and heating up another TV dinner. There's nothing wrong with working until eight or nine o'clock, but try not to be the one who locks up the office *every* night. And just because you work late, it doesn't mean your nights have to be empty. Mind you, we're not saying it's necessarily depressing to be alone. Solitude can be a great thing sometimes—but too much of it can get to you after a while. You'll know you've had an overdose of solitude or have been working too hard when you start talking to the TV sit-com characters, or when you fall asleep hunched over your lap-top computer.

Our theory, then—which is certainly not scientifically proven, but may strike a chord in some of you nevertheless—is that some of you workaholics are putting in those marathon days at the office because there's nothing in your life right now to tempt you away from your work. Others of you are so genuinely passionate about your work that you barely have time to *think* about what you'll do with your leisure time.

That's what's so great about the bar and club scene. It doesn't require any advance planning, it provides you with instant companionship and social opportunities, and it's still there waiting for you no matter *what* time you finish working. You can drop in anytime.

If you feel self-conscious about going alone, ask your co-workers to unwind with you at a neighborhood pub. You don't have to be close friends to go bar-hopping together. Helpful hint for women: find out which bars the local softball teams hang out at.

You may already have a few favorites, or you might even be one of those night owls who's already done the whole circuit. On the other end of the spectrum, some of you might have been avoiding the bar scene altogether because you don't like to drink or because you assume all bars are loud, dark, and smoky. Well, they're not all that way—and nobody said you have to drink just because you're in a bar. They do serve Ginger Ale, you know.

There are as many different kinds of bars and clubs as there are restaurants. We've reviewed about a hundred bars and clubs throughout the tri-state area, and we've tried to give enough descriptive details to give you "the feel" of each one, as well as practical information about what to wear, the best times to go, and how much money to bring.

This is by no means a comprehensive listing of your bar/club options—in fact, we're only skimming the surface. But it's a good cross-section. Many of you, whether you live in New York, New Jersey, or Connecticut, probably work in Manhattan, so we've focused more heavily on the nightlife there. In addition to the drinking establishments we reviewed in Manhattan, there are certain neighborhoods that have "pockets" or "strips" of bars and nightclubs—sometimes three or four per block. For example, on the Upper West Side, there's an enclave of bars on Amsterdam Avenue between Seventy-ninth and Eighty-sixth Streets, and between Seventieth and Ninetieth Streets on Broadway and Columbus Avenue, as well as the area surrounding Columbia University.

On the Upper East Side, your best bets are First, Second, and Third Avenues, from the Sixties through the Nineties—especially Second Avenue from Seventy-Sixth through Ninety-Sixth streets.

You won't find as heavy a concentration of bars and clubs in the midtown, Chelsea, and Gramercy Park areas—they're more scattered throughout these neighborhoods.

When you're down in the Village, try Seventh Avenue South from Fourteenth Street down to Fourth Street; Greenwich Avenue; Eighth Street East of Sixth Avenue; Bleecker Street; and West Fourth Street from Sixth Avenue to Seventh Avenue South. In Soho, walk up and down West Broadway, Prince Street, and Broome Street to find a lot of interesting hangouts.

We were surprised to see how many places had closed down over the last couple of years—places that used to be jam-packed and much talked-about, like the Cat Club, B-Squared, Heat Wave, Glamorama, King Tut's Wah Wah Hut, The Island Club, M.K.'s, the Surf Club, The Tunnel, Private Eyes, and Forty Worth (which is now a gay men's leather bar called "The Altar")—just to name a few.

That just goes to show you: even the bars and clubs aren't recession-proof—and besides, the demographics are shifting (those baby-boomers who used to fill up all the bars and clubs are having babies of their own and leading more domestic life-styles). In fact, life-styles are changing among the younger set, too. Maybe for every bar or club that closed, a video store opened up?

Most of the bars and clubs we reviewed offer Happy Hour specials on a regular basis, but the days and times change so frequently that it would be impractical to include that information in this guide. You can easily find out when their Happy Hours are by calling ahead.

Warning: we urge you not to drive home from these drinking establishments unless you're sober. (And let someone else be the judge of whether you're sober or not; you can't be objective about it.) If you're in Manhattan, you're probably cabbing it anyway, but if you're in the suburbs, be smart about it. Take the "designated driver" approach—rotating among your circle of friends so that everyone gets their turn to let loose. Or leave your car parked overnight and take a cab or bus home—your car will be there in the morning, and you'll be able to drive it without risking your life and somebody else's.

Okay, with that said, let's get on with the reviews!

ADAM'S APPLE

WHERE: 1117 First Avenue
New York, NY
(212) 371-8650

WHEN: The club is open seven days a week from 11:30 a.m. to 4:00 a.m. October, November and December are peak months.

WHO: A melange of the unattached—Wall Street and Madison Avenue types, school teachers, secretaries, bus drivers—the gamut. Locals, the bridge and tunnel crowd, and tourists. Age range: 25 to 45.

AMBIENCE: Open now for twenty-one years, Adam's Apple was once touted as *the* singles place in Manhattan. Trends, venues, and scenes have changed in the city, but the place holds fast to its old guard East Side deportment. It is far from the cutting edge compared to trendier spots, but continues to be a popular meeting place for singles. There's an abundance of live and silk plants—to the tune of $750,000—a restaurant, a bar, three small to mid-sized dance floors, two of which are suspended in air, and two kitchens, an American and an Italian.

THREADS: The crowd is well dressed, but not over dressed or avant-garde.

COSTS: There is no cover charge, but there is a minimum of $12.00 in the disco. Mixed drinks range from $3.90 to $5.50; beer from $2.75 to $3.75. A dinner will cost you around $20.00 to $25.00.

SCOPE FACTOR: The mix is usually 65 percent women, 35 percent men. Wednesdays, Thursdays, and Fridays are your best bets. Cocktails are from 5:00 to 8:00 p.m., a good time to strike up conversations before the big crowds start to descend.

TUNES: Three DJs spin Top 40 hits.

ARMADILLO CLUB

WHERE: 2420 Broadway (corner of 89th Street)
New York, NY
(212) 496-1066

WHEN: The club is open Monday to Friday 4:00 p.m. to 4:00 a.m.; Saturday and Sunday 12:00 p.m. to 4:00 a.m. Kitchen closes at 1:00 a.m.

WHO: This is a lively gathering. On weeknights, there's a mostly neighborhood crowd. On weekends, a mixed crowd of non-yuppie professionals from all over, 21 to 61.

AMBIENCE: A southwestern motif is woven around a ceiling-high neon cactus. Relaxed. A completely Tex-Mex menu; try the fajitas and Southwest barbecue burger. Margaritas are a must.

THREADS: Laid-back looks.

COSTS: Drinks average $3.50 to $4.00, beer $3.50, dinner $10.00 to $16.00.

SCOPE FACTOR: Nice atmosphere for talking at the bar. The male-female ratio is even.

TUNES: A variety of modern music is featured.

AU BAR

WHERE: 41 East 58th Street
New York, NY
(212) 308-9455

WHEN: Seven days a week 9:00 p.m. to 4:00 a.m. It's always busy, so make reservations for dinner (the only kind of reservations you can make here).

WHO: Very wealthy European beautiful people.

AMBIENCE: Along the lines of an elegant English men's club. Très chic, très savoir faire, and très chèr. You could be in Monte Carlo when you're dancing. As you may have guessed, the menu is very continental. Getting in falls to the caprice of the famous New York rite of entrance, the Selective Door Process (always in effect, but of course).

THREADS: The upscale Euro-crowd dresses like an upscale Euro-crowd.

COSTS: If the Fates smile upon you and you are ushered in, the cover is $10 Sunday to Wednesday; $15 Thursday to Saturday. Drinks are $10 to $11; imported beer $5. A dinner with appropriate libations goes for around $75.

SCOPE FACTOR: Always good opportunities to meet people. Conversations are witty and debonair.

TUNES: Frank Sinatra to Frank Zappa.

AUSTRALIAN COUNTRY INN

WHERE: 1036 Fort Salonga Road
Northport, NY
(516) 754-4400

WHEN: Every day from 11:30 a.m. (except Saturday, when it's from 4:30 p.m.) "till when people leave." Free buffet Sunday night at the Boomerang Bar; also sundry specials, ladies' nights, and lots of activities. Holidays, especially Valentine's day, New Year's day, and Mother's day, are very busy.

WHO: From near and far, patrons gather to kick back and amuse themselves. The crowd is varied; age range is from 26 to 66.

AMBIENCE: Beautiful, non-glittery South Australian-style inn. The setting is poetic; lovely gardens and picturesque windows looking out at local wildlife, notably those koalas of the north, raccoons. And the menu is up to the surroundings, offering fine meat, fowl and seafood dishes such as Sydney Steamboat, a shellfish medley, and filet mignon sauteed in cassis liqueur. Down-Under drinks include koala koolers, grand passion cocktails, and didjeridoos (you'll also see a real didjeridu hanging about). There's lots of great music and two dance floors.

THREADS: Hoganesque, maritime-motifs, and sporty fits in fine; the guiding principle here is cozy and casual.

COSTS: Never a cover. Mixed drinks average in at $3.75; a very nice dinner is about $20.00.

SCOPE FACTOR: The inn does a lot of catering for singles groups. The Long Island Single Sailors (age requirement is over 30) come a-waltzin matilda on the first and third Thursday of every month. Not surprisingly, every night's a good night to meet singles.

TUNES: Live music on Friday, Saturday, and Sunday—Top 40 hits, steel drum, jazz. The essence of the inn's sage philosophy is "play what the room wants."

BAMBOO BERNIES

WHERE: 2268 Broadway
New York, NY 10024
(212) 580-0200

WHEN: 5:00 p.m. till 4:00 a.m., every day of the week. Gets the most crowded during the summer months and in December/January. Best time to get picked up: Tuesday, Thursday, Friday, and Saturday nights—especially Friday.

WHO: Diverse crowd, generally in the 21 to 31 age group. On week-nights you'll find a more local clientele, but on Fridays and Saturdays people trek in from other parts of town and from other cities. You'll be just as likely to meet an attorney as a construction worker here.

AMBIENCE: Tropical decor and wild, easygoing party atmosphere. No dance floor. Eat before you get here—unless you want a liquid dinner. The only thing served besides drinks is popcorn.

THREADS: Casual. Jeans are fine, but if you're coming straight from work, just stay in your office attire.

COSTS: No cover charge. Mixed drinks will cost you anywhere from $3.75 to $4.25; a beer costs $2.75 to $3.50, and wine by the glass is $2.75. For adventurous drinkers: try the Flaming Ipo Bowl, Shark Bite, or Zombie. (No, we won't spoil the surprise by saying what's in them!)

SCOPE FACTOR: Guys and gals have an equally good chance of meeting a member of the opposite sex.

TUNES: Reggae, soul, and classic funky dance music.

BEACHTREE CAFE

WHERE: 292 Merrick Road
Amityville, NY
(516) 691-4423

WHEN: Weekdays from 11:30 a.m. to 2:00 a.m.; weekends, 12:00 p.m. to 3:00 a.m. Sunday brunch is served from noon till 3:30 p.m., late-night menu till 1:00 a.m.; happy hour with a free buffet, Monday to Friday, 5:00 to 7:00 p.m. Holidays are very busy.

WHO: Nice demographic and age mix at the restaurant. When colleges break, an early-twenties crowd takes over the full bar; at other times, patrons range from 25 to 45.

AMBIENCE: Fun-activated atmosphere in a modern, cozy, Long-Island-contemporary setting: soft sculptures, ceiling fans, stained glass, and all that jazz. There is something going on every night: Monday is game-show madness; Tuesday and Sunday, karaoke; live music on Wednesday, Friday, and Saturday. New to-dos are often added. The surf-and-turf menu ranges from burgers to lobster tails, and there are plenty of frozen drinks, from Mudslides to Banana Banshees.

THREADS: Campus chic, outfitting by L.L. Bean, Banana Republic, or J Crew; be neat but casual.

COSTS: There's no cover. Drinks are generally about $3.50

SCOPE FACTOR: Lots of singles at the bar on weeknights, with a good male-to-female ratio.

TUNES: Modern music in a diverse array.

BEAR BAR

WHERE: 2156 Broadway
New York, NY
(212) 362-2145

WHEN: Every weekday from 5:00 p.m. till 4:00 a.m., and weekends from noon till 4:00 a.m. Best singles nights: Thursdays, Fridays, and Saturdays. Guys, if you're going to throw your money around and keep the girls supplied with drinks: go on ladies' nights (Monday, Tuesday and Wednesday). It usually gets the most crowded on Wednesday and Friday nights. This place is busy all year round. If you want to meet someone here, the later the better.

WHO: Out-of-towners on the weekends; mostly locals on weeknights. If you're under 30, you'll feel right at home. Lots of Fordham law grad students, Columbia business and medical students, young stockbrokers, and folks from the entertainment industry hang out here.

AMBIENCE: Crowded and crazy watering hole with upstate New York lodge decor. Very friendly and very lively. Talk loud to be heard. Grab a bite to eat before you get here—no food served.

THREADS: Strictly jeans and T-shirts. (Of course, they won't kick you out if you haven't had a chance to change out of your work clothes.)

COSTS: Beer can be really cheap: from 50¢ to $3.75. A glass of wine is $3.00, and mixed drinks range from $3.75 to $6.00. What to get really happy on: Bear Juice and Moose Juice.

SCOPE FACTOR: Neither sex is outnumbered here. Just be friendly and you'll have no trouble meeting someone.

TUNES: Classic rock with a smattering of new stuff.

BENTLEY'S

WHERE: 25 East 40th Street
New York, NY
(212) 684-2540

WHEN: Thursdays from 6:00 p.m. till 2:00 a.m.; Fridays from 5:00 p.m. till 4:00 a.m.; Saturdays from 10:30 p.m. till 4:30 a.m.

WHO: Very ethnic, well-to-do clientele; serious dancers.

AMBIENCE: Two mirrored dance floors and a super-sharp sound system accentuate the main purpose of this place: DANCE the night away!

THREADS: Dress-to-kill

COSTS: $5.00 to $10.00; free on Fridays from 5:00 to 9:00 p.m.

SCOPE FACTOR: Great socializing and dancing opportunities

TUNES: DJ music; Thursday is Reggae-Soca-Calypso night

BIRDLAND

WHERE: 2745 Broadway (105th Street)
New York, NY
(212) 749-2228

WHEN: All week, restaurant 5:00 p.m. to 12:00 a.m.; 1:00 a.m. on the weekend. Sets: 9:00 p.m., 11:00 p.m., 1:00 a.m. Sunday brunch with music 12:00 to 4:00 p.m.

WHO: Sophisticated and mixed crowd of jazz and blues lovers, twenties to fifties. Three decades ago they would have been called cool cats and hipsters.

AMBIENCE: Modern jazz club. Cool and sleek. The linear namesake of that haven of jazz giants, the world-famous Birdland that once stood at Times Square. Eras are different, but there's lots of hot music here, too. The bar is big and there's also an upstairs. Cuisine is Cajun and good.

THREADS: Casual to night-life chic.

COSTS: On weekdays: tables $5.00 cover, $5.00 minimum; bar no cover, $5.00 minimum. On weekends: tables $10.00 cover, $10.00 minimum; bar $5.00 and $5.00; upstairs no cover, $10.00 minimum. Mixed drinks $3.50 to $6.00, beer $3.50, dinner for two $40.00 to $50.00.

SCOPE FACTOR: Strike it up at the bar. Sultry, contemplative or sizzling vibes fill the air, and it reflects in people's mood and dialogues. Sunday brunches ($9.95) make urbane first or second dates.

TUNES: Live jazz Friday to Tuesday; blues Wednesday and Thursday.

THE BOOMER CLUB

WHERE: At the Clarion Hotel
50 Kenney Place

Saddle Brook, NJ
(201) 843-0600

WHEN: Friday and Saturday 8:30 p.m. to 2:30 a.m. Comedy night on Thursday.

WHO: Hotel guests, New Yorkers, area residents, motorists who happen in—a mélange, as is the age range.

AMBIENCE: Hotel disco. Two dance floors. There's bar food and snacks and a restaurant downstairs.

THREADS: From suit and tie to casual.

COSTS: The cover after 9:30 p.m. is $5.00. Drinks are priced like hotel disco drinks.

SCOPE FACTOR: One cosmopolitan young Clifton woman said, "It's far from happening," but others have reported that it's good for singles. There are usually more women than men here.

TUNES: DJs do a time warp: starting with the fifties, they move up a decade every hour.

BORDER CAFE

WHERE: 2637 Broadway
New York, NY
(212) 864-3037

WHEN: Weekdays from 3:30 in the afternoon till the wee hours of the morning; Sundays from noon. The dining room opens at 4:00 p.m. and closes at 11:00 p.m.; snacks and appetizers are served till midnight. As for Sunday brunch: get there between noon and 4 p.m. Most popular night: Friday. Fall is the busiest time of year.

WHO: Neighborhood folks and Columbia students—plus, lots of different ethnic groups are represented from the International Youth Hostel. Great blend of people from all walks of life—well, maybe not all.

AMBIENCE: Casual southwestern decor and fun, lively atmosphere. Watch sports on the wide-screen TVs. The food is southwestern, too—nachos, cajun chicken fingers, salsa and chips, fried chicken, chicken borracho, fajitas, barbecued ribs, and more yummy stuff.

THREADS: Don't dress up for this one; be casual.

COSTS: After 10:00 p.m., you pay $2.00 to get in—which is almost like paying nothing at all, especially when you consider the fact that a draft beer only costs a buck, and mixed drinks can be as cheap as $2.00, which is also what a glass of wine costs. And would you believe that beer refills only cost a quarter at the bar after 10:00 p.m.? One more surprising fact: ten-ounce frozen margaritas can be had for $1.50 apiece at the bar.

SCOPE FACTOR: Wednesday, Thursday, and Saturday nights are especially good opportunities to mingle with singles—and women have a slightly better chance of finding guys (two-to-three ratio).

TUNES: Rock from the 1960s through the present, and some rhythm & blues.

THE BOULEVARD

WHERE: 2373 Broadway (88th Street)
New York, NY
(212) 874-7400

WHEN: Monday to Wednesday 11:30 a.m. to 12:00 p.m.; Thursday to Saturday till 1:00 a.m.; Sunday 11:00 a.m. to 12:00 p.m. Last call at the bar when the kitchen closes.

WHO: Melange of neighborhood people (yuppies and non-), European tourists, out-of-towners and around-the-towners. Age at the bar ranges from twenties to fifties.

AMBIENCE: Modern Upper West Side motif. Lots of hand-painted urban caricature murals. Two floors. A good-sized bar, sort of a tapered triangle, is downstairs. The menu is contemporary, Italian, Tex-Mex, burgers, and barbecue.

THREADS: Casual.

COSTS: Drinks average $4, beer $3, dinner from $12 to $21.

SCOPE FACTOR: Weekends the bars are busy with mostly singles.

TUNES: A variety of CDs are played.

BRAZIL 2000

WHERE: 127 West 72nd Street
New York, NY
(212) 877-7730

WHEN: Tuesday to Sunday 4:30 p.m. to 2:00 a.m. (kitchen), 2:30 to 3:00 a.m. (bar). Happy hour 4:30 to 7:00 p.m. Live Brazilian jazz Wednesday to Saturday. Carnival ball every year at the end of February.

WHO: A mix of local and Tri-state aficionados of Brazilian music and food. The majority (70 percent) are in their late thirties to fifties; most of the remaining 30 percent are mid-twenties to early thirties.

AMBIENCE: Modern Brazilian-Italian lines *con sensa tropicale*, from canopies of green to murals of toucans and parrots. The club and music aspect have been added fairly recently to the restaurant, and are proving popular. The space is good-sized. There's a small bar and dance floor, which can get steamy when the fiery jazz and *carnivale* tunes start going. The Brazilian and Portuguese cuisine is delicious. And for drinks, try the *caipirinha*, Brazil's national concoction, and *batidas*.

THREADS: Casual. On music nights, though, there are some elegant and electrifying outfits and light-fabric Ipanema looks. For carnival, the costumery can get elaborate.

SCOPE FACTOR: Good-looking singles; some nights there are more men, some nights more women, but usually the ratio is pretty much even. The atmosphere is romantic, even sensual (Brazilian things sort of lend themselves to this.)

COSTS: No minimum, no cover. Drinks $4.50, beer $3.25, dinner generally $14.00 to $24.00 (entree, appetizer, wine).

TUNES: *Jazz Brasiliana.*

BRIDIE'S PUB

WHERE: 63-28 Woodhaven Boulevard
Rego Park, NY
(718) 426-8580

WHO: Locals, mostly in their twenties and thirties. Men like to congregate at the bar and watch sports on TV, but lots of women come here, too.

AMBIENCE: Cozy Irish bar with a couple of wooden booths across from the bar, mock Tiffany lamps, a jukebox, and lively conversation. There's a separate dining room adjacent to the bar. You can have a good, hearty dinner for a reasonable price—or just munch on finger foods at the bar.

COSTS: Drinks can be had for $3.00 to $5.00; entrees cost $7.00 to $15.00; and appetizers are priced from $2.50 to $4.50

SCOPE FACTOR: You probably wouldn't be comfortable coming here by yourself — but if you come with a group of friends, you might wind up expanding that group by the end of the evening.

TUNES: Great jukebox, with an emphasis on classic rock.

BRIGHTFELLOW'S

WHERE: 2565 Hempstead Turnpike (where the Turnpike meets Wantagh Parkway)
East Meadow, NY
(516) 579-2131

WHEN: Every day noon to 4:00 a.m. The kitchen is open till 2:30 a.m. Happy hour is Monday to Friday 4:00 to 8:00 p.m. Ladies' night is on Wednesday (this also continues to be one of the busiest nights). Live music on Thursday.

WHO: Young, diverse crowd from all over the island, the city, and elsewhere, 24 to 28.

AMBIENCE: Modern Long Island meeting spot and club. Fun. There are thirty-six TV screens scattered around, airing sports and dance stuff. Two dance floors, one big, one small. And if you get hungry, you can eat late here. The full menu runs from burgers to continental. Good London Broil and daily specials.

THREADS: Young-casual and "lookin' fine, goin' to dance" looks.

COSTS: Cover $3.00 to $5.00, some nights no cover. Drinks average $3.25, beer $2.75, dinner $10.00 to $15.00.

SCOPE FACTOR: Definite on singles circuits; women usually outnumber men two-to-one.

TUNES: DJs spin dance, Top 40 hits. Live cover rock bands on Thursday.

CAFE IGUANA

WHERE: 235 Park Avenue South
New York, NY
(212) 529-4770

WHEN: Weekdays from 11:30 a.m. till 4:00 a.m., and weekends from noon to 4:00 a.m. Sunday brunch is served from noon till 4:00 p.m., and there's also a midnight brunch, served nightly from 11:30 p.m. till 2:00 a.m. This bar/restaurant is busiest in the fall and winter months.

WHO: Midtown work crowd. Lots of professionals—especially at lunchtime and right after work. The youngest patrons are in their early twenties, and you'll find that a good portion of the crowd are in their thirties and forties—but the later it gets, the younger the crowd gets.

AMBIENCE: Fun and festive atmosphere, with a loud hum of conversation filling all three levels. It's a Southwestern-themed place with a lively combination of terra cotta, peach, and seafoam. When you enter the place, you'll be greeted by Richard Burton Iguana, a ten-foot brass reptile who hovers over the entrance, and Ava Gardner Iguana, the sixteen-foot mascot, who's made of crystal, suspended from the ceiling over the bar. Also near the entrance is the Iguana Store, which sells T-shirts, sweatshirts, jackets, iguana pins, post cards, beach umbrellas and towels, and baseball caps and sun-visors. There's plenty of good eating here: Tex-Mex, grilled, and barbecued specialties. As for specialty drinks, try their Iguanarita, margarita, Sex on the Beach, and Long Island iced tea.

When the level of action gets really frenzied, you'll probably have to wait outside for a little while, or inch your way into the bar—but if you're a nine-to-fiver and you drop in right after work you'll get a table.

THREADS: Everyone's pretty well dressed—and you'll see some flashy outfits here. It would be hard to be overdressed for this place.

COSTS: The only times there's a cover charge ($2.00) are Thursday, Friday, and Saturday nights. Mixed drinks cost $6.00, a beer costs $4.00, and a glass of wine costs $4.00 to $5.00.

SCOPE FACTOR: There are always a lot of singles here, so it's just a matter of striking up conversations till you hit it off with someone. Talk loud!

TUNES: The DJs start spinning records at 8:00 every night. You'll hear a wide variety of music.

CAFE SOCIETY

WHERE: 915 Broadway at 21st Street
New York, NY
(212) 529-8282

WHEN: The disco opens at 11:00 p.m., but you can eat dinner from 7:00 p.m. Saturday or enjoy Friday's Happy Hour from 5:00 to 7:00 p.m.

WHO: Cafe Society's name tells all; the crowd tends to be filled with those who are part of the city club scene.

AMBIENCE: This midtown hot spot looks like a cross between the inside of a nuclear reactor and a catering hall: a large open space filled with neon-lit beams and eating areas that overlook the dance floor. After 11:00 p.m., the decor is enhanced with male and female dancers, live on pedestals. Cafe Society is one of New York City's most trendy hot spots. The club has two floors and a basement. The first level has the dance floor, bar, and main dining area. The second floor has an additional bar, and all of the dinner tables overlook the dance floor area. The basement is filled with pool tables

If you enter after 11:00 p.m. on Friday or Saturday, you will wait on line for at least thirty minutes. As with most hot spots, if you tip the bouncer enough, entrance is easy

THREADS: Black is the color for this place. If you're not wearing something black, you're in the minority. Other than that, it's dress up and be trendy

COSTS: Admission is $10.00. A word of advice: eat dinner there (food is excellent Italian) and scope the crowd. You must make reservations for dinner, but it's worth it. Dinner is under $20.00 per person, and once you're in, admission is free. It's a little expensive to get buzzed here—$7.00 for beers and $9.00 for mixed drinks

SCOPE FACTOR: Women outnumber the men two to one. This bar may have more women in black mini skirts than any other in New York City.

TUNES: Disco, disco, disco. This place is loud and the music is always blasting

---

CARMINE'S

WHERE: 2450 Broadway (between 90th & 91st Streets)
New York, NY
(212) 362-2200

WHEN: Monday to Thursday 4:30 to 11:00 p.m. (kitchen), 2:00 a.m. (bar); Friday and Saturday till 12:00 a.m. (kitchen), 3:00 a.m. (bar); Sunday 2:00 to 10:00 p.m. (kitchen), 1:00 a.m. (bar). Very busy, especially weekends.

WHO: A collage of good-looking people—professionals, yuppies, the gamut. Early in the week, mostly a neighborhood crowd; toward the end of the week the crowd is from all over. At the bar, the age range is twenties to forties.

AMBIENCE: Old-world rustic, classic Little Italy unveiled on the Upper West Side. Both the restaurant and the downstairs full bar (food is also served here) are very popular. People mill outside to get in every weekend evening. The menu is Southern Italian; portions a true *abbondanza*.

THREADS: *Patroni* are smartly dressed, attires from casual to chic.

COSTS: Drinks average $4.00, beer $3.50, a dinner is around $20.00.

SCOPE FACTOR: The bar *e molto buono* to meet people, especially weekends. Most are parked barside specifically to hang out, a few are imbibing while waiting for tables.

TUNES: CDs. Jerry Vale, Tony Bennett, Old Blue Eyes, and other *paisans* start the evening, followed by opera arias. By midnight the music gets spiced up with a diverse array.

CASEY'S DANCE HALL & SALOON

WHERE: 1584 York Avenue (at 83rd Street)
New York, NY
(212) 570-5454

WHEN: The saloon is open Monday through Saturday; there's dancing on Thursday, Friday, and Saturday nights. The later the better.

WHO: Mostly upper-east-siders; young professionals.

AMBIENCE: Neon and surf boards mixed up with an Irish charm describes this upper East side hangout. Decent-sized dance floor, but it does get crowded.

MOOD: "Lut's party." If Spuds McKenzie had a New York City hangout, it would be Casey's.

THREADS: Pick up a J Crew catalog and shake it. Pictures of a Casey's crowd will fall out.

COSTS: $10.00 on Saturday night. However, if you enter the doors in a group of seven to ten, people have been known to make a deal with the bouncer. A beer will cost you $4.00.

SCOPE FACTOR: Good-looking Yuppies. Women slightly outnumber the men. Lots of room around the dance floor for eye contact and light conversation.

TUNES: Mostly rock and roll. Mixed with modern dance music and all the old ones you know and love. After thirty minutes on the dance floor your ears will start to ring, but the noise level in the bar area is tolerable.

CHATFIELDS AT THE PARK RIDGE MARRIOTT

WHERE: 300 Brae Boulevard
Park Ridge, NJ
(201) 307-0800

WHEN: Weekdays from 4:30 in the afternoon till 2:00 in the morning, and Saturdays from 8:00 p.m. till 3:00 a.m.

WHO: Wide variety of people from many different neighborhoods.

AMBIENCE: Bright, attractive decor that lends itself both to socializing and private conversations. All kinds of events and entertainment take place at this hotel bar—live band performances, DJ music and dancing, reggae parties, Monday night football on the big screen, and matchmaking parties sponsored by organizations like Calculated Couples and Club Singles.

THREADS: Casual, but people dress nicely here.

COSTS: Sometimes there's a cover charge, but never on Fridays—which is an especially good night for singles to go. Drink prices vary: on Monday nights you get draft beers for $1.50 apiece and hotdogs for free.

SCOPE FACTOR: The best times to meet someone are Thursday, Friday, and Saturday nights—or on those evenings when the matchmaking parties are hosted there.

TUNES: Lots of different kinds of DJ music and live bands.

CHILES

WHERE: 590 Hartford Road
New Britain, CT
(203) 229-0155

WHEN: Seven days a week 11:00 a.m. till 11:00 p.m. (Sunday to Thursday), 12:00 a.m. (Friday and Saturday). Happy hour Monday to Friday 4:00 to 6:00 p.m. The full bar is busiest after 9:00 p.m. and Fridays.

WHO: Mostly a local crowd 22 to 50. Thick with the after-work crew for happy hour.

AMBIENCE: Southwestern look; lots of plants, tiles and knickknacks. Friendly atmosphere. The Tex-Mex menu is big on burgers, ribs and fajitas; great buffalo wings. Bartenders get very creative with the house specialty top-shelf margaritas; if you have a yen for cranberry, melon, banana or just about any flavor margarita, they'll make it.

THREADS: Aside from the office-clad, it's a blend of L.L. Bean and jeans and sweatshirts.

COSTS: Mixed drinks $3.00, brew $2.00 to $3.15, dinner $6.00 to $12.00.

SCOPE FACTOR: Quiet and relaxed, nice for striking up a conversation; the male-female ratio at the bar (and in the restaurant) is about even.

TUNES: One of those looped tapes of pop music.

CHINA CLUB

WHERE: 2130 Broadway (75th Street)
New York, NY
(212) 877-1166

WHEN: Monday to Saturday 10:00 p.m. to 4:00 a.m. Every Wednesday there's a celebrity jam session. The later the better.

WHO: A showbiz crowd, 25 to 45. Lots of people from the music industry and modeling agencies.

AMBIENCE: Still going strong after seven years, the China Club is a favored haunt of rockers. Comfortable. Blue and black, dark wood bar, Chinese touches, salt-water aquarium, and guitars on the wall, including one of Eric Clapton's. There's also a VIP room with couch seating. Eat first because no food is served.

THREADS: Neat, casual, and laid back.

COSTS: The cover is $10.00, drinks average $4.50, beer $3.00 (imported $3.50).

SCOPE FACTOR: Male-female ratio is usually even. You might wind up saying to someone, "Aren't you . . .?" Good place to meet other singles.

TUNES: Live and DJ music—R&R, R&B. Big names jam on Wednesday.

CITY

(formerly SHOUT!)

WHERE: 124 West 43rd Street
New York, NY
(212) 869-2088

WHEN: Wednesday through Friday from 5:00 p.m. till the wee hours of the morning, and Saturday from 9:00 p.m. till same. Most popular nights to hang out there are Saturdays and Thursdays during happy hour. Complimentary buffet is available from 5:30 to 7:30 p.m. on Wednesday and Friday. Spring and fall are the most active seasons here.

WHO: Local midtown work crowd, and middle- to upper-class yuppies ages 25 to 40. This club has a loyal following of regulars. On weekends you'll find Manhattanites and people from the surrounding boroughs and towns.

AMBIENCE: Modern decor, scantily furnished to allow for vast dancing space. In fact, CITY has the largest dance floor and lighting system in the city.

THREADS: On weekends people show up in their dressy dancing clothes. During the week you'll see lots of suits and business outfits.

COSTS: Cover charge of $5.00 before 8:00 p.m., which includes one drink and complimentary buffet. After 8:00, the cover charge is still $5.00, but that's just for admission. The price goes up to $10.00 on Saturdays after 8:00. Beer is $3.50 for domestic, $4.00 for imported; mixed drinks cost $3.75 apiece; a glass of wine costs $3.50.

SCOPE FACTOR: There a nice even mix of men and women, so go ask your dream guy or gal to dance.

TUNES: Top 40 hits from the sixties through the present. There's live entertainment every Wednesday night.

COPACABANA

WHERE: 10 East 60th Street
New York, NY
(212) 755-6010

WHEN: Tuesday 6:00 p.m. to 3:00 a.m.; Friday 6:00 p.m. to 4:00 a.m.; Saturday 9:30 p.m. to 4:00 a.m.; other nights are for private parties. There's a free buffet Tuesday and Friday from 6:00 to 8:00 p.m.

WHO: A mixed crowd of Latin music lovers from the tri-state area. Women must be 21, men 25 to get in.

AMBIENCE: Nice art deco. Romantic. *Caliente.* Dancing is impassioned, and there's plenty of room to merigue, salsa, and lambada.

THREADS: The crowd is well-dressed.

COSTS: The cover: after 7:00 p.m. on Tuesday $5.00 for ladies, $10.00 for men; Friday 6:00 to 9:00 p.m. $5.00, afterwards women $10.00, men $15.00; Saturday 9:30 to 11:00 p.m. ladies free, $10.00 after, men $15.00 all night. A drink averages $4.25, a beer $2.75.

SCOPE FACTOR: Latin music *tu sabe*: Meeting is in the air all three nights. You don't hear real Latin music in elevators, do you? Guess why.

TUNES: Latino downstairs, Americano disco upstairs.

COYOTE CAFE & SALOON

WHERE: 50 Water Street
South Norwalk, CT
(203) 854-9630

WHEN: Sunday to Thursday 11:00 to 1:00 a.m., Friday and Saturday till 2:00

a.m. Caters to live music. Summer's the busiest season, but evenings jam year-round.

WHO: Artists, musicians, college crews, yuppies, 21 to 45, from the area. A lot of businesspeople after work and lunch time.

AMBIENCE: Arizona eccentric, a Tex-Mex theme. Fun, friendly, lively and popular. There's a conservative-sized dance floor in front of the stage. Bands include Funkestra, Milk, acoustic musician Doug Allen, and Stylie. The menu is Tex-Mex, *claro,* and margaritas are plentiful.

THREADS: Yuppified and semi-tropical to plain ole casual. It's also a good place to wear your thunderbird bolo or squash blossom necklace.

COSTS: Usually no cover except for bigger bands; then it's $4.00. Drinks $3.25, draft to imports $2.00 to $3.25, dinner $10.00 to $12.00. There are also specials on drinks.

SCOPE FACTOR: Great spot for singles. The *hombres-mujeres* ratio varies.

TUNES: Live music every night, with DJs spinning in between. R&B, R&R, reggae, dance and acoustic.

CRACKER BARREL PUB

WHERE: 30 Main Street
Tariffville, CT
(203) 651-0596

WHEN: Friday and Saturday the bar is open from 11:00 till 2:00 a.m. and the dining room from 11:00 a.m. till 10:00 p.m.. Sunday, both the bar and dining room are open from 11:00 a.m. to 11:00 p.m. Monday the bar's open from 11:00 a.m. to 11:00 p.m. and the dining room from 11:00 a.m. till 10:00 p.m. Tuesday through Thursday the bar is open from 11:00 a.m. till 1:00 a.m., and the dining room from 11:00 a.m. till 10:00 p.m.. Fall and winter are the busiest seasons.

WHO: There's a loyal following of regulars, but happy hours bring lots of new faces. You'll find a very mixed crowd here during lunch and at Friday happy hours—people in their twenties, thirties, and forties, both blue-collar and white-collar.

AMBIENCE: Charming, cozy, pub-like atmosphere, exposed-brick walls. There's an outdoor deck, which is popular during the warmer months. There's no dance floor—but that doesn't stop some people from dancing anyway. You won't starve here: you can satisfy your growling stomach with a wide variety of finger foods. Potato skins and Buffalo wings are among the highlights. Or, if you want to feast on a whole dinner, there's prime rib, baked stuffed shrimp, and changing daily specials.

THREADS: Dress is casual; people don't come here to see and be seen.

COSTS: Never a cover charge, even when there's live entertainment. Sixty-cent hotdogs are served on football nights.

SCOPE FACTOR: Usually it's about half men, half women—but during TV football games, men dominate the bar. Ladies: might as well not bother trying to engage the men in conversation on football nights. Why compete for their attention? You *know* football has a good chance of winning!

TUNES: All kinds—top 40 hits, pop, jazz, oldies, country music. Live entertainment on Fridays and Saturdays.

THE "NEW" DANCETERIA

WHERE: 29 East 29th Street (between Madison and Park Avenues)
New York, NY
(212) 683-1046

WHEN: Open from 9:00 p.m. to 4:00 a.m.; the action doesn't really get going until midnight.

WHO: For the most part, this is a young crowd. They seem to be into the whole club scene: waiting for the bouncer to let them in, making out in dark corners, and drinking heavily.

AMBIENCE: Wouldn't win any interior design awards—not that the decor matters to the crowd. Black, grey, and red are the colors of this place, and there are two rooms, each with its own dance floor and bar. If you stand smack in the middle of the two dance floors, you can hear the conflicting music—rap blasting into your right ear, disco blasting into your left. There are balconies upstairs from which you can gaze down at the dance action.

THREADS: The fashions are trendy, not corporate—they probably came from Merry-Go-Round, not Brooks Brothers. You'll see a lot of black, some gaudy stuff, and tight minis.

COSTS: $7.00 before midnight, otherwise $10.00 to $15.00 to get in; $4.00 to $6.00 for mixed drinks. $1.00 drinks from 10:00 to 11:00 every night.

SCOPE FACTOR: There's a definite abundance of guys here—so gals will have a better chance of getting past the bouncer during those peak hours.

TUNES: Lots of rap, lots of disco, and some rock as the night progresses. Live bands perform onstage in the room with the big dance floor.

DANIELLE'S OF FOREST HILLS

WHERE: 70-28 Austin Street
Forest Hills, NY
(718) 268-4524

WHEN: The dance club is open on Thursdays, Fridays, and Saturdays from 11:00 p.m. till 4:00 a.m., and the restaurant is open seven days a week from 11:00 in the morning till 11:00 at night. The summer months (July and August) aren't as busy as the rest of the year.

WHO: It's a mixed crowd, with the majority ranging in age from 25 to 45. Lots of locals, and a good number of professionals.

AMBIENCE: Modern, glamorous decor and relaxed atmosphere. There are plenty of tables, so you can enjoy dinner (Italian cuisine) in a comfortable setting. Specialty drinks include Italian Ices, Pina Coladas, Long Island Iced Teas, and Woo-Woos. This is just as much a disco as it is a restaurant: there's a dance floor that measures twenty by fifteen feet.

THREADS: Casual but neat. Don't show up in sneakers or T-shirts.

COSTS: $5.00 cover charge; $4.00 for mixed drinks; $3.50 to $4.00 for a beer; $3.50 for a glass of wine. Dinner entrees cost $10.00 to $15.00.

SCOPE FACTOR: Go on Thursday, Friday, or Saturday to meet someone. Your chances are probably better if you're interested in the 30-plus population.

TUNES: Classic disco. They have live entertainment a couple of times a year.

DOCK'S

WHERE: 2427 Broadway (between 89th and 90th Streets)
New York, NY
(212) 724-5588
(There is also a Dock's at 633 Third Avenue; tel. (212) 986-8080.)

WHEN: Sunday to Thursday 11:30 a.m. to 11:00 p.m. (kitchen); Friday and Saturday till midnight. The bar closes an hour or so after the kitchen.

WHO: A well-heeled crowd spanning three generations. Ultra preppie.

AMBIENCE: Right between Jake's fish market and Murray's Sturgeon shop. Old world-style New York seafood restaurant and oyster bar. Airs of an exclusive chowder club. Very popular and always crowded. The cuisine is very good.

THREADS: Natty attire.

COSTS: Drinks and beer around the going price at most places; better spirits get up there in cost. Dinner is $20.00 to $40.00.

SCOPE FACTOR: There are usually a lot of people hanging out at the oyster bar, which is lively with dialogue and repartee. Some patrons are on the supercilious side, some are pleasant, some are outright friendly. Big hangout for the midtown work force.

TUNES: Background music. Mostly you get the sound of people conversing.

FUDDRUCKERS

WHERE: 725 Merrick Avenue
Westbury, NY
(516) 832-8323
(One of many locations throughout New York City and northern New Jersey.)

WHEN: Seven days; 11:00 a.m. to 10:00 p.m. during the week, to 11:00 to 12:00 p.m. on the weekends. Karaoke on Saturday 9:00 to 12:00 p.m.

WHO: A local crowd. Young families on the weekdays and Sundays; on Saturdays it's more singles, 22 to 35.

AMBIENCE: Simple cathedral ceiling, track lighting. Mostly a family restaurant, except Saturday nights, when it gets noisy. There's a full bar. Burgers, dogs, and stuff like that.

THREADS: Neat and casual.

COSTS: Drinks $3.00, bottled brew $2.00, tap $1.00.

SCOPE FACTOR: Come on Saturday night to increase your odds.

TUNES: Sing-along karaoke; otherwise music is low-key.

GECKO BAR

WHERE: 407 Amsterdam Avenue (near 80th Street)
New York, NY
(212) 799-0558

WHEN: Seven days a week 5:00 p.m. to 4:00 a.m. Happy hour every day 5:00 to 7:00 p.m. DJs spin records on weekends. It opened last New Year's Eve; the only day that the place isn't packed is Monday.

WHO: A very trendy, well-dressed crowd of varied ages. Gecko's is happening, so it draws patrons from all over like house lizards to a hot rock.

AMBIENCE: There's a big palm on the bar, an optimizer on the wall and five original gecko paintings, including American Gothic, George Washington, Mona Lisa, and Andy Warhol Gecko. Muse on whether that big gecko head mounted on the wall will loose its tongue to snare your olive. More reptilian decor is even now being added. The bar's specialty is pitchers of Kamikazes and, of course, Geckoaid and Gecko Punch.

There's a dance area, but dancing can get very tight with a full house.

Expect a short wait to get in on weekends after 10:30 p.m.

THREADS: The crowd is scaled fashionably Upper West Side chic.

COSTS: No cover. Domestic beer $2.75, imported $3.25, mixed drinks $3.50, Gecko special pitchers $15.00.

SCOPE FACTOR: Sophisticated, good-looking singles every night. The male-female ratio is even.

TUNES: Pop, rock, the breaking sounds. DJs do their thang on the weekend. The sound system is great.

GEORGETOWN SALOON

WHERE: 8 Main Street
Georgetown, CT
(203) 544-8003

WHEN: Mondays to Saturdays 11:30 a.m. to 1:00 a.m.; Sundays 1:30 to 11:00 p.m. Biggest crowds are in the spring and fall.

WHO: Clientele run the gamut from truck drivers to IBM employees, ages 20 onward.

AMBIENCE: Very comfortable, laid-back atmosphere with a Western flair. The menu features basic saloon fare—burgers, steaks, ribs, chili. For drinks, try the house spiked-coffee specialties. The dance floor is nice and mid-sized.

THREADS: Some people get dressed up, some wear cowboy gear.

COSTS: On nights with live music there is a cover of around $2.00. Bottled beer goes for $3.00; mixed drinks $3.50; a dinner averages $10.00 to $12.00.

SCOPE FACTOR: Live music nights are the best times to meet other singles. Men and women are evenly balanced.

TUNES: Live music Thursday, Friday and Saturday—country, Motown and rock.

GERONIMO'S BAMBA BAY

WHERE: 1454 Second Avenue (76th Street)
New York, NY
(212) 650-0561

WHEN: Sunday to Thursday 11:30 to 1:00 a.m.; Friday and Saturday till 4:00 a.m. (lunch starts at 11:30 a.m., dinner at 5:00 p.m.). Wednesday and Thursday are Ultimate Ladies Nights—women get free margaritas and beer all evening. Happy hour with free taco bar Monday to Friday 4:00 to 7:00 p.m. Friday and Saturday are real busy.

WHO: A wide range of friendly people, 25 to 40.

AMBIENCE: Tropical, fun and comfy. Say hi to the big statue of Geronimo the Apache Surfer. Nice-size space. Seven screens—it's not a sports bar, but keeps the coverage for big sports events. Extensive collection of music videos. Tables are moved out when people want to dance. Excellent Southwest and Tex-Mex cuisine.

THREADS: The crowd is well dressed but casual; suits and ties and jeans and sneakers are equally appropriate.

COSTS: Never a cover. Drinks and beer $3.00 to $4.00. A dinner goes for $8.00 to $10.00. The $8.95 weekend brunch includes unlimited margaritas.

SCOPE FACTOR: Great spot all week for singles; even balance of men and women.

TUNES: Live acoustic folk and soul Monday and Tuesday, DJs and dancing on Friday and Saturday. Rock, dance, pop, and soul.

GOLDEN SPUR DISCO

WHERE: 246 S. Highland Avenue
Ossining, NY
(914) 762-3501

WHEN: Seven days a week from 3:00 p.m. to 3:00 a.m. Live music on Wednesday, Friday, and Saturday. Spring is the busiest time.

WHO: A 30-and-over crowd from all over the region.

AMBIENCE: A country bar with all the bucolic trappings. There's plenty of line dancing and other countrified fun. A CD jukebox spins the tunes on the nights when there's no live bands. There are no real dinners, but there are snacks and hot dogs.

THREADS: Plaid and jeans would do just fine.

COSTS: No cover. A mixed drink averages $3.00, as does a glass of suds.

SCOPE FACTOR: Live music nights are the best time to strike it up.

TUNES: Good 'ole country music.

HI LIFE

WHERE: 477 Amsterdam Avenue (83rd Street)
New York, NY
(212) 787-7199

WHEN: Sunday to Tuesday 4:30 p.m. to 1:00 a.m.; Wednesday to Saturday 4:30 p.m. to 3:30 a.m. Kitchen closes at 11:15 p.m.

WHO: Mixed crowd from all over. Like other places on the Upper West Side, more locals weeknights, more "from elsewheres" weekends. The bar crowd ranges from mid-twenties to thirties.

AMBIENCE: Retro-style 1940s, 1950s bar and grill. Very serious about dinner till 11:30 p.m. when the place switches into a bar mode. The cuisine is tasty and mostly American. There are pasta and grilled specials. And the portions are good-sized.

THREADS: Casual to dressed-up.

COSTS: Drinks average $3.50, beer $3.00, a full dinner $15.00 to $20.00.

SCOPE FACTOR: Good spot for meeting people on weekend evenings.

TUNES: CD, cassette and DJ. Diverse array from dance and funk to rock and blues.

THE HOP

WHERE: 120 Union Boulevard
Totowa, NJ
(201) 942-8867

WHEN: Thursday to Sunday 7:00 p.m. to 3:00 a.m. Thursday is ladies' night and classic rock night; Friday, live music; Saturday, oldies; Sunday, Classic Showcase.

WHO: A lively crowd of locals, other Garden Staters, and out-of-staters. On oldies night the age range is 25 to 70; other nights it's 21 to 50.

AMBIENCE: Oldies decor, big space. This is one of the most popular dance clubs in the area. There are bikini contests and cheerleader squads, even special track act appearances. For eats, there are burgers, steak, pizza, and things like that.

THREADS: Campus finery, rock looks, fifties cruisin'.

SCOPE FACTOR: Saturday is mostly couples; otherwise, singles city.

COSTS: After 10:00 p.m., when there's a cover, $3.00 to $5.00. Beer and wine $3.00, drinks $4.00. Reduced prices during Hopomania, Thursday and Friday.

TUNES: Live and DJ, rock, dance, and oldies.

THE INSOMNIA HOTEL & BAR

WHERE: 462 Amsterdam Avenue (between 82nd and 83rd Streets)
New York, NY
(212) 874-9912

WHEN: Every day, check in at 5:00 p.m., check out at 4:00 a.m. Busy from near midnight till 3:00 a.m.

WHO: A mixed, late-night crowd that usually rolls in around 11:30 p.m. Avant-gardists and night owls, twenties to forties.

AMBIENCE: Opened at the beginning of this year. The sign outside asks, "Why Sleep?" There's a small lounge like you might find in an Upper West Side resident hotel or in a "lost on the highway motel in a town down South around twilight." Decor deliberate low-key. There are dollar shots per second—the bartender stands on the bar and pours it down your gullet—and there are Woo-Woos and Sex on the Beach too. People dance, even atop the pool table. No serious eats, but munch barside on popcorn and cheddar goldfish.

THREADS: Confirmed late-night looks.

COSTS: Drinks around $3.50, beers in $2.00 and $3.00 range; different liquor specials.

SCOPE FACTOR: Men are in the majority; the number of night owlettes varies.

TUNES: Progressive rock and dance tapes and CDs.

J'S NIGHTCLUB/RESTAURANT

WHERE: 2581 Broadway, 2nd Floor
New York, NY
(212) 666-3600

WHEN: Doesn't open till 7:00 p.m. on Saturdays and Sundays—but stays open till the wee hours of the morning. Monday through Friday, from 5:00 p.m. till whenever.

Most popular nights: Friday and Saturday. The only slow

months are June and September.

WHO: A broad cross-section of New Yorkers.

AMBIENCE: Casual, comfortable, living-room feel. They serve Continental/American grill.

THREADS: Whatever you feel like wearing (within reason, of course)

COSTS: No cover charge, despite the live entertainment. Mixed drinks will run you $4.00 to $7.00; beer $3.75 to $5.00; wine by the glass $4.00 to $7.50.

SCOPE FACTOR: It's usually a nice, even mix of guys and dolls—and you can meet just about every kind of person here. It's hard to say what the best times of the week are for single-hunting—it varies.

TUNES: Live entertainment every night of the week.

JUKEBOX

WHERE: 304 East 39th Street
New York, NY
(212) 685-1556

WHEN: Open from Wednesday through Saturday till 4:00 in the morning, starting at 5:00 p.m. on weeknights and at 9:00 p.m. on Saturdays.

Busiest time of year is November through December, and Friday is the most popular night of the week.

WHO: A wide mix of neighborhoods is represented here. Lots of nine-to-fivers hang out here after work.

AMBIENCE: A throwback to the 1950s and 1960s. Lots of old jukeboxes and signs, and lots of drinking and dancing. The dance floor is a decent size—twenty by twenty-five feet. There's a complimentary buffet for after-work partiers, from 5:00 to 7:00 p.m. Wednesday through Friday.

THREADS: It's casual, but you see a lot of suits and professional clothes because people come straight from the office.

COSTS: Until 7:00 p.m., there's no cover charge; after that, it's only $5.00.

SCOPE FACTOR: Your best bet is to drop in after work for the buffet on Wednesdays and Thursdays and hang out till about 11:00 p.m.

TUNES: Good ol' rock 'n roll from the fifties and sixties, plus some current pop music.

KCOU RADIO

WHERE: 430 Amsterdam Avenue (near 80th Street)
New York, NY
(212) 580-0556

WHEN: Every day 5:00 p.m. to 4:00 a.m. Busier towards the later hours.

WHO: During the week, mainly a neighborhood crowd, 30 to 50. On weekends, bridge and tunnelites and college crews, twenties to thirties. No yuppies in sight here.

AMBIENCE: Minimalism. No name outside, but if you look inside, you'll see it on the wall. Some African sculpture around. Casual and non-pretentious, a New Age bar. No eats and no chichi drinks. Rolling Rock is the favored bottled brew.

THREADS: Neat, casual, and non-glitzy.

COSTS: Drinks $3.25 to $3.75, beer $2.75. From 5:00 to 8:00 p.m., there's a two-for-one drink special.

SCOPE FACTOR: People come here because they like it basic. Conversations sans background buzz; male-female ratio pretty even.

TUNES: Diverse jukebox.

LA GREC'S STAATEN

WHERE: 697 Forest Avenue
Staten Island, NY
(718) 448-6000

WHEN: This club-restaurant-catering hall is open Tuesday to Sunday. Lunch Tuesday to Friday, 11:30 a.m. to 3:30 p.m. Live music and dancing Wednesday to Saturday 10:00 p.m. to 3:00 a.m. December gets real busy.

WHO: The dance crowd is a mix of locals, Brooklynites, and Jerseyites, ages 25 to 50.

AMBIENCE: Nice colonial feel. During live music nights a medium-sized dance floor is used, and snacks and appetizers like fried calamari are served.

THREADS: The crowd is not overdressed; sports jackets, nice slacks, and dresses predominate.

COSTS: No cover. A mixed drink goes for $3.00; beer $2.50.

SCOPE FACTOR: Wednesday, Friday, and Saturday are good meeting nights.

TUNES: A wide range of danceable music.

LA TIENDA CAFE

WHERE: West Street, Route 202
Litchfield, CT
(203) 567-8778

WHEN: Every day from 11:30 a.m. till the wee hours of the morning

WHO: Locals from Litchfield and surrounding towns, plus weekenders from New York. All ages, all walks of life.

AMBIENCE: Very friendly and casual Mexican restaurant/bar with moderate prices. They've won *Connecticut Magazine*'s Best Mexican Restaurant in Litchfield County for the past eight years—which is how long they've been in business. Besides Mexican food, they serve some American dishes, including ribs.

THREADS: Casual

COSTS: Food is moderately priced, but if you're going just to drink, mixed drinks are $3.00 to $4.50, beer is $1.75 to $2.50, and wine is $3.00 a glass.

SCOPE FACTOR: The owners recommend going in the late afternoon and evenings to meet other singles. Most popular nights are Fridays, Saturdays and Sundays. Usually a well-balanced mix of men and women.

TUNES: There's some background music, but music isn't a focal point here.

L.I. EXCHANGE

WHERE: At the Huntington Hilton
598 Broadhollow Road
Melville, NY
(516) 845-1000

WHEN: Tuesday 5:00 p.m. to 4:00 a.m.; Friday 4:00 p.m. to 4:00 a.m.; Saturday and Sunday 9:00 p.m. to 4:00 a.m. Happy hour with free hot and cold buffet Tuesday 5:00 to 11:00 p.m.; Friday 4:00 to 8:00 p.m. October, November, and December are the busiest months.

WHO: During happy hour, suits and ties and yuppies; otherwise, a nice looking dance crowd of all ages from around the island.

AMBIENCE: High-tech and high-energy dance club. Two big dance floors. Shot girls move through the crowd, and then there are those shots of jello for fun-drink lovers.

THREADS: The code is proper attire. Well-dressed but not club-crawling outlandish.

COSTS: The cover: after 8:00 p.m. on Friday $5.00, after 10:00 p.m. $10.00; Saturday $10.00; Sunday $5.00; Tuesday (thirty-and-over night) no cover. People in the hospitality industry—bar and restaurants, hotel personnel—are admitted free on Sunday. Drinks go for $4.00 to $5.00; there are half-price specials.

SCOPE FACTOR: Tuesday, especially in the summer, is usually the optimal night for meeting other singles.

TUNES: On Tuesday and Friday there are hustle hours; the rest of the time it's big-tempo dance music.

LIMELIGHT

WHERE: 660 Sixth Avenue
New York, NY
(212) 807-7850

WHEN: Seven days a week 10:00 p.m. to 4:00 or 4:30 a.m.

WHO: *The* salmagundi of crowds, an urban chop suey—yuppies, rappers, cujeens, cujettes, homees, crossdressers and drag queens, the bridge and tunnel crowd, tourists, uptowners, downtowners, clubcrawlers, artistes . . . The Limelight caters to both straight and gay patrons. Age spectrum 18 to 50.

AMBIENCE: A deconsecrated church with much of its ecclesiastical features intact. Some may find this too bizarre, but New York guidebooks always seem to include the place for this very reason. Capacious it is—stained glass windows, five bars, four dance floors, a chapel draped in flowers, a fantasia room and lots of little rooms with constantly changing themes. And it all moves through varying degrees of decadence. There's no food, but habitues eat at nearby Lox Around The Clock when they get hungry.

THREADS: Everything goes; see WHO.

COSTS: The cover: weeknights and Sunday $12.00; Friday and Saturday $15.00. Drinks $5.00, beer $4.00.

SCOPE FACTOR: There's a stream of singles here every night, especially Friday and Saturday.

TUNES: Downtown sounds, dance, the gamut. Live music Tuesday and Sunday.

MAIN STREET USA COMEDY CAFE

WHERE: 146 Main Street
Hackensack, NJ
(201) 488-5888

WHEN: Open evenings and nights on Wednesday and Saturday, and all day on Thursday and Friday

WHO: Professionals aged 25 and up, from a wide variety of neighborhoods.

AMBIENCE: Casual, intimate, and very relaxed. There's a small dance floor (about twelve by fourteen feet), and comedy routines are performed three nights a week. The place can be rented for private parties. Light snacks and Continental cuisine are served.

THREADS: Some casual, some corporate—depends whether you're coming straight from work or going home to change first.

COSTS: If you're coming for the comedy show, the cover charge is $12.00; otherwise there's no cover. Drinks cost anywhere from $3.00.

SCOPE FACTOR: Guys, you'll be slightly outnumbered—so take advantage! The best nights to socialize here would be Thursday and Friday.

TUNES: Dance music.

MARIO'S PLACE

WHERE: 36 Railroad Place
Westport, CT
(203) 226-0308

WHEN: Seven days a week 11:30 a.m. to 12:00 a.m. (weekdays), 1:00 a.m. (Friday and Saturday), 11:00 p.m. (Sunday).

WHO: Lots of professionals and commuters from all over, twenties to fifties. It's right across from the railroad station.

AMBIENCE: Nice and hang-outish. Lot of wood. Full bar. The menu is Italian and American; prime ribs are very popular.

THREADS: *Dopo Lavoro*: Straight from work and yuppie casual looks.

COSTS: Meals are even-priced, drinks $3.00 to $4.00, beer $2.00.

SCOPE FACTOR: The bar "happens" on the commuter and after-work meetings circuit

TUNES: Piped-in Sinatraesque.

MARTY & LENNY'S DISCO

WHERE: 50 LeCount Place
New Rochelle, NY
(914) 576-2244

WHEN: Wednesday to Saturday 9:00 p.m. on. Hopping in the summer.

WHO: The young-twenties local crowd, except on Friday teen night, when the sixteen-, seventeen- and eighteen-year-olds take over.

AMBIENCE: Westchester dance club outfitting—the paneling, the rugs, the mirrors. Big dance floor. No food-food, but bar snacks. Teenagers get their own venue on Friday nights; no alcohol is served then, and the DJs dazzle with Hot 97 tracks.

THREADS: Casual and neat.

COSTS: The cover ranges from $5.00 to $20.00; teen night is on the higher end because it's boozeless. On the other three nights drinks average $2.75, beer $2.50 (draft $2.00).

SCOPE FACTOR: Young dating fever.

TUNES: DJ-driven music. Hot 97 tracks on Friday, R&R on Saturday, new wave on Wednesday and Thursday.

MAXWELL'S

WHERE: 1039 Washington Street
Hoboken, NJ
(201) 798-4064

WHEN: Tuesday to Friday 4:00 p.m. to midnight; Saturday and Sunday 10:00 a.m. to 3:00 a.m. Live entertainment every night. Crowds thin down in July and August.

WHO: Patrons are largely young, hip followers of the alternative music scene; they come from throughout the tri-state area and as far as D.C. The look of the crowd changes with the band performing that night. Age ranges from 21 to 45.

AMBIENCE: Relaxed pub decor, an interesting blend of trendy and homey. Maxwell's is a launching pad for many an alternative band. When the big ones like REM, Nirvana, and Bo Dallas and the Wild Magnolias play the New York area, they often play a night here, so Maxwell's has become known as a small place with big bands. There is also a room with a DJ, but basically there's little dancing. The menu offers

American eats—buffalo chicken wings, good soups—and pasta John Courage is the preferred ale of the house.

THREADS: Who's playing often governs what to wear. Minimalist, existentialist, beat, and "I'm sitting reading Le Figaro with my capuccino while thinking of deconstructist art" looks can all be appropriate

COSTS: Cover ranges from $6.00 to $10.00. A drink goes for $3.00, beer $2.50, a full dinner $11.00 to $12.00.

SCOPE FACTOR: Start grooving before the music starts. Thursdays, Fridays and Saturdays are best.

TUNES: Alternative, Cajun, zydeco, folk, and C&W.

NELL'S

WHERE: 246 W. 14th Street (between 7th and 8th Avenues)
New York, NY
(212) 675-1567

WHEN: Seven days a week, 10:00 p.m. to 4:00 a.m. Monday is new talent night; Tuesday, "Boom" night (new bands); Friday, Eurohouse.

WHO: An elegant crowd; many ages from many locales.

AMBIENCE: Much like a turn-of-the-century English club—Victorian-style furniture, antiques, mirrors. Very comfortable and cozy. There's live jazz upstairs and a dance floor downstairs. Your hostess is actress-singer Nell Campbell, one of the stars of both the stage and screen versions of "The Rocky Horror Show." The relaxed menu offers lots of appetizers, burgers, grilled chicken, steak, and sundries.

THREADS: Come dressed in your best club finery. No jeans, no sneakers.

COSTS: The cover is $12.00 on Friday, Saturday and Sunday; other nights it's $6.00. Abe Lincoln and a few bits will get you most mixed drinks; without the bits for a beer. Dinners average $10.00 to $15.00.

SCOPE FACTOR: The atmosphere is most congenial and conducive to meeting people. Hot nights: Wednesdays and Sundays.

TUNES: Jazz and dance music, plus new bands.

NICK'S GROVE

WHERE: 209 East 84th Street
New York, NY
(212) 744-5003

WHEN: Tuesday through Saturday from 10:00 a.m. till 4:00 a.m. Fall and winter are the busiest seasons, and Thursday through Saturday are the most popular nights.

WHO: Depends on when you go there; usually there's a mix of locals and New Yorkers from other neighborhoods, mostly between ages 25 and 35.

AMBIENCE: This is a stylish but relaxed place for drinking and hanging out. It has a good-sized dance floor (twenty by thirty feet), but it's not a dance club in the true sense of the word. You can call it the upper east side's "mini-disco."

THREADS: In the summer it's very casual, but during winter months you'll see a wide range of outfits.

COSTS: Cover charge is $5.00, mixed drinks cost $4.50 and up, beer is $3.50 and up, and the house wine is $4.50 by the glass.

SCOPE FACTOR: Friday and Saturday nights. On Saturdays after 11:00, it really gets popular.

TUNES: Pop dance music. Occasionally they have live entertainment.

180°

WHERE: 570 Amsterdam Avenue
New York, NY
(212) 580-7755

WHEN: Monday through Friday from 4:00 p.m. to 4:00 a.m., and Saturday and Sunday from noon till 4:00 a.m.

WHO: Mostly neighborhood folks—all ages, all professions.

AMBIENCE: A casual hangout for drinking and socializing. No dance floor.

THREADS: Casual, or corporate if you're coming straight from work.

COSTS: $4.50 for mixed drinks, $3.00 to $3.50 for a beer, and $3.50 for a glass of wine

SCOPE FACTOR: Any night's a good night to meet people, but Monday and Friday are the most popular nights to hang out here.

TUNES: Varied.

ONSTAGE DANCE CLUB

WHERE: 70 Beach
Staten Island, NY
(718) 442-5692 (recording), (718) 447-9518 (real person)

WHEN: Friday and Saturday, 10:00 p.m. to 4:00 a.m.

WHO: Local, very young crowd 18 to 21 (about the age range of the whole strip here).

AMBIENCE: Old movie theater, now a techno and other effects rock-dance club. No food.

THREADS: Casual.

COSTS: No cover. Beer and drinks go for around $3.00 a pop.

SCOPE FACTOR: Young singles dating circuit outpost.

TUNES: Rock and dance, DJ and live.

PALLADIUM

WHERE: 126 East 14th Street
New York, NY
(212) 473-7171

WHEN: Tuesday to Saturday 10:00 p.m. to 4:00 a.m.

WHO: Club crawlers, boroughites, out-of-towners, SoHo-, CoHo- and NoHo-types and people who look like they were on that Obsession commercial—"I am you, you are me, he is she, we are they"—and even regular joes and jills converge and spread out across the giant space and its many nooks and crannies. Age range generally from twenties to forties.

AMBIENCE: A sprawling, high-tech, mega-temple of cool with an art-heavy environment. Celeb events, networking parties, downtown dos. For a while the Palladium as a loud glitter palace was on the wane, but the word is out on the circuit that it's gotten good again. Lots of live music now ranging from Menudo and Patty LaBelle to techno sounds, industrial alternative, and other-dimensional.

THREADS: Downtown club attire, chic, all the way to Saturday Night Live's "Sprockets" style. "Hi, I'm Dieter, your host."

COSTS: The cover: Tuesday and Wednesday $5.00; Thursday $10.00; Friday and Saturday $15.00. Drinks are in the mid-price range.

SCOPE FACTOR: It's loud, but you can find a nook somewhere to converse. The meeting rate is good, the male-female ratio fluctuates. Check what's going on to get a bead on the crowd.

TUNES: Dance, techno, mechanico, alternative to alternatives, pop, R&B—wide spectrum.

PATZO

WHERE: 2330 Broadway (corner of 85th Street)
New York, NY
(212) 496-9240

WHEN: Monday to Friday 11:30 a.m. to 1:00 a.m. (kitchen), 2:00 a.m. (bar). Saturday and Sunday, brunch 11:00 a.m. to 4:30 p.m., dinner 5:00 p.m. to 1:00 a.m., 2:00 a.m. (bar).

WHO: Mostly neighborhood yuppies, thirties to fifties. Big crowd.

AMBIENCE: Bustling restaurant and meeting place. Very eclectic exterior: adobe square fused with a modernistic Italo-Mexican tower, which has a great swiggle line. There's a large bar downstairs and a service bar upstairs. Good Italian fare, with most regions represented. Pasta is served in big tureen-like bowls.

THREADS: Nice casual.

COSTS: Drinks average $3.75, beer $2.75, dinner $12.00 to $18.00. Great recession-buster weekend brunch $3.95.

SCOPE FACTOR: The big downstairs bar, a hang-out, is a good spot to strike up a conversation.

TUNES: Background pop.

PEDRO'S

WHERE: 301 East 91st Street
New York, NY
(212) 831-1788

WHEN: Monday through Saturday from 5:00 p.m. till 4:00 a.m., and Sunday from 4:00 p.m. to 4:00 a.m. Busiest time of year is during the winter, especially around the Christmas and New Year season, when partying activity is at its peak.

WHO: Lots of regulars, but there's usually a combination of locals and people from a wide variety of other neighborhoods. All walks of life—students, professionals, etc. Some nights it's mostly students, some nights it turns into a preppie hangout. Try different nights of the week and find your element.

AMBIENCE: A true neighborhood bar—crowded, compact, and relaxed. One regular summed it up like this: "Cold beer, close quarters, and friendly people." It's nothing fancy, but there's an interesting array of objects hanging from the ceiling and on the walls (which is covered with Mexican money wallpaper): college pennants, bras, and boxer shorts, just to name a few. Is the hanging underwear meant to be suggestive? Probably not—just eye-catching.

For diversions and amusement, there's a mini-bowling game, and lots of sports-spectating goes on at the bar TV.

You can't order food here, but Pedro's offers menus from other, nearby restaurants—so you can order food to be delivered!

THREADS: Doesn't really matter what you wear; nobody will care.

COSTS: Mixed drinks can be as cheap as $2.50, up to $5.50; beer is $3.00 for domestic, $3.50 for imported; white wine by the glass costs $3.25. Specialty drinks: Kamikazes, banana daiquiris, and Woo Woos.

SCOPE FACTOR: Nice, even mix of guys and gals—try it on a Thursday, Friday, or Saturday night.

TUNES: Whatever gets selected on the jukebox.

PERFECT TOMMMY'S

WHERE: 511 Amsterdam Avenue (between 84th and 85th Streets)
New York, NY
(212) 787-7474

WHEN: Seven days a week, 5:00 p.m. to 4:00 a.m. Happy hour is 5:00 to 8:00 p.m. Human Bar Fly Wednesday (see below) starts at 11:00 p.m. (but get there early) to 1:00 a.m. It's always busy.

WHO: Artists, musicians, yuppies, West and East Siders: a nice mix, twenties to forties. The press on human bar flies is bringing an even greater diversity of people to the place.

AMBIENCE: Great layout and wild fun. Wall murals lead you into the upstairs—a full-length mirrored bar and a completely open space. Downstairs there's a marble-top bar, a pool table, and a mid-sized dance floor. And, most importantly, the site for Wednesdays's human bar fly craze. Anyone can enter the competition. Clad in a special velcro suit, you take off from a twenty-yard runway, spring off a trampoline and plop, you're on a ten-by-ten mat on the wall in all sorts of poses. The winner gets a bottle of Moet and a chance at the nationals. There's no food, but some bar snacks. For specialty drinks, try a Perfect Tommmy or flaming shot.

THREADS: Casual "set to party" looks.

COSTS: Cover $3.00. Mixed drinks $3.50 to $4.00, beer $3.00.

SCOPE FACTOR: This is perhaps *the* best place for singles on the Upper West Side. The male-female ratio is usually even, except for Tuesdays and weekends, when it tilts toward more women.

TUNES: DJ-propelled dance music Tuesday to Saturday.

PLANET HOLLYWOOD

WHERE: 140 West 57th Street
New York, NY
(212) 333-7827

WHEN: Monday to Friday 11:00 a.m. to 1:00 a.m.; Saturday and Sunday 11:30 a.m. to 1:00 a.m. The bar closes at 1:45 a.m.

WHO: A fun crowd of local patrons, bridge and tunnelites, and domestic and international tourists. The age range is generally twenties to forties.

AMBIENCE: Groovy. California dreaming. The bar is designed to provide a "you're in the pool" effect—pool handrails, back wall water blue, surfboard. Rooms include the Blimp Room, set in an upper and lower blimp; Marilyn Room (VIP), function room, screening room, and sound room. There's no dancing, but you can watch movies and music videos in the last two. The cuisine is Californian—why natch—with a little Mexican, Chinese, and Italian. Specialty drinks are silver-screen-themed: Try the Terminator.

THREADS: You'll see an after-theater crowd with furs and a person right behind with jeans and sneakers or Pacifica-clad. Laid-back casual.

COSTS: Never a cover. Drinks around $4.00, beer $3.25, dinner $12.00 to $20.00.

SCOPE FACTOR: Saturday and Sunday evenings are your best bets. The movie soundtracks are not loud, so conversation's simpatico.

TUNES: Hollywoodesque.

Q-CLUB INTERNATIONAL

WHERE: 93-37 150th Street
Jamaica, NY
(718) 262-0733

WHEN: Thursday through Sunday from 10:30 a.m. till 4:00 a.m.

WHO: People come here from a wide variety of neighborhoods.

AMBIENCE: Classy, contemporary decor with a Caribbean flair. Plenty of room to dance—there are two large dance floors, measuring sixty by eighty feet and thirty by forty feet. The menu is filled with a wide variety of international and Caribbean specialties. The club has live entertainment and periodically shabba ranks.

A word of advice: Make reservations if you're planning to have dinner there.

THREADS: Dress to kill

COSTS: Cover charge is $10.00 to $15.00; mixed drinks will run you from $8.00 to $12.00; beer costs $4.00 or $5.00; wine by the glass is $5.00 and up; and you can celebrate with a bottle of champagne that can cost as little as $18.00 and as much as $275.00

Specialty drinks: Sex on the Beach, Long Island Tropical Ice Tea; Q-Club International Special

SCOPE FACTOR: Thursday and Sunday nights are especially good times to meet singles. Women slightly outnumber the men.

TUNES: Reggae and house music.

QUARTER MOON SALOON

WHERE: 442 Amsterdam Avenue (81st Street)
New York, NY
(212) 580-9080

WHEN: Seven days a week 1:00 p.m. to 4:00 a.m. Happy hour Monday to Friday 1:00 to 8:00 p.m.

WHO: Upper-middle-class, clean-cut yuppies from the neighborhood and beyond; ages mainly twenties and thirty-something.

AMBIENCE: Casual and fun. Great copper bar lanterns. You can shoot pool, flipper out on pinball, or pop a pop-a-shot. Dancing isn't rampant, but people do when the mood seizes them. No vittles, but free popcorn. Try the specialty Moon Shot: a mix of vodkas, melon and juice, and bang, zoom, how claire de lune.

THREADS: Very casual.

COSTS: Mixed drinks $4.00, beer $2.75.

SCOPE FACTOR: Sparing's good every night, 'specially Thursday, Friday, and Saturday.

TUNES: CD jukebox with a wide range of selections.

RACCOON LODGE

WHERE: 480 Amsterdam Avenue (83rd Street)
New York, NY
(212) 874-9984

(There is also a Raccoon Lodge at 59 Warren Street, telephone: (212) 766-9656, and 1439 York, telephone: (212) 650-1775.)

WHEN: Monday to Friday 11:00 a.m. to 4:00 a.m.; Saturday and Sunday 1:00 p.m. to 4:00 a.m. The place is not that big, and on summer weekends gets tightly packed.

WHO: Largely a young, rollicking twenties crowd. On weekends and in the summer, the boroughs, New Jersey, and Long Island are well represented, as are colleges during breaks.

AMBIENCE: This lodge has all the trappings of a hangout and frat house—the old Mobil red Pegasus, metal beer signs, license plates, a wide stack of decoy ducks—lightly peppered with Honeymooners' nostalgia. There are two busy pinball machines, a pool table, and a TV sunk into the wall. You can dance next to the bar if there's any room. At night, especially in the warm months, the sound level of the crowd hits high decibels.

THREADS: T-shirts and jeans, satin-sheen tour and club jackets, baseball caps worn catcher-style—hanging out gear. Occasionally you'll find some ladies wandering in dressed more along nineties femme fatale lines and men à la Ivy League.

COSTS: No cover. The average mixed drink is $3.00; beer $2.50.

SCOPE FACTOR: Get there before 10:00 p.m. on weekends if you want enough space to carry on a dialogue. The wooden settee along the window is a good refuge for talking when the crowd gets too thick.

TUNES: There's no live music, but the speakers fill the lodge with classic rock, modern rock, and recent hits.

RASCAL'S

WHERE: 12 East 22nd Street
New York, NY
(212) 420-1777

WHEN: Open Monday to Friday, 11:30 a.m. till 11:00 p.m. Monday, 12:30 a.m. Tuesday, 2:00 a.m. Wednesday, 3:00 a.m. Thursday, 4:00 a.m. Friday. Saturday 7:00 p.m. to 4:00 a.m. Happy hour on weekdays with free buffet, 5:00 to 7:00 p.m. Bustles on the weekends.

WHO: After-work and corporate crowd during happy hour. Other times a mixed crowd, 25 to 35. (You must be 23 or over to get in.)

AMBIENCE: Lots of wood, peanut barrels and sawdust on the floor. Good-sized dance floor. The American menu is extensive (kitchen's open till 3:00 a.m. on weekends).

THREADS: No sneakers or T-shirts. You won't be out of place in a suit.

COSTS: Cover on Friday and Saturday is $7.00. Drinks and beer $4.00 to $5.00. A dinner will cost you around $20.00.

SCOPE FACTOR: Good number of singles here.

TUNES: DJs spin records on the weekends—dance, Motown, and pop.

ROCK 'N ROLL CAFE

WHERE: 149 Bleecker Street
New York, NY
(212) 677-7630

WHEN: Monday through Saturday. Opens at 6:00 p.m., and closes at 2:00 a.m. except on Friday and Saturday, when it stays open till 4:00 a.m.

WHO: Wide variety of people, both locals and tourists. Mostly it's hip people in their twenties and thirties who like rock 'n roll.

AMBIENCE: Rock 'n roll nostalgia through and through. Pictures of current and classic celebrities. Live bands perform nightly. The dance floor is small but functional (ten feet square). They serve lots of good munchies: burgers, chicken fingers and wings, mozzarella sticks, potato skins, and nachos.

THREADS: Casual or after-work clothes

COSTS: Cover charge ranges between $5.00 and $7.00; mixed drinks cost $4.00 to $5.00; beer is $3.00 to $3.50; and wine is $4.00 a glass. Frozen drinks and shots are popular.

SCOPE FACTOR: Good meeting place any night of the week

TUNES: Classic rock 'n roll

ROSELAND

WHERE: 239 West 52nd Street
New York, NY
(212) 247-0200

WHEN: Ballroom dancing Thursday and Sunday 2:30 to 11:00 p.m. Mexican-Latin music Saturday 7:00 p.m. to 3:00 a.m.

WHO: Those fleet of feet, tourists, and a whole mix, 20 and up.

AMBIENCE: This is New York's legendary ballroom, trying to deal with the change of eras, propelled up into the nineties. Nostalgia, though, is still in the air. *Big* place—2,500 capacity. There's a deli and two bars to fuel up between dances.

THREADS: Some people are dressed for "Eine Kleine Nachtmusik," some like disco inferno, and some for shades in between.

SCOPE FACTOR: On Thursday it's mostly mature couples cheek to cheek. Sunday is the day for singles 20 to 50.

COSTS: A $5.00 cover, except Sunday, when it's $10.00. Drinks $4.00, beer $2.75, a meal $10.00.

TUNES: An array of dance music. There's a live band Sunday; otherwise it's DJ-driven.

RUSTY SCUPPER'S

WHERE: 501 Long Wharf Drive
New Haven, CT
(203) 777-5711

WHEN: Monday to Saturday 11:30 to 1:00 a.m. (bar), restaurant closes at 10:00 p.m. weekdays, 11:00 p.m. weekends. Sunday brunch 11:00 a.m. to 2:00 p.m.

WHO: Largely a mix of businesspeople from nearby office centers, locals and motorists on the way to Providence, Boston, or New York; age range thirties to fifties.

AMBIENCE: Somewhat like a Fitzwillie's. Plants, simple lines, and harbor views. The popular deck opens and live music starts in the summer. There's a jukebox and two TV screens flashing music videos and other things. The American menu ranges from burgers to fish, with a lot of mesquite-grilled dishes.

THREADS: Most patrons are attired à la corporate America or in jeans, but some get really dressed up.

COSTS: Mixed drinks average $3.25, beer $2.50, dinner $14.00

SCOPE FACTOR: Summer's the best time, but Friday and Saturday nights at the bar are normally good year-round for singles.

TUNES: Live Dixieland, small bands, and guitarists in the summer.

RYAN'S DAUGHTER

WHERE: 350 East 85th Street
New York, NY 10028
(212) 628-2613

WHEN: Daily from 10:00 a.m. till 4:00 a.m.. Summer months are a bit slower than the rest of the year.

WHO: Wide variety, but mostly professionals in their mid- and late twenties.

AMBIENCE: Traditional neighborhood bar with friendly atmosphere. Besides drinking you can play basketball, shoot pool, and play a game of darts. Eat before you come.

THREADS: Casual but not scruffy

COSTS: Mixed drinks cost from $3.25 to $3.75; beer costs from $2.75 to $4.00; wine by the glass is $3.25. Specialty drinks: Frozen margaritas and Irish coffee.

SCOPE FACTOR: Friday is the best action night; Thursday, Saturday, and Sunday are good, too. Good balance of guys and gals.

TUNES: The jukebox has a varied selection.

SAND CITY

WHERE: 10 Bayville Avenue
Bayville, NY
(516) 628-8729

WHEN: Seven days a week 2:00 p.m. to 4:00 a.m. Wednesday it's suds city, with fifty-cent draft beers. Summer is mega-busy.

WHO: In the winter, locals; in the summer, people from around the tri-state area. The crowd is in their twenties.

AMBIENCE: Mostly a summer place. Nice view of the Long Island Sound. Dance club look. Darts and shooting pool are popular. Food is served only in summer months—heavy in the seafood and chicken departments. This is also the time that the Tiki and Clam Bar come alive and frozen drinks start flowing.

THREADS: Anything from jeans to suits.

COSTS: Live music cover $3.00. Drinks and beer average $3.00 (except on half-dollar draft night). Dinner goes for $12.00 to $20.00.

SCOPE FACTOR: Wednesday is very popular—probably something to do with that hops stuff—and is the day that women outnumber men. Otherwise the ratio is fairly even.

TUNES: Dance and rock. DJs spin records Wednesday, Thursday, Friday and Saturday. Live music most weekends as the weather goes clement.

SILVER SCREEN NIGHT CLUB

WHERE: 34-48 Steinway Street
Long Island City, NY
(718) 786-8680

WHEN: Wednesdays from 9:30 p.m. till 4:00 a.m.; Fridays and Saturdays from 10:00 p.m. till 4:00 a.m.. Popular hangout year-round.

WHO: More than half of the clientele—about 60 percent—are regulars, and the other 40 percent come from a variety of neighborhoods.

For the most part, the age range is 25 to 35. Those who come here are party-minded, but they don't get super-rowdy (in other words, don't worry about fights breaking out and stuff like that). You'll find a lot of Greeks and Italians here, and a lot of professionals who are established or getting there.

AMBIENCE: Classy and modern, with futuristic lights and a large dance floor (four hundred square feet). Fun and festive. There are different theme nights that cater to different tastes. If you're into disco, go on a "Wild Wednesday" (you have to be at least 18). On Friday nights, it turns into "Club Berlin" with Nu music, and on Saturdays, the theme is the "Elite Club" for those 21 and over.

Live entertainment is performed about three times a month.

THREADS: On Wild Wednesdays, dress for fun. Saturdays, don't show up in jeans and sneakers.

COSTS: Depending on the event, the cover charge is between $5.00 and $10.00, but on Saturdays, women 23 and over and men 25 and over will get in for free until midnight. One-dollar drink specials are offered on Wednesdays till 11:00 p.m., and you can get a beer for a dollar on Saturdays until midnight. Otherwise, mixed drinks cost $5.00 to $6.00, beers are $4.00 (domestic) and $5.00 (imported), and wine is $4.00 a glass.

The club offers over fifty varieties of specialty drinks—some of the most popular ones are margaritas, pina coladas, iced teas, and "Jones Beach" drinks. They'll occasionally serve buffet-style food, and there are some nut mixes at the bar.

SCOPE FACTOR: If you're open to it, you have a pretty good chance of meeting someone any night of the week, especially from 11:00 p.m. till 2:00 a.m.

TUNES: Disco (classic and current) and progressive (Nu) music

SKI BAR

WHERE: 1825 Second Avenue
New York, NY
(212) 369-9635

WHEN: Every day from 5:00 p.m. till 3:00 a.m. If you pass by there on a Friday or Saturday night, you'll see a big crowd waiting outside.

WHO: A base clientele of local regulars as well as customers from all over the tri-state area and some out-of-towners. If you're in your mid-twenties to early thirties, you'll be part of the majority.

AMBIENCE: As the name suggests, skiing is the theme here—complete with ski lodge atmosphere, back-bowls, authentic ski paraphernalia, and even a piece of a mountain.

The bar sponsors trips to ski resorts throughout the world on a weekly and monthly basis.

You can't order food here, but they do have serving bowls filled with hot pretzels and popcorn.

THREADS: Casual—and don't forget your skis!

COSTS: Never a cover charge. Mixed drinks are $3.75 and up; a beer is $3.00; and wine costs $3.00 a glass.

Try their specialty drinks, the "Back-Bowl" and "Worldcup"—giant drinks shared by friends using long straws.

SCOPE FACTOR: Best time to meet the man/woman of your dreams: Tuesday through Saturday

TUNES: Wide mix of music.

SOB'S (Sounds of Brazil)

WHERE: 204 Varick Street
New York, NY
(212) 243-4940

WHEN: Monday through Friday from 5:00 to 8:00 p.m. is happy hour. The club is open from Monday through Saturday from 8:00 p.m. till 3:00 a.m. (dinner is served till midnight). Christmas and New Year's Eve are the busiest days of the year.

WHO: An international crowd—lots of tourists and a good number of upscale executives (there are a lot of ad agencies in the area) and professionals. Of course you'll find a lot of music lovers here, too.

AMBIENCE: Even in the winter it feels like summer in this tropical thatched bar with palm trees and Caribbean murals. There's a dance floor (twenty by twenty feet) and a stage where live entertainment is performed every evening.

To really get into the mood of the place, enjoy a Brazilian or Caribbean-style dinner. Or, if you prefer, order American standards like hamburgers and sandwiches. SOB's features over fifty tropical drinks—some favorites are margaritas, pina coladas, and caipirinhas (Brazil's national drink).

THREADS: Some are casual, some dressy. You'll see a lot of corporate attire during happy hour.

COST: The cover charge ranges from $7.00 to $16.00, depending on the act. Mixed drinks can be had for $3.00 to $6.00; beer costs $3.00 to $4.00; wine by the glass is $3.00 to $4.00.

SCOPE FACTOR: Women are slightly outnumbered here, so they'll have an easier time finding a dance partner. Singles can come here alone and not feel out of place; you probably won't be standing by yourself for long.

TUNES: Brazilian Samba, jazz, Caribbean music, R & B, zydeco, and Soca

SPACE AT CHASE

WHERE: 98 Third Avenue (at 12th Street)
New York, NY
(212) 475-1407

WHEN: 9:00 p.m. till 4:00 a.m.

WHO: Mostly locals in their twenties who like to drink and tune-in to live bands.

AMBIENCE: A basic club with a room in the back for the live bands and their followers, and a bar and a couple of wooden booths up front. This is a comfortable, laid-back hangout with no pretenses.

THREADS: No need to put a lot of thought into getting dressed for this place.

COSTS: $10.00 cover charge when there's a live band playing, or $5.00 if you can get hold of an invite. Drinks are $3.50 to $4.50.

SCOPE FACTOR: You can meet people here if you're open to it, and guys are usually more abundant than gals.

TUNES: Rock, rock, and more rock.

THE SPORTING CLUB

WHERE: 99 Hudson Street
New York, NY
(212) 219-0900

WHEN: Every day of the week, from 11:30 a.m.. Closing time is between midnight and 2:00 a.m., depending on the day.

WHO: A mixture of locals and people visiting from other neighborhoods, mostly in their twenties and thirties. Wall Streeters, lawyers, athletes—a wide variety.

AMBIENCE: The main focus of this restaurant/sports bar is food, drink, and sports. There are eleven TV screens to make your head spin from all the sporting events! There's no dance floor per se, but if the music really moves you, the wood floors around the bar will serve your purposes.

You won't go hungry here. Choose among numerous offerings. ribs, burgers, fresh fish, lobster, pasta, steaks, salads, sandwiches, pizza, nachos, chicken wings, etc.

THREADS: Corporate or casual. No tank tops, and no shorts in the winter months.

COSTS: No cover charge. Mixed drinks cost from $3.00 to $4.00; wine is $3.00 a glass; beer usually costs $3.00, except on Thursday and Friday nights when you can get a draft for 75¢. Popular drinks are margaritas, hot exotic drinks, and shots (especially Jell-o shots).

SCOPE FACTOR: Best opportunities for singles: Monday through Friday nights and Sundays during the day.

Ladies, you have the advantage here: what easier place than a sports bar to be outnumbered by the male species? Of course, they may prefer to watch the game. . . .

TUNES: Rock from the fifties to the present, oldies, disco—a wide mix.

STRATOS

WHERE: At the Radisson Hotel Islandia
3635 Expressway Drive
Hauppauge, NY
(516) 232-3000

WHEN: Friday 4:30 p.m. to 4:00 a.m., Saturday 8:00 p.m. to 4:00 a.m. Happy hour Friday with butler-passed hors d'oeurves till 7:00 p.m., and live entertainment till 8:00 p.m.

WHO: A varied crowd from all over (few are from the hotel) 25 to 35, except for happy hour, when it's corporate cabaret.

AMBIENCE: Nice modern room with lots of seating and a sunken mid-sized dance floor. The menu offers appetizers and entrees from quesadillas to burgers and chicken parmigiana.

THREADS: Jeans, sneakers are a no-no; people are pretty dressed up.

COSTS: No cover. Drinks $4.00, beer $3.25, dinner $12.00 to $15.00.

SCOPE FACTOR: The place has proved popular for meeting people. On Saturday there are more women than men; Friday's ratios are unpredictable.

TUNES: Classic disco, top 40 hits, requests. Friday's entertainment till 8:00 p.m. is a very versatile one-woman band. There's also other live music once or twice a month.

STRUGGLE'S JAZZ CLUB

WHERE: 10 Dempsey Avenue
Edgewater, NJ
(201) 224-2244

WHEN: Fridays and Saturdays from 7:00 p.m. till 3:00 a.m.

WHO: Upscale clientele, successful professionals, and jazz lovers of all ages—but most are in their forties.

AMBIENCE: This is a sophisticated jazz club that presents live jazz concerts by world-renowned musicians. It's also a restaurant, serving Italian cuisine.

THREADS: Don't come in looking frumpy; this is an upscale crowd with an upscale wardrobe.

COSTS: There's always a cover charge to get in, but it varies with the performance event. Mixed drinks cost $5.00, beer costs $4.00, and wine is $4.00 a glass.

SCOPE FACTOR: You won't always find a lot of singles here, but if you enjoy jazz in a classy setting, try it anyway. You just never know who might be there.

TUNES: In case we didn't make the point already—jazz, jazz, jazz.

TATOU

WHERE: 151 East 50th Street
New York, NY
(212) 753-1144

WHEN: Lunch is served from 11:30 a.m. to 4:00 p.m., Monday through Friday; dinner is served from 5:30 p.m. to midnight, Monday through Saturday. The dance floor opens up at 10:30 nightly. Reservations are recommended.

WHO: If you're someone who gets intimidated by the rich and famous, you might not be comfortable here. A lot of celebrities have been known to frequent this supper club—okay, let's name-drop: Anthony Quinn, Ben Gazzara, Liza Minelli, Raul Julia, and even Princess Caroline of Monaco. But don't worry: not *everyone* who hangs out here is famous, or a member of high society.

AMBIENCE: The decor is grand in this custom-built replica of a nineteenth-century New Orleans-style opera house. Picture a thirty-foot domed ceiling with a majestic chandelier hanging from the center, a theater stage and proscenium arch, sconces on the walls, and lots of pink brocade and velvet—and you'll get some sense of what this ritzy supper club is like.

Upon entering, the first thing you see is the crowded bar. Past that is the dining room, with the stage at the rear.

The cuisine is Creole-Southern accented American, which, if you've never experienced it, includes such dishes as honey-mustard roasted salmon, pan-roasted loin of lamb with okra and tomato stew, and barbecued rock cornish hen with jalapeno spoonbread.

THREADS: Jacket required. You'll want to choose your outfit carefully—there are a lot of "beautiful people" who come here to see and be seen.

COSTS: You don't have to be super-rich to dine at Tatou: Entrees start at $13.75 and go up to $25.00; appetizers range from $5.00 to $12.50. You can get a complete three-course pre-theater dinner with music for $25.00 if you come before 7:00 p.m.

SCOPE FACTOR: Your best chance to meet someone is after 10:30 p.m., when the dancing gets in gear.

TUNES: Live music performed by the Tatou Rhythm and Blues Band and by various jazz and R&B ensembles. Monday night is Amateur Night.

TAYLOR'S/CACTUS CLUB/THE LAST RESORT

WHERE: 2310 W. Route 70
Cherry Hill, NJ
(609) 486-1001

WHEN: Tuesday and Wednesday from 5:00 p.m. till 1:00 a.m., Thursday and Friday from 5:00 p.m. till 2:00 a.m., Saturday from 8:00 p.m. till 2:00 a.m. Happy hour starts at 5:00 p.m. on Thursday and Friday and goes on till 9:00 p.m.

WHO: Most of the people who come here are from South Jersey and Southeast Pennsylvania. A lot of white-collar professionals, mainly in the 21 to 40 age group. That age range broadens to include a forty-plus faction during happy hours. On Wednesday and Thursday nights there's a younger crowd.

AMBIENCE: Taylor's is a two-level art-deco-style building with an exciting array of special effects. For example, there's a full-color, computer-driven laser show with state-of-the-art sound, light, and video system. There's a sophisticated clientele here, and the pace is high-energy. There's a spacious dance floor that measures thirty by thirty feet.

Upstairs from Taylor's is a new hangout called The Last Resort, which is more casual but also buzzing with activity. It has an eccentric "vacation-world" decor with a fake swimming pool, aging neon signs, a carved totem pole, dancing pink flamingos, and a plastic moosehead.

The Crazy Cactus Club! is an open-air restaurant/nightclub, located directly in front of Taylor's, that serves dinner and late night snacks—buffalo wings, salads, burgers, sandwiches, pizza, and grilled specialties. The atmosphere is laid back and casual.

Special events are sometimes sponsored—such as the "Hottest Tan in the East Finals."

You won't have trouble finding this prominent complex: its fifty-foot tower is surrounded by eight brightly colored neon rings that make the nightclub visible for miles.

THREADS: Casual but fashionable. People tend to dress up more for happy hours and weekends.

COSTS: The $5.00 cover charge entitles you to go back and forth between Taylor's and The Crazy Cactus Club! as often as you wish. Wednesday is ladies night—ladies get in for free. There are usually specials being offered, but when there aren't, mixed drinks cost between $3.50 and $4.75; beer costs $2.75 to $3.25; wine is $3.25 by the glass. All drinks are half price during happy hour. Wednesday is "Crazy Quarters Night: 50¢ for draft beer, and 75¢ for mixed drinks from 9:00 p.m. till midnight. On Thursday and Friday nights, regular drinks cost $1.00 apiece from 9:00 to 11:00 p.m.

SCOPE FACTOR: There's a good mix of men and women; the best time to meet and mingle is during happy hour on Thursday and Friday.

TUNES: Live rock on Tuesdays, post-modern rock on Thursdays, and dance music on Wednesdays, Fridays, and Saturdays

TIFFANY CAFE

WHERE: 6550 Jericho Turnpike
Commack, NY
(516) 499-2244

WHEN: Seven days a week from 5:00 p.m. on. Live music every night. A snug refuge in the winter, which is the busiest season.

WHO: The crowd, 25 to 45, comes from around the island and the boroughs.

AMBIENCE: Romantic and intimate, all booths for two or four. There's also a full bar and a big screen for football, baseball, and National Trivia Showdown. The menu offers a wide range of good food, from pasta and seafood to cheeseboard and fondue. And the bar mixes up some mean oriole cookies.

THREADS: L.L. Bean; neat, fresh-scrubbed looks.

COSTS: No cover. Table minimum Sunday through Thursday is $5.00, Friday and Saturday, $10.00. Drinks $3.25, beer $2.00 to $3.00, dinner for two around $30.00.

SCOPE FACTOR: Mostly a couples place right now, but there are some singles. Good spot for first or second date.

TUNES: Soft rock.

TIMEPIECE CAFE

WHERE: 351 Merrick Road
Rockville Centre, NY
(516) 766-2244

WHEN: Weekdays and Sundays from 5:00 p.m. to 12:30 a.m., Fridays and Saturdays until 1:30 a.m. March is the busiest month of the year for the bar and restaurant.

WHO: A good number of families at the restaurant, a young dating crowd at the bar; most hailing from Manhattan, Brooklyn, and Bayside.

AMBIENCE: Romantic and homey—dark wood, nice carpeting, oil paintings, reading racks replete with original *Life* magazines. Board games and a party room add to the feel. A number of dating services recommend Timepiece as a good choice for a first date. The menu offers fine cuisine Americana; barbecued baby-back ribs are the house specialty. Leading the list of fun drinks are oriole cookies, and the jello shots come in a different flavor every night.

THREADS: Neither yuppie nor ostentatiously upscale; the de rigeur "casual but neat" reigns.

COSTS: No cover, but a table minimum. Mixed drinks average $4.50.

SCOPE FACTOR: Young, congenial singles command the bar on weeknights. The mix is good.

TUNES: Live mellow-rock seven nights a week, starting about 8:00 p.m. When the feet start to swing, the lobby doubles as a dance floor.

WEST END GATE CAFE

WHERE: 2911 Broadway
New York, NY
(212) 662-8830

WHEN: Seven days a week. The kitchen is open from 11:30 a.m. till 11:00 p.m., and the bar stays open till 4:00 a.m.

WHO: Locals and visitors from other neighborhoods, from varied backgrounds. Students and professors from Columbia, blue collar, white collar—there's a wide mix.

AMBIENCE: Comfortable and casual. This is a no-pretense place to hang out and listen to music. A wide variety of food is served at very decent prices.

THREADS: Not high-fashion; casual.

COSTS: There's a cover charge, which varies between $4.00 and $7.00; $3.00 to $4.25 for mixed drinks; $3.25 for a beer; $2.50 for a glass of house wine.

SCOPE FACTOR: If you want a lot of people to choose from: Thursday, Friday and Saturday are the most popular, crowded nights.

TUNES: Funk, rock, jazz, and blues. Live entertainment two or three nights a week.

WETLANDS PRESERVE

WHERE: 161 Hudson Street
New York, NY
(212) 966-4225

WHEN: Sunday through Friday from 5:00 p.m. till 4:00 a.m., and Saturday from 9:00 p.m. till 4:00 a.m.

WHO: This club tends to attract a young crowd—people in their early twenties, for the most part. Great place to meet Grateful Dead fans.

AMBIENCE: A very down-to-earth place with a fun atmosphere and no pretenses, no attitude problems. There is a dance floor, and live entertainment every night of the week.

Vegetarian finger foods are served, like pizza, empanadas, and salsa & chips.

Wetlands is an environmentally conscious club: it sponsors several solidarity and action group lectures and benefits under its Eco-Program—such as the Wetlands Rainforest Action Group, networking parties for social causes, and Save the Earth Society.

THREADS: Very casual; a bit dressier on Friday nights

COSTS: The cover charge varies—the highest it goes is $15.00. Mixed drinks cost from $3.25 to $3.50, and beer costs from $2.75 to $3.50. Specialty drinks are priced slightly higher: $4.00 to $5.00.

SCOPE FACTOR: Any night's a good night to meet someone, but Thursday through Saturday are the busiest nights.

TUNES: Rock, funk, reggae, and psychedelic music.

WHISPERS

WHERE: At the Smithtown Sheraton
Vanderbilt Motor Parkway
Smithtown, NY
(516) 231-1100

WHEN: Wednesday, Thursday, Saturday, Sunday 8:00 p.m. to 4:00 a.m.; Friday 5:00 p.m. till 4:00 a.m.

WHO: Large local crowd. Some people, though, are far-and-widers. Average age during the week is 35 to 40; gets younger on the weekend.

AMBIENCE: Wood, brass, full array of dance lighting, video screens. Friendly atmosphere. Big dance floor. Although it's not promoted, if you get hungry, they can send down to the Garden Cafe for meals.

THREADS: Casual to dressed-up. No jeans or sneakers. Dress shirts for men.

COSTS: Cover on Wednesday, Friday and Saturday is $5.00. Drinks average $4.00, beer $3.25.

SCOPE FACTOR: Friday is the best time for singles (Saturday is heavy on couples).

TUNES: DJs keep it rolling with dance and top 40 hits with other music mixed in. Live C&W on Wednesday and Oldies on Friday.

WILDLIFE

WHERE: 355 Amsterdam Avenue (77th Street)
New York, NY
(212) 724-3600

WHEN: Every day 5:00 p.m. to 4:00 a.m. Thursday through Saturday are peak days.

WHO: People from all over leaning toward the yuppie side, 23 (which is the minimum entry age) on up.

AMBIENCE: Santa Fe lost in downtown Nairobi. Friendly. Big bar room with really nice African masks, an African bull head and a skull (from Maxilla and Mandible). Since it opened last August, it's been mobbed. The lack of trendification and gimmicketry plus the reputation of the owner has accounted for its success. Rolling Rock is the main brew. (Too bad they don't have Tuskers; it would be great here.) No food, just bar snacks, but there are plans to open a sidewalk cafe. The crowd hum is especially loud on Thursday, Friday, and Saturday nights.

THREADS: All sorts of relaxed-looking ensembles. Banana Republic tags fit in fine.

COSTS: No cover. Drinks average $4.00, beer $3.00.

SCOPE FACTOR: Whole lotta people here. Find a spot where you can carry on a conversation.

TUNES: Although it's not a spot for dancing, DJs spin a great mix from Motown and rock to Afropop.

WILSON'S

WHERE: 201 West 79th Street
New York, NY
(212) 769-0100

WHEN: Seven days a week, generally 4:00 p.m. to 4:00 a.m. (bar). Opens earlier for brunch on weekends. Live music Monday, Tuesday, and Wednesday.

WHO: A usually lively crowd of sophisticates, sports and entertainment celebs, neighborhood regulars, patrons from the ABC and CBS studios, and soap stars. The age scene leans toward 30 and over.

AMBIENCE: Set in an ornate cinnabar building, near to Charivari's, Wilson's is conservatively chic. Open atmosphere and high ceilings. It's fairly large, but imbues coziness nonetheless. The restaurant area is normally buzzing, as is the full bar. People dance, too. Good pastas and fresh-grilled seafood (the menu is continental with an Italian flair).

THREADS: Casual chic, though you'll also see degrees of chic-chic.

COSTS: The live music cover is usually $10.00. Drinks $3.00 to $5.00, draft $2.50 (there are daily special drinks), dinner $12.00 to $20.00.

SCOPE FACTOR: The bar and its environs are good places to strike it up; the ratio is about 55 percent male, 45 percent female.

TUNES: Dance, pop, and jazzier stuff.

WINE GALLERY

WHERE: 70-20 Austin Street
Forest Hills, NY
(718) 544-0894

WHEN: From noon (lunch is served) until 2:00 a.m., seven days a week. Fridays and Saturdays after 9:00 p.m. are your best bets if you want to meet someone.

WHO: Mostly Forest-Hillians, Rego-Parkers, and Kew-Gardenites, spanning two generations. Lots of high school kids claim this as their hangout, but singles and couples in their twenties, thirties, forties, and fifties love coming here too.

AMBIENCE: Friendly and fun, with cozy lighting, duplexed dining room, and a small, intimate bar with a couple of video games. This is a good, casual place to drop in after the movies (there are four theaters within a three-block radius) for some wine and cheese—or stay longer and enjoy a complete dinner. The food's pretty good.

THREADS: Don't wear anything *too* fancy, but you can get a little dressed up without feeling out of place—the locals tend to be fashion-conscious.

COSTS: Wine is $3.00 to $4.00 a glass; mixed drinks average $3.50 or so. Dinner can cost as little as $6.00 (standard burger or cheese platter) and up to $15.00 for seafood or chicken specialties.

SCOPE FACTOR: Single guys often sit solo at the bar, and tables are pretty close together in the dining areas, so you and your friends might hook up with another group.

TUNES: Soft rock, top 40, and, as the night progresses, dance music.

DATING SERVICES & MATCHMAKING PARTIES

Dating services can be a great way to hook up with someone. Although some of you may be turned off by the idea of paying someone to find you a date, it is a viable option, one you shouldn't dismiss too hastily. After all, when you think about it, what's so terrible about letting someone else do the legwork for you?

Lots of singles, just like you, are too busy to socialize very often. When you finally have a free evening, you don't want to spend it searching for that ideal mate—because you'll probably have to go through some kind of process of elimination. So why not let someone screen out the prospects for you? Just think of it as the same kind of arrangement you have with an employment agency who tries to find you a suitable job, or with a real estate agent who tries to find you the perfect apartment.

For some reason, some people believe that a dating service is the last resort, that joining one would indicate some level of desperation.

We'd like to try to dispel that myth. Why would you have to be more desperate to join a dating service than to place a personal ad or to hit the bar scene? If you want to meet people you should try every avenue.

Forget those myths you may have heard, like "Only losers sign up with dating services." People who make comments like that are either expressing their own fear of the unknown or basing their opinion on someone else's negative experience. Don't ever assume you'll have a negative experience just because somebody else did. If your friend broke his leg skiing, are you going to avoid the slopes because the same thing might happen to you?

And take therapy as an example. Remember the days when it wasn't acceptable to see a therapist? Back in those days, people felt compelled to harbor this deep dark secret even from their friends. We've come a long way since then. A weekly visit to the therapist is about as commonplace as a weekly workout at the gym.

It's the same thing with dating services. People used to shy away from them because they thought you had to be desperate to sign up. Or they were put off by the idea of paying somebody money to get them a date. But guess what? Whatever doubts and fears you have about joining a dating service, you can bet everyone else went through the same internal battles before going through with it. If you examine your objections one by one, you may find that they're easy to overcome. Instead of perceiving people who join dating services as "desperate," perceive them as the kind of people who "take the bull by the horns" and aggressively try to fulfill their needs. Why not just see it as a personal investment in your future?

When you join a dating service, you're usually asked to fill out an application, or biographical profile, which sometimes asks probing questions about the applicant's moral values, future goals, religious preferences, and lifestyle. The more detailed the profile, the better—because when you give them a lot of information about yourself, the dating service can get a better sense of who you are and who to match you up with.

At some dating services, singles are asked to come in for a personal interview after filling out the profile; others conduct the interview over the phone. The agencies have different ways of determining compatibility between members: they may use trained psychologists to counsel each client; they may rely on computers to match clients with similar characteristics; or they may sell lists of names and descriptions and let clients choose for themselves. Video dating services, where you will be videotaped as you answer questions about yourself, are a relatively new approach. If you're not camera-shy, this can be an excellent way to let someone "meet" you even before you've met them.

Membership costs vary greatly—of the dating services we've researched, the cost ranges from $25.00 to $250.00 for a one-year membership. So you see, singles at all levels of the economic scale can afford this method of meeting people.

Many of the dating service owners we interviewed gave us some impressive statistics about the number of marriages that resulted from the services' matchmaking efforts. We won't report them here, because the numbers won't mean as much to you as the personal accounts told by satisfied customers.

So we'll tell you about Joanne, who met her husband Albert through a dating service called Compatibility Plus.

Joanne had been dating for a long time in the hopes of finding someone who would turn out to be "marriage material." At age 39 she was starting to get a little worried that she wasn't going to find anyone to share her life with. She definitely felt receptive to settling down.

So she signed up with Compatibility Plus, and during her first three years of membership, she developed serious relationships with two of the men she was matched up with. But it wasn't until she met Albert that marriage became a real prospect for her.

On the evening of their first date, there was a snowstorm, Joanne recalled. "We sat in my living room and talked, and four and a half hours later, he left." Maybe that was Mother Nature's way of giving them a chance to really get to know each other.

"But Albert wasn't going to come back after the first date," she said good-naturedly. (Now that they're married, she can afford to be good-natured about it.) "He thought I was nice, but not quite right for him."

So what happened to change his mind? Well, he got an extra little push. Iris Feller, vice president of Compatibility Plus, urged the hesitant Albert to go back for two more dates before reaching his final verdict about Joanne.

"By the third time, he was hooked," Joanne reported happily. Her instincts had told her all along that Albert was right for her—and at least it didn't take him long to come around! "I can tell whether I like someone just from talking to him on the phone once," Joanne said.

She and Albert have been married for three years, and they've purchased a condominium in Hightstown, New Jersey. Albert loves to joke about the way they met; he tells people: "My wife cost me ninety-five dollars!"

The strangest coincidence about the way Joanne and Albert's paths crossed is that they lived on the same block for eighteen years as kids—but they never met in all that time they were neighbors! It wasn't until many years later that the dating service "reunited" them.

One cautionary word about dating services, though, before we launch into the list: do be careful when it comes to that first date with someone. Dating services can't possibly guarantee the integrity and stability of every client. Someone may present himself as a very nice, normal person during an initial interview, but that doesn't mean he's showing his true colors. We're not trying to make you feel paranoid about the people you'll meet; we're just suggesting that you be sensible about everything before you really get to know someone. Err on the side of caution.

For example, arrange the first meeting to take place in a public place, like a restaurant, movie theater, or museum—not your apartment. Or, as some dating services encourage, get to know someone through telephone conversations and/or letters before actually meeting them.

On to the listing! . . .

DATING SERVICES

THE BENNERS

WHERE: 281 E. 205th Street
Bronx, NY 10467
(212) 881-3037

WHAT: Here's how this works. You order a photo bulletin from The Benners, which includes names, addresses, and information about other members. Matches are made by comparing location, age group, backgrounds, and special interests. The Benners have been offering matchmaking services for over forty years.

WHO: There are about a thousand members of all ages, from a wide variety of backgrounds.

HOW MUCH: The photo bulletin can be ordered for $5.00 if you're a man or $3.00 if you're a woman. There are additional fees depending on how many contacts you request.

BETWEEN FRIENDS OF AMERICA, INC.

WHERE: 79 East Putnam Avenue
Greenwich, CT 06830
(203) 622-9041
(There are branches all over the United States.)

WHAT: A personalized dating service founded in 1982 that, according to a spokesperson, provides a "dignified, discreet, non-embarrassing way for unattached adults to meet." Between Friends doesn't use any computers or videos—just personal interviews.

WHO: There are fourteen thousand members nationwide, as young as 18 and as old as 85!

HOW MUCH: You can choose among eight membership plans—call for costs.

CHOICES VIDEO DATING CLUB

WHERE: 49 Riverside Avenue
Westport, CT 06880
(203) 226-2299

WHAT: This video dating service keeps a library of club members' personal profiles and videos on file. All members are allowed to go through the library files—but all information is kept confidential except for members' first names. If someone is interested in a particular member's file, the owner of the dating service (Terrie Poly) contacts that person and reviews the interested member's personal profile with him or her. Then, if there's interest on both sides, Terrie gives each one the other's phone number. This video dating service was started in January 1991.

WHO: Members are mostly people in their thirties and forties.

HOW MUCH: Contact Terrie Poly for information about membership procedures and costs.

COMPATIBILITY PLUS

WHERE: P.O. Box 3337
Wayne, NJ 07470
(201) 256-0202

WHAT: Psychologists at this fifteen-year-old dating service match potentially compatible singles based on the following: social profiles, which members fill out; long conversations between members and staffers at Compatibility Plus; and a feedback system after matches have been made. The detailed three-page social profile asks about such issues as race, religion; strength of religious convictions; preferred type of dating activity; smoking and drinking habits; personality traits (you're asked to check one box for each of thirty-three adjectives); and personal values and goals. After your matches have been picked for you, you'll receive their biographies before meeting them face to face.

WHO: Single professionals who are looking for solid, long-term relationships. There are about 2,800 members—mostly women ages 21 to 45 and men from 26 to 55.

HOW MUCH: Annual membership costs $245.00—with a guaranteed minimum of fifteen introductions per year.

CROSSROADS

WHERE: 321 East 43rd Street
New York, NY 10017
(212) 972-3594

WHAT: If you join CROSSROADS, you'll meet other singles in relaxed, personal settings, as well as through networking. You can attend different kinds of theme-oriented events. For example, you might want to sign up for one of their intimate, "by-invitation only" parties (at restaurants or in private homes); recreational events like skiing trips and tennis get-togethers; seminars; and concerts and other cultural events. All applicants are thoroughly screened and interviewed, and the CROSSROADS staff draws up the guest lists for all events in advance, matching up personal applications to coordinate compatible groups of people.

WHO: Members come from the tri-state area and Pennsylvania and are between the ages of 19 and 70. They are businesspeople, professionals, and academics with above-average levels of cultural and social awareness; over 95 percent have college degrees.

HOW MUCH: There are a few membership plans to choose from (full-service, limited-service, short-range, etc.). A full-service trial membership for a year—which entitles you to all the benefits—is $350.00.

DATELINE

WHERE: Locations in nine states, one of which is:
51 Shelton Road
Monroe, CT 06468
(203) 261-2908

WHAT: In its twenty years in business, this dating service has made more than a hundred thousand matches, and has resulted in thousands of marriages all over the country. Members fill out an application form (and are encouraged to include a recent photo, too), and within two to four weeks, they'll hook you up with your first match. Introductions are hand-picked for compatibility.

WHO: There are twenty-three thousand members all over the U.S., ages 20 to 80.

HOW MUCH: Costs are $25.00 for a three-month membership, $37.00 for six months, and $60.00 for a year.

DENISE WINSTON PERSONAL INTRODUCTIONS

WHERE: 200 East 61st Street
New York, NY 10021
(212) 935-9350

WHAT: You can rest easy about being fixed up with someone through this agency—they're not going to be ex-convicts, carriers of sexually-transmitted diseases, or embezzlers. All applicants have to pass investigation of their criminal, medical, and financial records in order to be accepted as members. Denise Winston uses a personal, confidential, and intimate approach to matchmaking. No computers or videos are used—just bios and photos.

The owner of this four-year-old dating service claims a high rate of success: more than a third of the members have reported meeting someone through Denise Winston with whom they developed relationships that lasted at least three months.

WHO: This is a select group of well-educated, successful, emotionally mature, well-groomed singles who have a genuine desire to get married. There are several hundred members, ranging in age from 23 to 83.

HOW MUCH: How much depends on the membership plan selected; contact Denise Winston for details.

FIELD'S EXCLUSIVE SERVICE, INC.

WHERE: 41 East 42nd Street, Room 1600
New York, NY 10017
(212) 391-2233

WHAT: Anyone who's seen "Fiddler on the Roof" will understand what we mean when we say that this dating service brings to mind the song "Tradition." Owner Dan Field calls his service a "marriage brokerage," and he's the third generation to carry on this tradition—which was founded by Grandpa Joe, a Russian emigrant and rabbi, as far back as 1920. Field will give you a list of forty to fifty names of people of all races, religions, and backgrounds—and you're free to contact anyone on that list who seems appealing. The owner recommends getting to know someone by letter for a while before contacting them. If you don't think anyone on that list will be compatible with you, he'll give you another list. But look out: sometimes well-meaning but meddlesome parents fill out application forms for their unsuspecting children! Tell Field's you don't want any applications someone's parents have filled out.

WHO: About eighty thousand people ages 18 and up have used Field's services.

HOW MUCH: The fee starts at $50.00 and depends on the level of service and the number of matches provided.

FRIENDSHIPS UNLIMITED

WHERE: P.O. Box 350
Brooklyn, NY 11202

WHAT: This one's been around for quite a while—since 1978. It's a computerized pen-pal service that brings people together from all areas of the world. You'll have to write a letter requesting an application, which will ask you personal information like age, hobbies, interests, occupation, and educational background. When you've sent back your completed application, the organization will do a computerized match-up of your characteristics with those of other members. Then they'll send you a list of at least five names and addresses. No phone numbers are given out initially, and no photos are exchanged. According to the founder of Friendships Unlimited, over 8,700 of its members have gotten married since the organization was founded.

WHO: Members include people from all over the world—more than twenty-four thousand of them, to be exact. The service reports members as young as 16 and as old as 89.

HOW MUCH: The owner reports that, because of their "tremendous response," they've actually reduced the membership fee to $15.00 a year (from $25.00) for men—and women don't have to pay any fee.

HANDICAP INTRODUCTIONS

WHERE: 152 Brigantine Road
P.O. Box 1215

Manahawkin, NJ 08050
(609) 660-0606

WHAT: This is a network of both handicapped and non-handicapped people who don't let their own or others' handicaps get in the way of an active social life. It's been around for about a decade. Members fill out detailed applications about themselves. The organization uses computers to eliminate obvious mismatches like incompatibility of age, height, or attitude toward marriage. After this process of elimination, a Ph.D.-level psychologist does the rest of the matchmaking process. At least six referrals are guaranteed for each six-month membership period.

WHO: Handicap Introductions has 650 members from ages 18 to 89. Not all members have handicaps—for example, one young lawyer from Florida who had spent four years in a wheelchair recovering from a car accident developed a whole new perspective on life and learned to look beyond the handicap at the person inside. "I now know that many of the most beautiful people in the world are handicapped," he said. "They have a beauty and tranquility that transcends the shallow physical idea of beauty that I grew up with. I want to meet someone like that."

HOW MUCH: Costs are $75.00 for six months or $125.00 a year if the member is employed; if he or she is on disability, the membership fee is $55.00 for half a year and $75.00 for a year.

THE INTRODUCTIONS CLUB, INC.

WHERE: 170 West End Avenue
New York, NY 10023
(212) 877-0728

WHAT: This is a personalized matchmaking service for single Jewish professionals, run by Dr. Barbara Chasen, a Ph.D. psychologist/psychoanalyst. All matchmaking is based on the personal interviews conducted with each member.

WHO: There are several hundred members ranging in age from 30 to 55 (women: 30 to 49, men: 35 to 55). Members must be single Jewish professionals with a high level of education.

HOW MUCH: Membership fees vary; contact Dr. Chasen for price quotes.

JEWISH DATING SERVICE

WHERE: There are several locations throughout the tri-state area, one of which is:

1260 New Britain Avenue, Suite 203
West Hartford, CT 06110
(203) 561-3250

WHAT: Matchmakers at this ten-year-old dating service have their Masters in Counseling, and they'll interview you to find out what kind of a person you are and what kind of person you're looking for. They'll also ask you to fill out an application. No computers are used. As you can probably figure out from the name, this service caters to Jewish clients only. Members are guaranteed a minimum of twelve matches.

WHO: Membership has reached about four thousand, and you'll find Jewish singles of all ages—from 20 to 70.

HOW MUCH: A two-year membership costs between $600.00 and $800.00—or you could opt for monthly memberships.

SOLUTION FOR SINGLES

WHERE: 2468 Lemoine Avenue
Fort Lee, NJ 07024
(201) 944-6171

659 Eagle Rock Ave.
West Orange, NJ 07052
(201) 669-8080

WHAT: This is a personalized dating service where the counselors sit down with each member and work closely with them to get to know their interests, tastes, and way of life. No computers or video tapes are used. After you've described yourself and what you're looking for in a mate, the counselors show you photos of other, potentially compatible members and discuss their profiles with you. Once you've started dating another member, the counselors will be available to give you advice on certain aspects of dating and relationships.

WHO: Members are college graduates and professional working people age 25 and up.

HOW MUCH: Membership plans range from $950.00 to $1,100.00.

SPECIAL SINGLES

WHERE: P.O. Box 903
Village Station, NY 10014
(212) 645-7378

WHAT: If you're physically disabled, call for a brochure, and you'll receive a personal profile to fill out. Instead of disclosing your name, you can use a code number to ensure anonymity. The idea is to send out as many profiles as possible to get several responses, and then you can screen out the ones you don't think you'd want to meet.

WHO: There are thirty members—limited to the tri-state area—ranging in age from twenties to sixties.

HOW MUCH: The cost is $75.00 for a one-year membership.

TOGETHER

WHERE: There are thirty-five locations nationwide (and in London and Toronto), but here's the address of the branch office we contacted:
457 Main Street
The Atrium Building
Danbury, CT
(203) 744-0665

WHAT: This is a seventeen-year-old dating service that brings people together by conducting in-depth personal interviews and asking all members to fill out a confidential "Compatibility Evaluation Guide" questionnaire. You'll probably meet your first match about ten days after you join TOGETHER.

NOTE: TOGETHER also has a travel club that organizes group trips to Caribbean destinations, Mexico, the Rocky Mountains, and other fun places. If you want information about these travel opportunities, contact The TOGETHER Traveler, 154 Winsted/Norfolk Road, Winsted, Connecticut 06098; tel. 1-800-942-9675.

WHO: Members are anywhere from 21 to 78 years old. In New York and Connecticut alone there are about five thousand members.

HOW MUCH: There are different kinds of membership plans, but the average cost is around $1,000.00 for annual membership.

VISUAL PREFERENCE LTD.

WHERE: 34 South Broadway
White Plains, NY 10601
(914) 683-1411
Connecticut: (203) 353-1400
New York: (212) 627-8677

WHAT: There are two ways you can get hooked up with someone through this dating service: video matchups and photo exchanges. Now in its sixth year, Visual Preference will work with you to produce a videotape on which you answer some questions about yourself. That video will be mailed to members whose profiles suggest they might be compatible with you. Or, you can exchange photos and written profiles. You might be interested to know that the president of this dating service introduced the concept of video dating to New York back in 1974.

WHO: Members are professionals and businesspeople whose romantic goals aren't being met through other social settings.

HOW MUCH: There are a few membership plans to choose from, one costing $25.00 a week. But take advantage of their free consultation (make an appointment).

VITAL ENCOUNTERS

WHERE: P.O. Box 2519
Stamford, CT 06906
(203) 975-94893

WHAT: A matching service that serves only singles aged fifty and over. Matchmaking is done in a very non-threatening way: a newsletter is published four times a year, and it contains personal ads from singles throughout the tri-state area. If someone's ad seems appealing to you, you can respond to that ad. You can also place your own ad in the newsletter. There's no need to include addresses; you will be assigned a code number, and responses will be sent to the attention of that number. Vital Encounters will forward the responses to you.

HOW MUCH: The cost is $20.00 for a one-year subscription, $10.00 for a single issue. It costs $20.00 to advertise (up to 55 words) in four issues, $15.00 to advertise in two issues, and $10.00 to advertise in one issue.

MATCHMAKING PARTIES

This is a great concept, and there are quite a few organizations that host these events. Some of them combine the festive, nonthreatening atmosphere of a party with the dating service concept of matchmaking (you'll see exactly what we mean when you read the listings); others are less structured and simply bring hundreds of singles together—by invitation or through publicity—to a club or restaurant, or even to someone's apartment.

If you're hesitant to join a social club that meets on a regular basis or dubious about signing up with a dating service because the idea of a long-term membership commitment doesn't appeal to you, you'll want to attend one of these matchmaking parties. There are no obligations beyond that one evening, and you can talk to whomever you want to. There'll be a huge gathering of people to choose from, and if you go with a friend, you can rescue each other from awkward conversations or situations.

CALCULATED COUPLES

WHERE: Corporate Headquarters:
Innovations in Corporations, Inc.
3370 N. Hayden Road, Suite 123-296
Scottsdale, AZ 85251
(800) 44-MATCH

WHAT: Here's how this one works: You fill out a personal-profile questionnaire, and the information is matched to a minimum of three other singles' personal profiles. Those will be the three people you have to find at the Calculated Couples matchmaking party (everyone will be wearing a badge with a personal identification number on it). The nice thing about this approach is that, even if you're not attracted to or don't hit it off with the three people whose numbers you've been assigned, there's a whole roomful of other singles you can mingle with.

WHO: Participants are singles from all walks of life, ages 22 to 55. This is a nationwide service, but if you attend a Calculated Couples matchmaking party in, say, Long Island, chances are you'd be mingling with fellow-New Yorkers.

HOW MUCH: There are no membership fees, but it costs $5.00 to attend each party.

CONNECTICUT CONTACTS

WHERE: 64 East Grand Avenue
New Haven, CT 06513
(203) 468-1144

WHAT: This isn't a dating service in the strict sense of the word. Connecticut Contacts hosts two dances a week: "Ladies' Choice" every Friday night at the Pinecrest Country Club in Shelton, and "Singles' Sunday" every—well, you can guess which night—at the Colonial Tavern in Oxford. You'll dance to top 40 hits and soft rock, and you can help yourself to the hot and cold hors d'oeuvres buffet. The dance parties aren't the same every week—there are different themes like "Karaoke Night," "Italian Festival," "Polynesian Party," "Super '70s," Poolside Party," and the like.

WHO: Participants are singles in their late twenties, thirties, forties, and fifties. There are twelve thousand people on the organization's mailing list—but don't expect to see them all at every event!

HOW MUCH: Admission to dances is $8.00; there are no other costs.

DISCOVERY CENTER

WHERE: 200 West 72nd Street, Suite 68A
New York, NY 10023
(800) 777-0338

WHAT: Discovery Center offers a three-hour social opportunity called "Party Meet," which has a format designed to help you socialize in a comfortable but structured way. First you exchange small talk with six to eight people in each group. Conversations are initiated by the leader of the group—a singles expert—who introduces new, provocative subjects for discussion as you rotate to the different groups. The cost of attending a Party Meet is $24.00.

The Discovery Center also hosts a wide array of classes and events, such as skills improvement seminars (photography, computers, etc.), wine tasting classes, and whitewater rafting.

LE JUDA

WHERE: 381 Park Avenue South, Suite 1112
New York, NY 10016
(212) 213-5515

WHAT: Le Juda sponsors weekly dances and parties at various clubs, hotels, and Jewish Centers in the tri-state area. When you attend an event, you can register to become a member or put your name on the mailing list to receive monthly mailings from the organization. An example of a typical event is "Some Enchanted Evening," hosted at CI, a Park Avenue nightspot. The event was designed so Jewish singles in their twenties and thirties could enjoy cocktails and quiet conversation in an intimate, upscale setting. Le Juda also sponsors numerous theme parties ("After-Work Party," "Moonlight Boat Party," etc.) and weekend trips. This organization has been in business for over fifteen years.

WHO: There are twenty thousand names on the mailing list. Most of the members range in age from 22 to 49.

HOW MUCH: There's no membership cost. Party admission is about $12.00 or $15.00, depending on the event.

THE LEARNING ANNEX

WHERE: 2330 Broadway
New York, NY 10024
(212) 580-2828

WHAT: The Learning Annex offers two party concepts designed to help participants meet people in a relaxed atmosphere: "Progressive Dinner Parties"—where diners change seats after every course so everyone gets a chance to converse with everyone else—and "Getting To Know You" parties—which use a series of easy writing/communication exercises in small groups to explore attitudes and feelings about romance and relationships. The Learning Annex is also a great place to take a class in just about anything.

WHO: Singles in their twenties to sixties; some have found out about the matchmaking parties while taking other courses at the Learning Annex.

HOW MUCH: The cost of attending is $29.00.

MANHATTAN SINGLES, LTD.

WHERE: 200 E. 78th Street, Suite 9D
New York, NY 10021
(212) 744-8515

WHAT: This organization mails out about twelve thousand invitations for its annual singles events, which usually bring in about four hundred people per event. You can expect buffet, DJ music, dancing, and lots of socializing. This year's singles get-togethers were held at, among other places, Casey's Dance Hall & Saloon (1584 York Avenue) and at Tavern on the Green (Central Park at the West 67th Street entrance). If you're between 28 and 48, you can be on the mailing list.

WHO: Participants are singles aged 28 to 48 from the tri-state area, including many professionals and upscale singles.

HOW MUCH: Events cost $15.00 to $20.00, which includes admission and buffet (drinks cost extra).

HEALTH & FITNESS CLUBS

Don't underestimate the social potential of health and fitness clubs. Sure, they're great places to burn off those calories and tone those muscles, but they also happen to be excellent meeting places for singles.

Being surrounded by all those biceps and thighs, it's hard to concentrate on your aerobic exercises—but you can always strike up a conversation later at the lounge with that gorgeous person you spotted on the Stairmaster! Become a member and you'll have the opportunity to see the same people over and over—in case you're too shy to approach them the first time around.

If you've never set foot inside a health club, let's make something clear for you right now: You don't have to look like Jane Fonda or Arnold Schwarzenegger to fit in. People of all shapes and sizes work out at these places, and there are exercise routines and classes for people at all levels of fitness.

Many health clubs have swimming pools and racquetball courts; some even have cocktail lounges and dance floors. You could conceivably spend a whole day at one of these clubs, alternating between working out on the Nautilus equipment, swimming, playing racquetball or squash, having snacks at the juice bar, and even sunning yourself on the roof deck.

If you're a single parent, ask about their child-care services; many health clubs are offering babysitting and group child care at reasonable rates.

Ask a friend to take you along on "guest night," if he or she is a member of a health club, so you can see what it's all about before committing yourself to membership. But we'd suggest that you join, because you can't really get a sense of what it would be like on a regular basis just from dropping in once. Besides, paying annual membership in the hundreds of dollars definitely gives you the incentive to be disciplined about staying fit!

BODY BY SERGE GYM INC.

WHERE: 692 Greenwich Street
New York, NY 10014
(212) 675-1179
Accessible to the Sixth, Seventh, and Eighth Avenue subway lines (E, F, and #1, 2, and 3); or take the Path train from Jersey. There's plenty of parking nearby.

WHAT: This is a fully-equipped health club with free weights, Nautilus equipment, Stairmasters, stationary bicycles—plus a sun-tanning bed, lockers, and showers. There are five personal trainers; they don't give class instruction. When you feel you've burned up enough calories, allow yourself a visit to the snack bar.

WHO: Members are mostly guys (about 70 percent)—but the good news is, mostly single guys. About 80 percent of the club's 250 members are single, and a lot of professional people work out here. There's a mixed Lower West Side membership group.

WHEN: Monday, Wednesday, and Friday from 6:30 in the morning till 10:00 at night; Tuesday and Thursday from 10:00 a.m. to 10:00 p.m.; and Saturday and Sunday from 10:00 a.m. till 6:00 p.m. Go after work (if you work nine to five) if you're looking to meet someone.

HOW MUCH: Costs are $550.00 for one year; $390.00 for six months; $275.00 for three months; $200.00 for two months; $125.00 for one month; or $10.00 a day if you don't want to make a long-term commitment. Costs for personal training: $50.00 for one session; $540.00 for twelve sessions; $960.00 for twenty-four sessions; $35.00 per session if you commit to more than thirty-six sessions. Sun-tanning sessions: $10.00 for twenty minutes; $15.00 for thirty minutes; or $150.00 for eleven half-hour sessions. Locker rental: $7.00 or $10.00 a month (depending on the size); $40.00 or $55.00 for six months; $75.00 or $100.00 for a year.

Body By Serge has an annual membership installment plan, in case you don't want to lay out the whole sum at the beginning. You'd make a down payment of $250.00, and then pay $100.00 each month for four months.

BODY IMAGE HEALTH CLUB

WHERE: Route 6
Mahopac, NY 10541
(914) 628-1015
Drive, because it's not close to public transportation. Free parking available.

WHAT: The club offers nautilus equipment and free weights. There's no class instruction, but there are ten fitness instructors who can give you personal attention.

WHO: 70 percent male; 30 percent female—and about three-quarters of the members are single. You don't have to be a member to use the equipment.

WHEN: The club is open from 9:00 a.m. till 11:00 p.m. every day. The best chance of meeting someone is in the evenings. There have actually been several engagements between members who have met at this workout facility.

HOW MUCH: $299.00 for annual membership.

BQE RACQUETBALL & FITNESS CENTER

WHERE: 26-50 BQE Expressway West
Woodside, NY 11377
(718) 545-8900
Take the N train to Northern Boulevard, or bring your car and park for free.

WHAT: You won't believe what a singles' hangout this is! Even without the exercise facilities, you could hang out here and meet someone in the lounge—at any time of day or night. But there are a lot of exercise facilities: a forty-four-foot indoor pool, Nautilus/Universal circuits (over a hundred machines), free weights, fourteen racquetball courts, a separate women's gym, and a cardiovascular section. If you come alone and want to play racquetball, BQE will match you up with a partner.

Other amenities include a unisex salon where you can have your hair done, get a facial, and have a massage; men's and women's sauna and steam rooms, a pro shop, a chiropractic wellness center, and free nursery service.

Class instruction is offered in calisthenics, aerobics, and karate—or you can get one-on-one training. There are twenty Nautilus trainers and fifteen aerobics instructors.

You could spend hours here: first do a good workout, play a game of racquetball, or take a class—then you can take a dip in the pool before having dinner at the restaurant or drinks at the lounge. If you've still got energy left, you can dance the night away at the BQE disco.

WHO: There are about ten thousand members, about half of them single. Women aren't outnumbered here.

WHEN: The club is open around the clock every day of the week

HOW MUCH: Membership costs $299.00 for a year and $499.00 for two years. You have to be a member to be admitted into the club, unless a member brings you as a guest (there's a $9.95 guest fee).

CARMEL FITNESS & POOL CLUB

WHERE: Old Route 6
Carmel, NY 10512

(914) 225-0888
Not accessible via public transportation. Free parking available.

WHAT: There's an indoor pool, indoor tennis and racquetball courts, Nautilus equipment, and cardiovascular machines. Group and private tennis and racquetball lessons are offered, and you can rent equipment. Courts should be reserved up to a week in advance.

Parties and leagues are sponsored.

WHEN: 7:00 a.m. till 11:00 p.m.

HOW MUCH: Membership costs $55.00 a month. Tennis is $10.00 an hour for members, $32.00 an hour for non-members; racquetball is free for members, $15.00 an hour for non-members. Tennis and racquetball lessons are $35.00 to $45.00 an hour.

CLUB FIT

WHERE: Lee Boulevard
Jefferson Valley, NY 10535
(914) 245-4040

North State Road
Briarcliff Manor, NY
(914) 762-3444

1 North Broadway
White Plains, NY
(914) 946-0404

Westchester County buses can take you to any of these locations. Parking is free.

WHAT: At Club Fit you can play indoor and outdoor tennis or racquetball, swim laps in the pool, jog around the indoor track, play volleyball and basketball in the gym, and work out at the Fitness & Cardio Center. You can rent racquetball equipment, but bring your own tennis racquet and balls. There are eight tennis courts and six racquetball courts.

Aerobic dance and exercise classes are offered, as well as tennis and racquetball instruction—both individual and group. A word of advice: reserve courts up to a week in advance.

In addition to the workout facilities Club Fit has a whirlpool, massage parlor, locker rooms, a boutique, hair salon, nursery, and a cafe.

"Single Mingles" are sponsored for non-members.

WHEN: Hours are 6:00 a.m. till 11:00 p.m. The best time to meet singles is after 4:00 p.m.

HOW MUCH: There are a number of different memberships to take advantage of: individual membership, couple membership, family membership, senior membership (60 and over), junior membership (17 and under), college membership for out-of-town college students; and premium individual or premium couple membership—which entitles you to full access to all three Club Fit facilities. We won't mention all the different prices here, but a regular individual membership costs $300.00 for initiation and $67.00 monthly thereafter.

It costs $8.00 an hour to play tennis, but use of racquetball courts is free with membership.

THE DIAGONAL CLUB, INC.

WHERE: 556 North Country Road
St. James, NY 11780
(516) 862-8888
Located near the Long Island Railroad St. James station. Free parking facilities.

WHAT: This is more than just a health & fitness club: it's a social scene and a business networking club.

Special get-togethers are hosted, such as dinner cruises, parties at local bars, social events at the club, and seminars.

Over fifty classes a week are offered at The Diagonal Club by twelve instructors (two of whom are exercise physiologists): Step classes, toning classes, kick boxing, high-energy fitness, hi-lo combo; and free personal one-on-one training with membership.

Equipment includes Nautilus, Stairmasters, treadmills, Lifecycles, rowers, Nordic Traks, and a large free-weight area. Nonmembers can use the equipment if they call a day in advance to reserve.

Free daycare services are offered. Drinks and snacks are sold. The club also offers massage therapy, facials, and manicures, for an additional fee.

WHO: At last count there were 1,100 members—half male/half female. A high percentage (about 70 percent) is single. For the most part the membership is made up of affluent local people with considerable discretionary income.

WHEN: The club is open Monday through Friday from 6:00 a.m. till 10:00 p.m. Best time for singles: evenings between 5:00 and 10:00 p.m.

HOW MUCH: Memberships range in price from $250.00 to $600.00 a year.

THE FITNESS CONNECTION

WHERE: 1320 Stony Brook Road
Stony Brook, NY 11790
(516) 751 3959

347A Nesconset Highway
Hauppauge, NY 11788
(516) 265-9838

Both locations are near the Long Island Railroad, and local buses also stop there. There's free parking.

WHAT: Fully equipped with Nautilus machines, free weights, a heated whirlpool and steam room, an indoor UVA tanning salon, and nursery facilities. Refreshments are available at the snack bar. The cardiovascular center has computerized Aerobicycles, rowing machines, Stairmasters, Nordic Traks, and Monarch exercise bikes.

The Fitness Connection has twenty-five instructors and offers classes in aerobics (beginner, intermediate, and advanced); and the staff will monitor your weight settings and chart your progress in the Nautilus program. Over sixty-five classes are offered each week. They also have a wellness council that promotes seminars on health-related topics like weight loss, stress reduction, and giving up smoking.

That's not all. Special activities are sponsored for members, like an annual picnic, Christmas party, beach parties, golf outings, ski trips, workshops, "Summer Fun Party," "Spring into Shape Party," Halloween party, and "Membership Appreciation Night."

WHO: The Stony Brook location has about 2,500 members, and the Hauppague location—which is new—already has 1,000 members. There's an even mix of men and women, and you'll find more singles than marrieds here (about 60 percent singles). The owner reports that there have been several marriages between people who have met at The Fitness Connection.

WHEN: The facilities are open every day, a hundred hours a week. Any time's a good time to meet other singles.

HOW MUCH: You'll pay from $15.00 to $30.00 a month, and $275.00 to $375.00 a year. Call and ask to receive a brochure; when you bring in that brochure, you're eligible for a free fitness evaluation and workout.

FLEX APPEAL GYM

(Formerly known as Sports Conditioning of Brooklyn, Inc.)

WHERE: 505 Ovington Avenue
Brooklyn, NY 11209
(718) 745-5724

WHAT: The club's six instructors will train clients on all pieces of equipment (two and a half circuits of Nautilus, aerobic machines, Lifecycles, treadmills, step/stair climbers, ski machines, rowers, and recumbent bikes) and will monitor their progress.

One-on-one training is available, but no class instruction.

WHO: There are 150 members, with an equal number of men and women.

WHEN: Hours are Monday, Tuesday, Thursday, and Friday from 10:00 a.m. till 9:00 p.m.; Wednesday from 5:30 p.m. till 9:00 p.m.; and Saturday from 9:30 a.m. till 3:00 p.m.

HOW MUCH: The cost of membership is $435.00 a year; there are no contracts or payment plans. Memberships can also be purchased for shorter periods of time (monthly, three-month, and six-month memberships). One-on-one training is offered for $25.00 an hour or $120.00 a month.

GREENWICH YWCA

WHERE: 259 East Putnam Avenue
Greenwich, CT 06830
(203) 869-6501
Accessible by bus and train—call to find out which bus or train to take from your location. Parking is free.

WHAT: At this YWCA you'll find a gym, dance studio, tennis courts, and a pool—plus classrooms and meeting rooms. They offer instruction in aerobics (step and rebound), ballet, tennis, swimming, volleyball, and badminton. There's also a snack bar.

WHO: You'll come across people of all ages here, both single and married. The ratio of men to women, or singles to marrieds, depends on the activity you choose.

WHEN: Monday through Friday from 7:30 in the morning till 10:00 at night, and Saturday from 9:00 a.m. to 4:00 p.m.. Best times to meet other singles would be early mornings, lunchtime, and during evening volleyball and badminton sessions.

HOW MUCH: A one-year membership costs $50.00. You can come as a guest for the first three visits, but after that the Y requires that you join as a member.

HEIGHTS CLUB INC.

WHERE: 85 Livingston Street
Brooklyn, NY 11201
(718) 875-8131
Take the F train to Court Street.

WHAT: The Heights Club has a pool, Camstar and Cybex machines, Stairmasters, treadmills, and free weights—plus sauna and steam rooms, massage parlor, and a juice bar. There are fifteen instructors offering step classes, training in high- and low-impact aerobics, calisthenics, yoga, boxing, karate, and streamlining. One-on-one training is available, too.

WHO: Women are slightly outnumbered (three-to-two ratio). There are about 1,800 members.

WHEN: The club is open sixteen hours a day, every day.

HOW MUCH: Annual membership is $250.00

KEW GARDENS HEALTH AND FITNESS CENTER

WHERE: 119-40 Metropolitan Avenue
Kew Gardens, NY 11415
(718) 847-9690
Take the E or F train and then walk up Continental Avenue to Metropolitan Avenue (there's also a local bus that takes you from the intersection of Continental Avenue and Queens Boulevard to Metropolitan Avenue. There are no parking facilities

WHAT: This facility is equipped with resistance weight machines, Lifecycles, Stairmasters, treadmills, rowing machines, sauna, tanning room, and free weights. Instruction is offered in step aerobics, high- and low-impact aerobics, muscle toning, and circuit training. There are six instructors. You can also get one-on-one training, fitness evaluations, and consultation on personalized fitness and weight reduction programs. Massages and facials are offered, too

Holiday parties are sponsored for members

WHO: This club has a membership of about five hundred, about 75 percent of which is singles. Men and women usually come here in equal numbers

WHEN: The center is open Monday through Friday from 6:30 a.m. till 10:00 p.m.; Saturday from 9:00 a.m. till 6:00 p.m., and Sunday from 10:00 a.m. till 6:00 p.m. Evenings are your best bet for meeting someone, because that's when it gets the most crowded

HOW MUCH: It costs $350.00 a year to be a member; there's a $10.00 guest fee.

PALMS POOL & RACQUET CLUB

WHERE: 101 Quintard Street
Staten Island, NY 10305
(718) 816-1717
Accessible by subway and bus. Free parking available

WHAT: There's a fifty-foot pool, a jacuzzi, steam room and sauna in each locker room, a tanning room, racquetball courts, Lifecycles, Liferowers, treadmills, Stairmasters, Lifesteps, Nordic Trak, Nautilus equipment, and free weights. Babysitting services are offered, and there is a snack bar.

You can take body toning classes and step aerobics; there are eight instructors.

WHO: A wide variety of people belong to the club, including lots of singles.

WHEN: Hours are Monday through Thursday, 9:00 a.m. till 11:00 p.m.; Friday from 9:00 a.m. to 9:00 p.m.; Saturday from 9:00 a.m. till 7:00 p.m.; and Sunday from 9:00 a.m. to 5:00 p.m. Your best socializing opportunities would be from 5:00 to 9:30 p.m.

HOW MUCH: You'll pay $500.00 for a thirteen-month membership. (If you don't want to pay it all in one lump sum, you can put down a hundred dollars and then pay $40.00 a month.)

ULTRAFIT HEALTH & FITNESS CENTER

WHERE: 1000 North Main Street
Brewster, NY 10509
(914) 279-7415
Located near the Metro North Brewster station. Parking facilities are free.

WHAT: The center has a full line of Universal equipment, free weights, and cardiovascular equipment. Classes are offered in aerobics, stretching, karate, body sculpting, weight training, and Nisei Gojo Rye training. There are eight or nine instructors.

Special events are sponsored from time to time, such as a summer picnic, karate tournaments, and Christmas parties.

The atmosphere at Ultrafit is very relaxed and easygoing. There's a juice bar, which offers some energy snacks.

WHEN: Hours are Monday through Thursday from 9:00 a.m. till 10:00 p.m.; Fridays from 9:00 a.m. till 8:00 p.m.

WHO: There are between 300 and 375 members, with about two men for every woman.

HOW MUCH: Membership costs $40.00 a month; $100.00 for three months, or $360.00 for an annual membership. Nonmembers can reserve the use of equipment on a daily basis and pay a fee.

VERTICAL CLUB

WHERE: 330 East 61st Street
New York, NY 10021
(212) 355-5100
(This is one of four Manhattan locations)

WHEN: Weekdays from 6:00 a.m. till 11:00 p.m.; weekends from 9:00 a.m. till 9:00 p.m.

WHAT: This is a very social health club, frequented by lots of singles—and it's been voted one of the three best clubs in the country by a health and fitness magazine. Celebrities hang out here, too.

The Vertical Club's facilities include an Olympic-size pool, indoor track, sauna, steam room, whirlpool, racquetball, tennis, and squash courts, a rock-climbing wall, and Nautilus and Universal workout equipment. A good place to seek out some conversation when you've finished working out is the sundeck on the roof, or the juice bar.

You can also sign up for one-on-one or group instruction in step aerobics, dance, stretch, plus squash and tennis.

Occasionally the club hosts casual get-togethers for its members.

HOW MUCH: Executive membership costs $899.00 per year; tennis membership, $4,000.00 per year.

WESTCHESTER ATHLETIC CLUB

WHERE: 950 Broadway
Thornwood, NY 10594
(914) 747-1300
Bring your car and park it for free, or take the train (Metro North) or bus.

WHAT: Workout equipment includes Nautilus and Eagle Cybex machines, treadmills, Stairmasters, rowers, Versaclimber, and stationary bikes. This club also has racquetball and basketball courts. Replenish your energy stores at the snack bar.

They offer a number of classes every day of the week—such as low-impact aerobics, muscle toning, exertone (breathing, stretching, and exercise techniques), cardiovascular exercise classes, and jazzercise a one-hour dance/fitness program consisting of warmup exercises, a choreographed aerobic segment, floorwork, and cool-down). There are ten to twelve instructors.

WHO: The male/female ratio is four to three. Lots of singles come here.

WHEN: The club is open Monday through Friday from 5:00 a.m. (does *anyone* get up that early?) till 10:00 p.m.; Saturday and Sunday from 9:00 a.m. to 5:00 p.m. If you're looking to meet someone, go between 5:00 and 8:00 in the evenings. Call for their class schedule.

HOW MUCH: A year's membership costs $425.00. There's an $8.00 guest fee.

DANCE INSTRUCTION

Always wanted to learn to dance? Or maybe you never cared until you got invited to be in your friend's wedding party—and then suddenly you wished you knew how to do a few dance steps. You imagine yourself dancing with the best man or with the maid of honor—in the middle of the wide-open dance floor, with the spotlights and a hundred pair of eyes focused on you—and you don't have the slightest idea of when to move your feet.

Even if you're not in the wedding party, it would be a shame if you had to sit on the sidelines and fake a headache whenever someone came over to ask you to dance.

Well, here's a thought. Take group lessons at one of your local dance schools, and you may end up with more than just a dance partner!

Group dance lessons can be a very enjoyable way to expand your circle of friends. Although many couples sign up together for dance lessons, you'll also find many singles who attend these classes alone.

Many of the dance schools host dance socials on a weekly or monthly basis, with DJ music, refreshments, and dance contests.

If you've got rhythm and you love moving to the music, signing up for dance lessons could be a perfect opportunity for you to meet new people while doing something you enjoy.

ARTHUR MURRAY

WHERE: Several locations throughout the tri-state area; here's one of them:
655 Jericho Turnpike (near the St. James train station)
St. James, NY 11780
(516) 862-6211

WHAT: At Arthur Murray dance studios, you can learn dances like the foxtrot, waltz, tango, mambo, chacha, swing, lindy, samba, hustle, rumba, and merengue. There are six instructors, and they'll allow up to thirty students per class for group lessons. You must sign up as a member to receive lessons. In a typical class the age range of participants is from 30 to 45. Both couples and singles come to learn, but singles are paired up.

Once a week students practice their dancing at the practice parties. The school also hosts a variety of dance socials and dance competitions.

WHEN: The studio is open from 1:30 until 10:30 p.m.

DANCE & ATHLETIC CLUB OF BRONXVILLE

WHERE: 72 Palmer Avenue
Bronxville, NY 10708
(914) 337-3542
By car, take the Cross County Parkway or the Bronx River Parkway. You can also get there by bus and by train (Harlem line).

WHAT: This fitness center offers two spacious dance studios and teaches classes in aerobics, exercise, ballet, tap, jazz, modern dance, karate, and yoga—from beginner to advanced, all ages. There are ten dance instructors.

The club also has a weight room with a state-of-the-art weight training circuit, free weights, treadmills, stair climbers, and stationary and computerized bicycles.

Other amenities: men's and women's locker rooms with showers and sauna, a juice bar and lounge, a boutique that sells activewear, and parking facilities. If you're a single parent, you can bring your child to this club—they offer babysitting services and classes for pre-schoolers.

WHEN: Club hours are Monday through Thursday from 6:00 a.m. to 10:00 p.m.; Friday from 6:00 a.m. to 8:00 p.m., Saturday from 9:00 am to 5:00 p.m., and Sunday from 9:00 a.m. to 3:00 p.m.

HOW MUCH: You'll pay $12.00 for each lesson you attend.

DANCE CITY

WHERE: 465 C Route 112
Patchogue, NY 11772
(516) 654-0150
Not accessible by public transportation, but free parking is available.

WHAT: Here you can learn all forms of ballroom dancing, both American and international, and attend dance parties every other Friday night from 9:00 p.m. Refreshments are served at the parties.

The classes generally attract people in their forties, and there are typically about three women for every man. (Guys: Get ready to be surrounded!) The highest number of students they'll accept in a class is fifteen, but it won't be less than six. There are seven instructors. You can either bring a partner or get paired up when you get there.

WHEN: Dance classes are held every Monday from 7:00 to 8:00 p.m., but you'd have to make an appointment for individual lessons. And don't forget: every other Friday night from 9:00 p.m., attend those dance parties.

HOW MUCH: Costs are $45.00 an hour for private lessons, $8.00 per person for the Monday night class, and $8.00 to attend the dance party (refreshments included).

DANCE EXTRAVAGANZA

WHERE: 99-20 Metropolitan Avenue
Forest Hills, NY 11375
(718) 520-1898
If you're not driving, take the Q23 or Q53 bus. If you don't live near a bus stop where that line runs, take the E, F, or R train to Continental Avenue and catch the bus there. Dance Extravaganza offers free parking.

WHAT: A place to learn ballroom, Latin, disco, lambada, and even belly dancing! There are five instructors, and in a typical class, you'd find students from their twenties to their fifties. The male/female ratio is about 40/60. You don't need to bring your own partner.

Every other week the instructors and students get together for a dance social. If you get really good, you can participate in competitions and showcases.

WHEN: The Dance Extravaganza is open every day from 3:00 to 10:00 p.m.

HOW MUCH: $199.00 will get you five lessons.

DANCE OBSESSION

WHERE: 18 Hempstead Turnpike
Farmingdale, NY 11735
(516) 753-2121
It's a five-minute walk from the Farmingdale train station (LIRR). If you're driving, you can park in front of the studio or at the shopping center next door.

WHAT: They teach social dancing, both American style and International style—and they specialize in competitive dancing. You'll learn to do the foxtrot, waltz, tango, quickstep, rumba, cha-cha, swing, hustle, samba, mambo, and merengue. There are eight instructors.

No need to bring a partner: there'll be other singles in the group. The average age in a typical group is 35, and there are about eight men for every ten women.

Right after the group class on Friday nights (at 10:15 p.m.), there's a dance social that runs till a quarter after midnight. There you can enjoy coffee, soda, and cakes in between dancing to a variety of music.

WHEN: The studio is open Tuesdays through Fridays from 1:00 to 11:00 p.m., and Saturdays from 1:00 to 6:00 p.m.

HOW MUCH: The cost of a group lesson is $10.00 per person, but you'll get your first lesson free and a discount on your first package deal. It costs $6.00 to attend the dance social.

DANCIN' TIME DANCE STUDIO

WHERE: 1029 Jericho Turnpike
Smithtown, NY 11787
(516) 864-9741
Not far from the Smithtown train station (LIRR). Free parking.

WHAT: This is a place to learn the fox trot, waltz, Viennese waltz, tango, rumba, cha-cha, swing, merengue, samba, hustle, disco, peabody, and quickstep. Most students are in their thirties and forties, and there are about twice as many women as men. Most get paired with other students in the class. There are six instructors, and they won't accept more than ten or less than four members per group.

Dance socials are hosted two Saturdays a month.

WHEN: The studio is open from 4:00 to 10:00 p.m. Call for a schedule of group lessons and dance socials.

HOW MUCH: Costs are $7.50 per person for a group lesson and $50.00 for a private lesson; $9.00 to attend a dance social.

DORIS AND JOHN'S INTERNATIONAL SCHOOL OF DANCING, INC.

WHERE: 5 Fifth Avenue & West Main Street
Bay Shore, NY 11706
(516) 665-1766
Accessible by Long Island Railroad and buses that run along Merrick Road. Free parking is available. (This is one of four locations.)

WHAT: The school offers ballroom, Latin, and disco dancing lessons. The age range of the students is 25 to 55; the ratio of men to women is typically two to one. (Finally, a dance school where women are outnumbered!) Classes have a minimum of ten students and a maximum of twenty. There are six instructors.

Dance socials are held on Friday and Saturday nights after class. On Fridays the party lasts from 10:00 p.m. till midnight and costs $7.50 per person. The Saturday party starts at 9:30 p.m. and goes on till 1:00 a.m.; the cost is $15.00 per couple.

FRED ASTAIRE DANCE STUDIO

WHERE: 25 W. Hartsdale Avenue
Hartsdale, NY 10530
(914) 949-2553
It's near the Metro North train station, but you'll have no problem parking your car in their ample free parking facilities. This is one of 240 Fred Astaire franchises.

WHAT: This is where you learn to dance like Fred Astaire and Ginger Rogers. Well, okay, maybe that's an exaggeration. But you will learn to master the steps of dances like the salsa, rumba, merengue, foxtrot, waltz, tango, and disco and Latin dancing.

Most students come solo and get paired up with other class members or instructors, but you won't necessarily get paired up with a member of the opposite sex, because women outnumber men by about two to one. The age range is typically 35 to 50. A class won't be larger than twelve students. There are six instructors.

Dance socials are hosted on the last Friday of every month, which the studio calls a "Practice & Guest Party" (you can bring a guest). The studio occasionally hosts special bashes, like the "Fred Astaire Hartsdale Evening at Glen Island Casino," where the really advanced students perform. There are also benefit performances, dancethons, and competitions between the Hartsdale and Manhattan Fred Astaire Dance Studios for all levels of dancers.

WHEN: Open from 1:30 to 10:30 p.m., Monday through Friday, and from 1:30 to 5:30 on Saturdays. Call for a calendar of events and a newsletter.

HOW MUCH: Costs are $18.50 per person for group instruction, $55.00 for a private lesson.

FRED ASTAIRE DANCE STUDIO

WHERE: 207-20 Northern Boulevard
Bayside, NY 11361
(718) 225-1980
Accessible to buses and the Long Island Railroad.

WHAT: This is one of 240 Fred Astaire franchises. The emphasis is on social ballroom dancing, Latin, and disco. The maximum number of students per class is thirty, and the minimum is six. There are four instructors.

A lot of singles take dancing lessons here; the age range is about 21 to 65, and there's a fairly even mix of male and female students.

In-studio dance parties are held here twice a month, and out-of-studio dance parties are held once a month.

WHEN: Studio hours are Monday through Friday from 1:00 till 10:00 p.m.

FRED ASTAIRE STUDIO

WHERE: 1445 Northern Boulevard
Manhasset, NY 11030
(516) 365-6155

4010 Hempstead Tpke
Bethpage, NY 11714
(516) 520-0102

WHEN: Daily from 2:00 p.m. till 11:00 p.m.

WHAT: Ballroom, Latin, disco, and lindy are taught here; the class size varies (there is no restriction on minimum and maximum number of students). There are twelve instructors. The age range is 30 to 65, and the male/female ratio is about 60/40. Most students register alone and get paired up with other members.

HOW MUCH: Group lessons cost $10.00 an hour, and a set of introductory lessons (one group and two private) costs $15.00.

PAUL PELLICORO'S DANCESPORT

WHERE: 1845 Broadway (at 60th Street)
New York, NY 10023
(212) 307-1111

WHAT: A huge, three-story ballroom and Latin dance studio where you can learn how to do the Argentine tango, salsa, fox trot, mambo, rumba, merengue, lindy, hustle, cha-cha, peabody, the quickstep, waltzes, and swing.

The instructors give both group and private lessons. Practice parties are hosted from time to time.

HOW MUCH: Take advantage of their introductory offer—$10.00 for three sessions, which include a group class, a private lesson, and dance party admission.

ROLYNN DANCE STUDIO

WHERE: 838 McLean Avenue
Yonkers, NY 10704
(914) 963-7720
Located right by one of the Central Avenue bus stops. No parking facilities.

WHEN: Call for appointment. (Lessons are by appointment only.)

WHAT: A wide variety of dances are taught here, including tap, jazz, ballet, aerobics, fox trot, waltz, tango, cha-cha, rumba, merengue, rock, and free-style. There are five instructors, and classes range from ten to fifty students. The age range is from 35 to 60, and men and women are evenly balanced. Most students bring their own partners, but sometimes they're just friends.

Dance socials are held regularly, especially on holidays: they hold a St. Patrick's Dance, a Halloween Party, and a Christmas Party.

HOW MUCH: Private lessons cost $25.00 an hour; group lessons $10.00 an hour.

RELIGIOUS ORGANIZATIONS

For those singles who have been brought up with strong ties to their religious denomination, we have put together a section on denominational dating services, social clubs, and travel organizations.

If the thought of meeting "the wrong person"—someone of a different faith—fills you with apprehension, you probably want to investigate these religious organizations, so you can narrow down your search for a partner to only those people who are "marriage material" or prospects for long-term commitment.

BRANFORD SINGLES FELLOWSHIP

WHERE: First Congregational Church of Branford
1009 Main Street
Branford, CT
(203) 488-5846
(203) 488-7201

WHAT: A wide variety of activities are hosted, including weekly meetings and discussions, lectures, dances, parties, suppers, game nights, and bus trips to local attractions.

Ask for Angela Graves when you call the church to get a schedule of activities.

WHO: Members are singles in their forties and older—men and women are pretty evenly mixed.

HOW MUCH: Membership is $5.00 a year, or $1.00 a week for members, $2.00 a week for non-members. Activities hosted outside of the church are held at additional cost.

CATHOLIC ALUMNI CLUB OF THE ARCHDIOCESE OF NY

WHERE: 83 Christopher Street
New York, NY 10014
(212) 243-6513 (message recorder)

WHAT: The objective of this club is to give single, Catholic college graduates an opportunity to meet friends of similar cultural, educational, and religious backgrounds. There are several other Catholic Alumni Clubs in the Midwest and in California, but the New York chapter has become the largest one. It traces back to 1958.

In an average month, about twenty activities take place, planned by six committees. Members are encouraged to sit on these committees, so if you're the kind of person who really likes to get involved in something, you might want to be part of these planning committees.

The Social Committee organizes dances, cocktail parties, and happy hours; the Religious Committee schedules speakers, panel discussions, and retreats; the Sports Committee plans resort weekends, camping and ski trips, hikes, picnics, swimming, bicycle riding, ice skating, horseback riding, golf, sailing, and beach parties; the Lively Art Committee organizes theater parties, evenings at the opera and ballet, visits to art galleries and museums, Sunday afternoon city excursions, and dinners; the Travel Committee puts together long weekend trips and summer vacations to various destinations; and the Community Service Committee plans excursions for underprivileged children and recreational activities for the elderly.

All events are generally scheduled near public transportation.

WHO: Members are mostly 30- to 45-year-old Catholic singles—but you'll find people anywhere from age 25 to 50 in this three-hundred-member congregation.

CATHOLIC SINGLES ASSOCIATION

WHERE: P.O. Box 406
Yonkers, NY 10704
(914) 423-8209

WHAT: Among the events sponsored at this association are dances, tennis parties, picnics, an annual moonlight sail, and an annual ski weekend. You can attend one event and see if you like it. If so, all you have to do is fill out the application for membership.

WHO: Most of the members are in their thirties and forties; a little over half are male.

HOW MUCH: The dances are $6.00 for members, $10.00 for nonmembers. Tennis parties are $20.00; the annual moonlight sail is $25.00. Members pay $10.00 for picnics, nonmembers, $13.00. The annual ski weekend costs $90.00 for members, $95.00 for nonmembers.

CHRIST CHURCH BAY RIDGE

WHERE: 7301 Ridge Boulevard
Brooklyn, NY 11209
(718) 745-3698
Take the Third Avenue bus or the double-R train to Seventy-seventh Street and Fourth Avenue, or the Sixty-ninth Street bus.

WHAT: This Episcopal church sponsors flea markets in the spring and fall, holiday food drives for the needy, a bi-monthly thrift shop, a Christmas Fair, and Lenten suppers. There's also a senior citizens group.

Sunday services are from 8:00 to 11:00 a.m. Special holiday services are held on Ash Wednesday and throughout Lent; on Holy Thursday, Good Friday, Easter Vigil/Easter Day, and on Ascension Day; for the Blessing of Pets (in October), Thanksgiving, Christmas Eve Pageant and 11:00 p.m. service), and on Christmas Day.

Christ Church Bay Ridge is also a meeting ground for many community groups that offer special services to the area, including Alcoholics Anonymous, children's exercise classes, high school retreats, school entry exam preparation classes, boy scouts and girl scouts, and other religious institutions.

WHO: The congregation has about 150 members of all ages.

CHRISTIAN DATING SERVICE

WHERE: P.O. Box 678
So. Orange, NJ 07079
(800) 723-LOVE

WHAT: Just fill out an application—they'll take care of the rest.

WHO: A wide range of ages, from 18 to 80. There is a total of six thousand members.

HOW MUCH: The lowest membership cost is $84.00; the highest is $720.00.

GATEWAY CATHEDRAL

WHERE: 200 Clarke Avenue
Brooklyn, NY
(718) 667-0300

WHAT: This is an interdenominational place of worship located one block from the Oakwood train stop. There are Sunday morning and mid-week services, bible study, outreach groups, counseling, opportunities to get involved in choir singing and drama, various outings, and a singles class.

WHO: Most of the members are in their thirties; there are 1,200 in the congregation.

HOW MUCH: Most of the activities are free—like choir singing, bible study, services, and outreach group participation.

JEWISH INTRODUCTIONS INTERNATIONAL

WHERE: Security Building
Suite 8110 Department 113
250 H Street
Blaine, Washington 98230
(604) 521-4805

WHAT: Here's how it works: you fill out a four-page questionnaire which you can either mail or fax back to the dating service. Within three days someone at the organization will call you with a list of introductions. No computers are used to do the matching; staff members match up the questionnaires based on similar values, attitudes, and temperament. A minimum of one introduction per month is guaranteed.

WHO: Members are Jewish singles aged 19 through 88—mostly well-educated professionals. There are members in more than a hundred U.S. and Canadian communities.

HOW MUCH: The regular six-month fee is $399.00; one year costs $499.00. Eighteen months costs $599.00, and twenty-four months $699.00. Ask about their specials.

NASSAU/SUFFOLK JEWISH SINGLES

WHERE: 39 Aster Street
Greenlawn, NY 11740
(516) 757-2434

WHAT: This organization brings Jewish singles together at house parties, which are hosted six to eight times a year. It also sponsors pool parties and holiday celebrations, also at private homes. People who volunteer the use of their homes and backyards are reimbursed.

WHO: Most who attend these house parties are 45 and older, and generally the turnout includes twice as many women as men. There's no formal membership, but if you attend one of these parties you'll be on the mailing list from then on.

HOW MUCH: It costs $15.00 to attend any party.

QUEENS JEWISH SINGLES

(Formerly part of the YM/YWHA of Northern Queens; currently receiving financial support from area synagogues.)

WHERE: 41-60 Kissena Boulevard
Flushing, NY 11355
(718) 460-5069

WHAT: This religious club offers a variety of programs for Jewish professionals, including sporting activities, trips (e.g., excursions to Great Adventure), Israeli dancing, Jewish content programs, exercise classes, support groups (such as for young widows and widowers), and individual counseling.

WHO: Members are Jewish singles ages 25 to 39; two-thirds of the members are men.

HOW MUCH: The cost of events varies: participation in major events costs $15.00, attendance at the Israeli Dance is $5.00, support group participation costs $7.00 (unless you purchase a package of four to six tickets—then you'll get a discount). Attending religious services is free.

SOUTH NASSAU JEWISH SINGLES

(A Division of the Beach YM-YWHA, Jewish Community Center)

WHERE: 310 National Boulevard
Long Beach, NY 11561
(516) 431-2929

WHAT: They sponsor recreational, social, and educational events for singles, like wine and cheese parties, dances, brunches, lectures, and discussion groups. An example of a lecture topic that has been presented is "Exciting Ways To Attract a Satisfying Relationship." There are also adult education classes that deal with issues other than relationships—such as "Mystical Aspects of Early Jewish History."

Members get together at least two or three times a month. Transportation is usually provided to events that take place off the premises.

WHO: Members are broken up into two age groups: 23 to 42 and 35-plus. In the 23 to 42 age group, the ratio of women to men is about three-to-two; and in the 35-plus group, about 70 percent are women. All of the members are single.

HOW MUCH: Annual membership is $45.00; the cost of attending dances is $10.00 for Y members and $14.00 for non-members; attending brunches costs $6.00 for members and $8.00 for guests; wine and cheese parties cost $6.00 for Y members and $10.00 for guests; and lectures cost $4.00 for Y members to attend and $6.00 for guests.

SUFFOLK YM/YWHA

WHERE: 74 Hauppauge Road
Commack, NY 11725
(516) 462-9800

WHAT: This is a group work Jewish community center whose primary function is to provide support groups for separated, divorced, and widowed singles. You can also attend their raps, socials, lectures, dances (which include buffet and DJ music), holiday parties, and volleyball tournaments.

To give you an example of the kinds of discussion groups you would encounter, there's the "Fishbowl Rap"—where participants get to ask members of the opposite sex any questions they've ever been curious about, and there's a rap group led by a professional image and communications consultant called "The New You: Getting Ready for the Social Scene." Other rap groups cover topics like loneliness, sexuality, risk-taking, ambivalence, and addictive relationships. Rap groups are often separated by age group (18 to 30, 28 to 42, 30-plus).

As far as the support groups go, you'd have to talk to a Y social worker before joining one. The Monday support group discusses the experience of losing a loved one. On Wednesdays there's a support group for the newly separated and divorced, and on Thursday nights, three groups in different stages of widowhood get together to talk about bereavement and returning to the social scene.

Members meet about three times a week; nonmembers are welcome to attend the events, too.

WHO: Members are mostly 35- to 55-year-old singles, with men slightly outnumbering the women (three-to-two ratio).

HOW MUCH: There's no membership fee, unless you want to join the Y to use their facilities (pool, track, weight room, etc.). As for the prices of singles' events: support groups are $2.00 for members, $6.00 for nonmembers; raps and socials are $4.00 for members, $6.00 for nonmembers; dances are $8.00 for members, $12.00 for nonmembers; brunch get-togethers are $3.00 for members, $6.00 for nonmembers.

TEMPLE SHAARAY TEFILA CENTER FOR JEWISH STUDIES

WHERE: 250 East 79th Street
New York, NY 10021-1294
(212) 535-8008

WHAT: A variety of courses are offered at this synagogue. Among them are "Talmudic Tradition and the Contemporary World," "The Heritage of Sephardic Jewry," "Zionism: Struggles Within," and "Psychology in the Bible: Mind, Mood and Madness." The center also offers a study series on Jewish literature, beginners' and intermediate Hebrew language courses, special music services, a Passover Seder Workshop, and the Rabbi's Roundtable Supper Seminars. You can also join the volunteer choir, which meets weekly to rehearse for performances on High Holidays, festivals, and occasional Shabbat evenings. On Sundays, the center offers Outreach Discussion Groups, which delve into issues such as interfaith marriages, access into the Jewish community for non-Jews, and theological differences between Judaism and Christianity.

WHO: Participants are young, middle-aged, and elderly people of the Jewish faith.

HOW MUCH: Lectures and courses range in price from $10.00 to $200.00.

UNITARIAN UNIVERSALIST CHURCH OF CENTRAL NASSAU

WHERE: 223 Stewart Avenue (at Nassau Boulevard)
Hempstead, NY
(516) 248-8855
(one block north of LIRR Nassau Boulevard Station on the Hempstead line)

WHAT: This Unitarian Church holds its weekly service on Sunday mornings at 11:00 and also sponsors a singles group called "The Gathering" which has become known as a safe, non-threatening way for singles of all ages to meet and get to know each other in a nurturing atmosphere. The church also hosts a special annual event called the "Harvest Fair," which draws people from all over Nassau County.

WHO: The congregation has 175 members, ranging in age from twenties to seventies; the majority are in their thirties, forties, and fifties.

HOW MUCH: Attendance is free.

UNITED SYNAGOGUE OF HOBOKEN

WHERE: 830 Hudson Street
Hoboken, NJ 07030
(201) 659-2614
(one block east of Washington Street, and eight and a half blocks from PATH trains)

WHAT: Services are on Friday evenings at 6:30 and Saturday mornings at 9:30, as well as on all major holidays. In addition, the United Synagogue of Hoboken Adult Jewish Learning Center (AJLC) offers a variety of eight-unit courses: Hebrew for beginners, a basic course in Jewish prayer, reading the book of exodus, an introduction to Kabbalah, the history of the Jews in Spain, and learning to chant from the Torah and the Haftorah.

The Singles Connection meets one Wednesday a month for an hour of entertainment, refreshments, and conversation. You don't have to be an AJLC member—just single. Besides the monthly get-togethers, the Singles Connection sponsors other activities—skating in Central park, nature hikes, Sunday brunches, billiards night at Willow Billiards, Shabbat dinners, and Hanukkah festivities. One night a week, instructions are given in international folk dancing.

WHO: There are members of all ages, but concentrated in the 30- to 45-year-old range.

HOW MUCH: Cost depends on the activity or course of study. Example: $15.00 for six weeks of international folk dancing lessons, or $3.00 per lesson; $3.00 to attend a Singles Connection meeting if you're not a member.

WESTPORT UNITARIAN SINGLES GROUP

WHERE: 10 Lyons Plain Road
Westport, CT 06880
(203) 227-1537

WHAT: This is a sixteen-year-old nonprofit organization run for and by singles. The group holds weekly meetings at the Unitarian Church from 7:30 to 10:45 p.m. The first hour is devoted to general socializing with tea, coffee, and cookies. At 8:30 the group separates into smaller groups for hour-long discussions on topics like reincarnation, the importance of humor in relationships, dreams and goals, and the effects past romantic relationships have had on the group members. Some participants may opt to pursue alternative activities rather than sit in on discussion groups—ballroom dancing lessons, disco dance lessons, group games like Trivial Pursuit or Pictionary, and lectures by various experts on individual growth and fitness

During the last hour of the meeting the whole group reconvenes in the main room for wine, soda, coffee, snacks, and conversation.

There are other activities worth noting: Friday dine-outs at various gourmet and ethnic restaurants, Monday night bridge tournaments for intermediate to advanced players, writer's workshops, evenings at the theater (followed or preceded by supper), hikes, bike rides, tennis, literature discussions, and musical get-togethers (singing, playing instruments, or just listening).

Every Sunday night, Westport Unitarian Singles joins over four hundred other singles at the Holiday Inn Crowne Plaza in Stamford, where they enjoy dancing, hors d'oeuvres, drinks, and DJ music.

How will you find out about all these activities? Westport Unitarian Singles Group publishes a monthly guide to events called "The Asparagus." Call to receive one.

WHO: Participants include Unitarian Church members of all ages.

HOW MUCH: Prices vary depending on the event, but attendance at the weekly meetings costs $5.00 for members and $8.00 for non-members.

ASSORTED RECREATIONAL ACTIVITIES

If you're an active single who likes variety, and the thought of movies and dinner every weekend bores you to tears, you'll be happy to read about the many diverse options on the following pages.

Although these are not especially targeted at singles, they offer ideal opportunities for you to expand your horizons and enhance the quality of your leisure time.

We've included billiard halls, bowling centers, racquet courts, and skating rinks—many of which host special events like bowling socials, tennis parties, and billiard tournaments.

Don't worry about being skilled at these activities; you don't have to be a pro. It's just good, clean fun—and if you go often enough, you just might become an expert!

BILLIARDS

AMSTERDAM BILLIARD CLUB

WHERE: 344 Amsterdam Avenue (between Seventy-sixth and Seventy-seventh Streets)
New York, NY 10024
(212) 496-8180
Take the number 1, 2, or 3 train to Seventy-second Street station and walk over from Broadway.

WHEN: The club is open from 11:00 a.m. every day. Closing time on Fridays and Saturdays is 5:00 a.m.; the rest of the week they close at 3:00 a.m. The most popular nights—and the best times for singles to hook up—are Thursday, Friday, and Saturday nights, or any night when there's a league taking place. Tuesday nights, starting at 7:30, the co-ed 8-Ball/9-Ball league plays. Or join the 14.1 Straight Pool league, 7:30 on Thursdays. Winners get prizes like cues, cue cases, books, and T-shirts.

WHAT: This club is frequented by a fun, upbeat, interesting crowd. It's a great place to people-watch. One of the owners aptly describes it as "the Cadillac of pool halls." There are thirty-one Brunswick Gold

Crown tables, a snack bar, and a cocktail lounge.

WHO: There are usually more men than women (three-to-two ratio), but you'll find an even mix on weekend nights.

HOW MUCH: Cost depends on the day and time of day, but on the average you'll pay about $10.00 an hour. The club offers free pool lessons for beginners every Monday night and for intermediate players every Wednesday night. There's a $35.00 registration fee each for the 8-Ball/9-Ball and 14.1 Straight Pool leagues. Also, from 11:00 a.m. till 6:00 p.m., seven days a week, up to four players can take part in the "Daytime Power Play" special offer, which entitles them to a maximum of seven hours' play for $15.00—$19.00 on weekends and holidays. Call the club to find out about other special deals.

BAILEY'S BILLIARDS

WHERE: 289 Springs Fireplace Road
East Hampton, NY 11937
(516) 329-9096
The East Hampton LIRR station is two miles away, so you're better off taking your car.

WHEN: The hall is open daily from noon till 2:00 a.m.

WHAT: Bailey's has sixteen nine-foot Brunswick Gold Crown tables, one twelve-foot snooker table and one Caroni billiard table. There's also a pinball machine and a twenty-two-foot shuffleboard game. Music comes out of the $8,000 sound system and the collection of over six hundred CDs.

The atmosphere is upscale, clean, and roomy. There's a no-smoking section. Bailey's won an honorable mention for "Best New Billiard Room" in the 1990 *Billiard Digest.*

The liveliest nights are Fridays and Saturdays, but the longest you'll have to wait for a table is usually fifteen minutes. Best time for singles: Thursday, Friday, and Saturday nights.

Snacks offered include chips, pretzels, soda, coffee, and tea.

WHO: There are slightly more men than women (three-to-two ratio).

HOW MUCH: Costs are $7.50 an hour for one player; $10.00 an hour for two players; $12.50 an hour for three people; and $15.00 an hour for a group of four. Women play for free till 9:00 p.m. on Thursdays. There's a two-for-one price for students on weekdays till 7:00 p.m.

BANK SHOT BILLIARDS CLUB

WHERE: 84 Washington Street
Hoboken, NJ 07030
(201) 217-1961
One block from Path station; one mile from the Lincoln Tunnel.

WHEN: The club is open Monday through Thursday from 2:00 p.m. till 1:00 a.m.; Fridays from 2:00 p.m. till 3:00 a.m.; Saturdays from noon till 3:00 a.m.; and Sundays from noon to midnight.

WHAT: There are ten nine-foot tables, video games, foosball, a jukebox, and a snack bar. Friday and Saturday nights are when it gets the most crowded; during peak times, you can wait up to half an hour for a table. If you're interested in joining a league, ask the management about the 8-Ball Winter League.

The decor is very elegant; this used to be a bank in the late 1800s and early 1900s, so the tables and lamps are antiques.

WHO: Men outnumber women by about three to one on a typical night.

HOW MUCH: You'll pay $6.00 for the first person before 6:00 p.m., plus $1.50 for each additional person. After 6:00 p.m., the rate is $12.00 an hour. On Tuesdays (Ladies Nite), there's a 25-percent discount for women.

BERGEN BILLIARDS

WHERE: 920 Bergen Avenue
Jersey City, NJ 07306
(201) 792-6760
Two blocks away from bus stop and train station.

WHEN: Hours are 12 noon till 2:00 a.m. daily.

WHAT: This one has twelve pool tables and three video games. Stereo music is played in the background. Although there's no snack bar, you can order take-out Chinese food from downstairs or get something delivered from a variety of other neighborhood eateries. There's also a snack machine.

Bergen Billiards gets the most crowded on Fridays and Saturdays; at that time, there's a slight wait for a table.

WHO: Patrons are predominantly Asian men (65 percent Asian, 90 percent male).

HOW MUCH: Cost is $9.00 an hour for three or more players.

THE BILLIARD CLUB INC.

WHERE: 220 West 19th Street
New York, NY 10011
(212) 206-7665
Take the 1 train (BMT line) to Eighteenth Street for the shortest walk from the station.

WHEN: Club hours are Sunday through Thursday, 10:00 a.m. till 3:00 a.m.—5:00 a.m. on Fridays and Saturdays. The best times for singles are 8:00 p.m. till midnight, especially on Fridays and Saturdays, when there tends to be an even mix of men and women. You might have to wait up to half an hour for a table at busy times.

WHAT: This billiards club has been attractively designed in the tradition of a European cafe. You can imagine how crowded it gets here, because even with thirty-three tables, there's a lot of waiting. But you'll enjoy socializing and listening to the music at the cocktail lounge and snack bar while you wait your turn, and you can also play video games.

WHO: Lots of singles come here, two-thirds of them members of the male persuasion.

HOW MUCH: If you get there early (before 7:00 p.m.), it's $5.00 per table, but if you want to be there when the place is humming with action, you'll pay $10.00 per table.

EAST MEADOW BILLIARDS

WHERE: 2339 Hempstead Turnpike
East Meadow, NY 11554
(516) 731-1880
This billiards club is right near the local bus stop and one and a half blocks from the train station (LIRR).

WHEN: Hours are 10:00 a.m. till 1:00 a.m. It's most crowded from 8:00 p.m. till closing, but you'd still only have to wait for a table for ten or fifteen minutes.

WHAT: There are twenty-one pocket tables, five video games, and two foosball tables. There's a snack bar but no cocktail lounge.

WHO: You'll usually find two men for every woman—but sometimes there's an even mix.

HOUSE OF LORDS

WHERE: 612 S. Oyster Bay Road
Hicksville, NY 11801

(516) 931-8454
Located near the LIRR Hicksville station.

WHEN: The hall is open from 10:00 a.m. till midnight and is most crowded on weekends. The best chance of getting a table is Sunday during the day and 5:00 to 9:00 p.m. on weekdays. At busy times you'll wait about fifteen minutes for a table.

WHAT: This place has a friendly atmosphere with modern decor and a stereo system. There are twenty-two tables and three video games. The snack bar serves coffee, soda, and candy.

WHO: There are three men for every woman.

HOW MUCH: Cost is $8.00 an hour for two players.

JACKS BILLIARDS

WHERE: 614 Ninth Avenue, 2nd Floor
New York, NY 10036
(212) 315-JACK
It's only two blocks from Port Authority, so you can get to Jacks on any bus or train that stops there.

WHEN: Jack's is open every day from noon till 4:00 a.m.

WHAT: Don't let the location fool you: this is a classy, plush establishment with imported carpets in muted colors, custom mahogany and Italian marble furniture, and a decorator lounge/alcove. They have ten Brunswick Gold Crown III tables, and the background music consists of sixties, seventies, and eighties rock. You can bring your own cassettes, if you'd like.

The longest you'll have to wait for a table is about fifteen minutes. Jacks gets the most crowded on Wednesday, Friday, and Saturday nights. Soda, juice, and coffee are available.

WHO: Patrons are businesspeople, theater-goers and couples. The male/female ratio is about three to two. Anyone who enters is monitored by closed-circuit television, so the clientele is respectable.

HOW MUCH: You'll pay $6.00 an hour for one person; $10.00 an hour for two people. Free private lessons are offered on Saturdays from 2:00 to 5:30 p.m.

JULIAN'S BILLIARDS ACADEMY INC.

WHERE: 138 East 14 Street
New York, NY 10003
(212) 475-9338
Take just about any subway line to Fourteenth Street (F, N, R, 4, 5, 6

trains), or take the crosstown bus on Fourteenth Street or the bus that runs south and north along Third Avenue.

WHEN: The academy is open daily from 10:30 a.m. till 3:00 a.m.

WHAT: This is like the McSorley's of billiard halls: women are allowed to hang out here but they'll probably feel out of their element. (For those of you who aren't familiar with McSorley's, it's a very down-to-earth beer hall that, until recently, didn't even have a ladies' room.) The ratio of men to women here, on the average, is about twenty-five to one.

There are twenty-nine pool tables and video game machines. No jukebox; no snack bar—but you can buy soda, candy, and cigarettes from the vending machines. The liveliest times are Wednesday through Saturday nights.

WHO: Most of the patrons are guys interested in playing some serious pool.

HOW MUCH: The fee is $5.00 an hour before 6:00 p.m.; but after 6:00 each extra person pays an additional $2.00 an hour.

MAMMOTH BILLIARDS

WHERE: 33-70 Prince Street
Flushing, NY 11354
(718) 463-6006
Five minute-walk from the number 7 train (Main Street stop) and from the bus stop.

WHEN: Mammoth is open around the clock, every day. It gets the most crowded on Fridays and Saturdays from 5:00 to 10:00 p.m., but there's hardly ever a wait for a table.

WHAT: There are twenty pool tables and three Ping-Pong games, plus eight video games. No snacks or drinks are served.

WHO: The scale is slightly tipped by the guys—about a three-to-two ratio.

MRS. POKEY'S BILLIARD GARDEN

WHERE: 1320 Stony Brook Road
Stony Brook, NY 11790
(516) 689-5992
Not close to trains or buses—you'll have to drive there.

WHEN: Hours are 7:00 p.m. till 1:00 a.m. nightly. The best time to meet singles is after 10:00 p.m.

WHAT: There are fifteen pool tables, foosball video games, and a snack bar. Mrs. Pokey's has a comfortable decor with wood paneling and plants. There's a friendly atmosphere and radio music (mostly tuned to WBAB).

WHO: Guys and gals come here in equal numbers.

HOW MUCH: The cost is $6.00 per game for two people, $8.50 for three, and $11.00 for four.

PALM BEACH BILLIARD CLUB

WHERE: 1310 Middle Country Road
Selden, NY 11784
(516) 736-0777
Bring your car or get a ride.

WHEN: The club is open seven days a week, 5:00 p.m. till 2:00 a.m. Leagues and tournaments are held on Monday and Tuesday nights. Weekend evenings are the most popular times to go. You usually won't have to wait for a table more than fifteen minutes. The best times to meet other singles are Friday, Saturday, and Sunday evenings.

WHAT: There are eighteen tables, plus video games and electric darts. No cocktail lounge, but there is a snack bar. This is an upscale but cozy atmosphere with Tiffany lamps and lots of memorabilia—so if you want more than just a basic game of billiards, check this place out. You don't even have to take part in the game to enjoy hanging out here—just sit back and enjoy the ambience and the music.

WHO: On a typical evening, there are six guys for every gal—ladies, what are you waiting for? The odds are with you!

HOW MUCH: You'll pay $6.00 per hour if you're playing against one opponent—$2.00 an hour for each additional player.

PLAYBOY BILLIARDS

WHERE: 1814 Coney Island Avenue (between Avenues N & O)
Brooklyn, NY 11230
(718) 645-0074
Located near bus stop and subway station.

WHEN: Hours are 10:00 p.m. till 1:00 a.m. from Sunday through Thursday, and till 2:30 a.m. on Fridays and Saturdays. It's crowded most evenings and weekends, but the wait for a table won't be longer than twenty minutes.

WHAT: Playboy Billiards has a comfortable atmosphere with fourteen Brunswick tables, two Ping-Pong tables, four video games, stereo music, and a snack machine. There's plenty of room to park.

WHO: Ladies—here's another one where you'll be outnumbered, so take your pick. On a typical night there'll be about twelve guys for each of you. Of course, some of them will be more interested in winning at pool than scoring with you.

POKEY'S BILLIARDS

WHERE: 325D William Floyd Parkway
Shirley, NY 11967
(516) 281-6751
No public transportation nearby—bring your car.

WHEN: The club is open from noon until 1:00 a.m. daily. Pokey's is most crowded during the winter, from 7:00 p.m. till 1:00 a.m. Waiting time for a table is about fifteen minutes at the busiest times.

WHAT: There are ten pool tables, video games, and a snack bar. The atmosphere is friendly, with wood paneling and oldies on the radio.

WHO: Patrons usually include an even mix of guys and gals.

HOW MUCH: The cost is $5.00 per game for two people, $7.50 for three people, and $10.00 for four.

ROYAL BILLIARDS

WHERE: 42-02 215th Street
Bayside, NY 11361
(718) 279-1847
Located near the Q13 bus stop, the Long Island Railroad station, and Northern Boulevard—which is a main bus route.

WHEN: Hours are 11:00 a.m. till 3:00 a.m. The place is pretty crowded every night. The best times for singles are ladies' nights (Monday and Tuesday), and Friday and Saturday evenings. The wait for a table is generally about fifteen minutes, but the management will often mix customers together at the tables to cut down on the waiting time.

WHAT: This is a happy and happening, clubby-type meeting place with thirty tables, video games, a jukebox and a 2000-watt sound system (radio, tapes, and CD). There's also a snack bar. The atmosphere is charged with the spirit of competition. Leagues and tournaments are held here.

WHO: Guys and gals come here in equal numbers. As for the staff—the owners describe them as "moral and cheerful people" who are also "a little crazy."

HOW MUCH: You'll pay $7.50 an hour per table.

SOCIETY BILLIARDS

WHERE: 10 East 21st Street
New York, NY 10010
(212) 529-8600
Take the N, R, F, or number 6 subway train to Twenty-third Street.

WHEN: The club is open weekdays, from 11:00 a.m. till midnight, and weekends till 3:00 a.m. Because there are so many tables, there's hardly ever a wait.

WHAT: This upscale billiards club has been featured in magazines, and caters to businesspeople and professionals. There are twenty-five tables. You'll be playing to music, and when you get hungry or thirsty, just go upstairs to Cafe Society (see Bars & Clubs).

WHO: There's a six-to-one ratio of men to women, on the average.

HOW MUCH: You'd expect such an upscale place to be a little pricey, but Society Billiards actually has the lowest prices in town. It costs $3.00 an hour per person before 7:00 p.m., and $4.00 an hour per person after 7:00. Free lessons are given during the day

---

SOUTH SHORE BILLIARDS

WHERE: 9101 Flatlands Avenue
Brooklyn, NY 11236
(718) 257-0504
Take the bus or drive your car

WHEN: The club is open noon till 2:00 a.m. daily. Friday nights are the best times for singles.

WHAT: This one has twenty-three pool tables, Ping-Pong tables, video games, a snack bar, and a video juke box. Saturday night is when it gets the most crowded, but you usually won't have to wait for a table.

WHO: Men outnumber women by about three to one on an average night

HOW MUCH: The club charges $8.00 an hour for two people.

UNDERGROUND BILLIARDS

WHERE: 259-27 Union Turnpike
Glen Oaks, NY 11004
(718) 343-6863

Located near an express bus stop (bus route goes from Queens to Manhattan). The local bus that runs up and down Union Turnpike will also get you there.

WHEN: Underground Billiards is open from 11:00 a.m. till 2:00 a.m. The best time to meet other singles is between 9:00 p.m. and 11:00 p.m., especially Saturday nights. Expect to wait about twenty minutes for a table at busy times

WHAT: This place has a casual, young, fun atmosphere. There are nineteen pool tables, four video games, and a jukebox. There is a snack bar, but no cocktail lounge.

WHO: On a typical evening there are seven men for every three women. Saturday nights it's about half and half.

HOW MUCH: The night rate is $7.50 per hour for the first person and $1.50 an hour for each additional person.

WESTCHESTER FAMILY BILLIARDS

WHERE: 965 Nepperhan Avenue
Yonkers, NY 10703
(914) 968-0211

WHEN: Hours are noon to midnight, seven days a week. The most popular nights are Friday and Saturday. At the busiest times, expect a ten- to twenty-minute wait for a table. Best times for singles to mingle: Wednesday through Sunday.

WHAT: This establishment has a nightclub atmosphere, minus the cocktails Twenty-six pool tables, video games, Ping-Pong table, and air hockey games. There's also a snack bar, big-screen TV, and music.

WHO: A pretty even mix of guys and gals—generally three-to-two. (Billiards still seems to be a more popular pastime with men than with women, so all you pool sharkettes out there take advantage of this great man-surplus!)

HOW MUCH: The club charges $10.00 an hour for two players and $2.00 additional for each extra player

---

WILLOW BILLIARDS CLUB & LOUNGE

WHERE: 1313 Willow Avenue
Hoboken, NJ 07030
(201) 420-4049
Three-minute walk from the Path train, and there's a bus stop on the corner.

WHEN: The club is open from noon till 2:00 a.m. Sunday through Thursday, and till 3:00 a.m. on the most popular nights (Fridays and Saturdays). At busy times you'll wait for a table no more than ten or fifteen minutes. The best time to meet other singles is on Wednesday nights and weekends—but you have pretty good opportunities to meet someone on just about any night. Ladies, you can play for free on Wednesday nights from 7:00 to 10:00 p.m.

WHAT: You'll feel cozy in this warm, upscale atmosphere—complete with exposed brick walls, wood paneling, lots of mirrors, and music. There are fourteen billiard tables (twelve Brunswick Gold Crown III and two custom Peter Vatalie tables), a full bar, and a snack bar that serves hot dogs. Plus, for sports fans—two big-screen TVs that keep you up-to-date on all sporting events.

WHO: The male/female ratio is about three-to-two.

HOW MUCH: The charge is $6.00 per person for the first hour and $2.00 for each additional hour.

BOWLING

ACE LANES

WHERE: 82-02 45th Avenue
Elmhurst, NY 11373
(718) 651-4343
Take the N or R train to Elmhurst Avenue, or drive—but there's no parking lot.

WHAT: There are twenty lanes here, plus a snack bar and a cocktail lounge.

WHEN: The best time for singles is 3:00 p.m. till 3:00 a.m.

HOW MUCH: You'll pay $3 a game.

BRUNSWICK WOODHAVEN LANES

WHERE: 72-25 Woodhaven Boulevard
Glendale, NY
(718) 896-1800
The closest subway station is the Woodhaven Boulevard stop on the G and R local line, but you'd have to take a bus from there up Woodhaven. The bus stops on the corner of Metropolitan Avenue and Woodhaven Boulevard. For you car owners, there's free parking—and no need to worry about your car; a security guard is on duty from 6:00 p.m. till midnight every night.

WHAT: This is a modern, bright, and cheerful bowling center with sixty lanes, a snack bar, and a cocktail lounge with satellite TV. Between games you can get rid of a few quarters in their large video game room. No question about it: the best time for singles is Saturday nights from midnight to 3:00 a.m. This "Moonlight Bowling" session turns into a big party with DJ music. Bowl and dance till you drop!

WHEN: Hours are 9:00 a.m. to midnight Monday through Thursday and Sunday; open till 3:00 a.m. on Friday and 4:00 a.m. on Saturday.

HOW MUCH: Cost depends on when you go. You'll pay 99¢ per game on Friday morning till noon; $3.00 per game in the evenings; $2.25 per game during the day on weekends.

If you want to book the bowling center for a large singles outing, they'll arrange a group price that includes buffet.

CORTLANDT LANES

WHERE: Route 202, Bear Mountain Exit
Peekskill, NY 10566
Take your car. Parking is free.

WHAT: Clean and bright with a friendly atmosphere, this bowling center has thirty-eight lanes, a snack bar and cocktail lounge, and video games. They have separate leagues for men and women, as well as mixed leagues, junior leagues, and Pee Wee leagues. There's also Bumper Bowling, and every Saturday night at 10:00 p.m. they offer "Spin the Wheel" bowling.

WHEN: Cortlandt Lanes is open daily from 9:00 a.m. till 1:00 a.m. The best times for singles are evenings after 9:30, or Sunday afternoons.

HOW MUCH: Cortlandt Lanes operates on a special "Pick a Price" policy; you take a computer ticket which gives any one of three prices: $2.25, $2.50, or $2.75 per game.

DEER PARK BOWL

WHERE: 849 Long Island Avenue
Deer Park, NY 11743
(516) 667-7750
Half a mile from the Deer Park train station (LIRR).

WHAT: Here you'll find sixteen lanes, a snack bar, a cocktail lounge, and video games. The best times for singles are Saturdays and Sundays.

WHEN: Deer Park Bowl is open every day from 9:00 a.m. till 1:00 a.m.

HOW MUCH: You'll pay $2.50 per game.

EAST ISLIP LANES

WHERE: 117 East Main Street
East Islip, NY
(516) 581-6200
Unless you want to walk three miles from the train station, take your car. Parking is free.

WHAT: This place has a pleasant, friendly atmosphere, forty lanes, a cocktail lounge, a snack bar, and video games. Several leagues play here: men's, ladies', mixed, and children's. The management would be willing to sponsor singles' leagues if enough people were interested in joining.

WHO: Men and women come here in equal numbers.

WHEN: The lanes are open daily from 9:00 a.m. till midnight.

HOW MUCH: The charge is $2.90 per game during open bowling; $2.50 per game for league players.

FARMINGDALE LANES

WHERE: 999 Conklin Street
Farmingdale, NY 11735
(516) 581-0065
There's a bus stop in front of the bowling alley, and the Farmingdale train station (LIRR) is three blocks away. By car, it's just off Route 110 near Southern State and LIE. Parking is free.

WHAT: This is a large bowling center with forty-eight lanes, a snack bar, a cocktail lounge (with a large TV screen), and video games. It has a friendly, warm atmosphere—especially on the weekends, which is the best time to meet fellow singles.

WHEN: Farmingdale Lanes is open practically around the clock—twenty hours a day.

HOW MUCH: The cost is $2.75 per game, except on Saturdays and Sundays during the day—then it's only 99¢ a game. Ask about special group rates.

LEEMARK LANES

WHERE: 423 88th Street
Brooklyn, NY 11209

(718) 238-BOWL
For those of you who don't know Brooklyn, this is the Bay Ridge section. The bus stop's on the corner, and the subway station is two blocks away. There's no parking lot.

WHAT: There are thirty-six lanes here, with automatic scoring, and they recently installed synthetic lanes. The place is fully equipped with a snack bar, a warm and cozy cocktail lounge, and video games. Friday, Saturday, and Sunday nights are the hottest times—there's disco bowling, singles leagues, and vacation leagues.

WHEN: You can play from 9:00 a.m. till the wee hours of the morning, seven days a week.

HOW MUCH: The charge is $3.50 per game.

MASPETH BOWL

WHERE: 53-01 74th Street
Maspeth, NY
(718) 651-1555
Drive, or take the E, F, G, R, or 7 train to the Roosevelt Avenue (Seventy-fourth Street) subway station.

WHAT: This bowling center came up with an interesting concept: Bowling Madness. Every Friday night, from midnight till 3:00 a.m., Maspeth Bowl turns into a disco/bowling alley. There's bowling and dancing to DJ music, and the cocktail lounge buzzes with activity. There's a live DJ on Saturday nights, too.

Leagues include men's, women's, mixed couples, juniors, "Pee Wees," and B.V.D. leagues—plus Bumper Bowling.

WHEN: 9:00 a.m. until midnight, every day (and, of course, until 3:00 a.m. on Bowling Madness Fridays).

HOW MUCH: $2.70 per game.

MELODY LANES

WHERE: 461 37th Street
Brooklyn, NY 11232
(718) 832-BOWL
Located two blocks from the subway station, and the bus stops on the corner. Free parking.

WHAT: This is run by the same folks as Leemark Lanes (described earlier), and there are a lot of similarities between the two. This one has recently installed synthetic lanes, too—twenty-six of them—and the same events are hosted here: singles leagues, vacation leagues, and disco bowling. Friday, Saturday, and Sunday nights are the happening nights.

WHEN: The place is open from 9:00 a.m. till the wee hours of the morning every day of the week.

HOW MUCH: The charge is $3.50 a game.

MELVILLE BOWL

WHERE: 895 Route 110
Melville, NY
(516) 271-1180
The bus runs along Route 110, so you can disboard right in front of the bowling alley. Or take your car—there's free parking.

WHAT: There are lots of lanes here—fifty-two, to be exact. They also have a cocktail lounge with a large-projection TV, and video games. The recommended times to hang out there and get to know someone are weekends and Monday evenings at 9:00. Unlike at bowling alleys, women aren't usually outnumbered here.

WHEN: Melville Bowl opens at 9:00 a.m. and closes at 2:00 a.m.

HOW MUCH: A game costs $2.75. Ask about special discount rates.

OAKDALE LANES

WHERE: 855 Montauk Highway
Oakdale, NY 11709
(516) 567-5700
Half a mile from the Oakdale railroad station (LIRR, Montauk branch), and the bus stops in front of the bowling alley.

WHAT: The staff is friendly and helpful at this thirty-two-lane bowling center. They'll help form a league for any group that's interested in developing one; there are time slots available on Mondays, Wednesdays, Fridays, Saturdays, and Sundays. There are other ways besides bowling to amuse yourself here: socializing at the snack bar or cocktail lounge, shooting pool at the pool table, or playing video games. There's also a jukebox. The best times to meet singles are evenings and weekends. Mixed leagues play on Wednesdays at 6:30. Lots of regulars come here and are on a first-name basis with the staff.

WHEN: Oakdale Lanes opens at 9:00 a.m. Mondays through Fridays, 8:00 a.m. on Sundays, and 11:00 a.m. on Saturdays. You can bowl till pretty late—

closing time depends on how long bowlers want to hang out.

HOW MUCH: The cost depends on the day. $2.65 per game is the standard price, but there's a special weekend rate of $1.00 a game from 2:00 to 7:30 p.m. on Saturdays, 8:00 a.m. to 6:00 p.m. on Sundays, and Mondays from 9:00 p.m. till closing.

PLAYDROME ROOSEVELT

WHERE: 427 Route 440
Jersey City, NJ
(201) 432-3535
Your best bet is to drive there. Parking is free.

WHAT: This is a newly renovated bowling center with forty-six lanes, automatic scoring, a snack bar, a cocktail lounge, and video games.

WHEN: Bowl from 10:00 a.m. till midnight every day of the week.

HOW MUCH: You'll pay $1.50 a game during the day, $2.25 a game in the evenings.

RAB'S BOWLING ON THE GREEN

WHERE: 55 Mill Road
Staten Island, NY 10306
(212) 351-4000
One block from bus stop. There's a parking lot on the premises.

WHAT: This establishment is a forty-two-lane bowling alley with lots of special events—ladies' leagues, mens' leagues, "Moonlight Bowls," "Rock 'n Bowls," "Disco Night," "Ladies' Night," and "Sing Along" night. There's a snack bar and a restaurant/cocktail lounge called Rab's Sports Cafe on the Green, plus video games that change monthly. The best times for singles to mingle are Tuesday nights (Sing-Along), and Thursday, Friday, and Saturday nights after 9:30. Both sexes are well-represented here.

Here's what to expect from the various special events: The Moonlight Bowling Dinner features a four-hour open bar, two hours of nighttime bowling, and live DJ music while you bowl. On Sing-Along nights you get to be a star. Participate in the talent show and you can win trophies, T shirts, or jackets. Then there's Ladies Night—D.J. music and dancing from 9:00 p.m. till 1:00 a.m.—and women spend only a dollar per drink! Friday nights at Rabs Sports Cafe are wild: dance to D.J. music and join in the limbo contest (winner gets a T shirt).

WHEN: Rab's is open from 10:00 a.m. to 2:00 a.m. every day except Fridays and Saturdays, when they don't close till 4:00 a.m.

HOW MUCH: The price for a game ranges from $1.50 to $2.75.

SHELL LANES

WHERE: 1 Bouck Court
Brooklyn, NY 11223
(718) 336-6700
A half block from bus and subway stops. No parking provided.

WHAT: This is a "classic" bowling alley—not a trendy-looking one—with thirty-two lanes, video games, and a cocktail lounge. The atmosphere is warm and friendly, and intimate. Bowling in the true sense of the word is the focus here; this bowling center attracts serious bowlers, not people who just want to hang out. There are usually just as many women as men here.

WHEN: Come on weekdays from 10:00 a.m. till midnight, and weekends from 9:00 a.m. till 2:30 a.m. The best time for singles is Saturday evenings.

HOW MUCH: You'll pay $2.50 per game.

34TH AVENUE BOWL

WHERE: 69-10 34th Avenue
Woodside, NY 11377
(718) 651-0940
Two blocks from the bus stop, and a ten-minute walk from the #7 line (Roosevelt Avenue subway station). Park your car for free.

WHAT: This bowling alley has thirty-five lanes and a cocktail lounge and snack bar.

WHEN: Come Sunday through Thursday, 9:00 a.m. till 1:00 a.m.; Friday and Saturday, 8:00 a.m. till 4:00 p.m. The best time for singles is on weekends.

HOW MUCH: You'll pay $2.50 per game.

RACQUET CLUBS

AMRITRAJ RACQUET & SPA

WHERE: 225 Howells Road
Bayshore, NY 11706
(516) 968-8668

WHAT: This place features indoor tennis and racquetball courts, a fitness center, a swimming pool, a whirlpool, and aerobics. Group and private instruction are offered for tennis and racquetball.

WHEN: It's open from 6:00 a.m. till 11:00 p.m.

HOW MUCH: Costs are as follows: $399.00 to $499.00 for annual membership; $35.00 an hour for the use of a tennis court, $16.00 an hour for the use of a racquetball court, $50.00 an hour for private tennis or racquetball lessons, and $54.00 an hour for group tennis or racquetball instruction.

CENTURY RACQUET CLUB

WHERE: 2600 Netherland Avenue
Bronx, NY
(212) 543-4700
Accessible by bus (Liberty Lines), subway, and the Hudson Line. If you come by car, you can park for just a dollar for three hours.

WHAT: The club has four indoor tennis courts, two squash courts, an Olympic-size pool, an aerobics room, pool and Ping-Pong tables, and locker facilities.

Tennis instruction is offered on an individual and group basis. Reserve courts at least a day in advance. When you purchase a season court, you become a designated member. Tennis racquets can be rented.

WHEN: This club is open from September through May. Hours of operation are: Monday through Thursday from 9:00 a.m. till 10:00 p.m.; Friday from 9:00 a.m. till 8:00 p.m.; and Saturday and Sunday from 8:00 a.m. till 10:00 p.m.

HOW MUCH: $225.00 for eight tennis lessons; $16.00 an hour for the use of a squash court. The cost for the use of a tennis court varies according to the time of day.

HARBOUR VIEW RACQUET CLUB

WHERE: Harbour View Island
Mamaroneck Avenue, off Route 1
Mamaroneck, NY
(914) 698-1634
Five-minute walk from the New Haven Railway Line. Parking is free.

WHAT: This is strictly a tennis club, with eight indoor clay courts. You can sign up for private or group lessons. There are eight instructors.

Occasional Saturday evening parties are hosted, as well as Round Robin tennis tournaments with refreshments.

Open time can be booked about a week in advance, but for the most part, courts are reserved for those who purchase seasonal court reservations.

WHEN: The club is open from October through May from 7:00 a.m. till 11:00 p.m.

HOW MUCH: Costs are as follows: private lessons, $62.00 to $72.00 an hour; group lessons, $285.00 to $365.00 for fourteen hourly sessions; court time, $37.00 to $45.00 an hour; racquet rental, $3.00, refundable on purchase of a racquet.

KINGS HIGHWAY TENNIS CLUB

WHERE: Kings Highway North
Darien, CT 06820
(203) 655-8769
Accessible via New Haven line and Amtrak. Parking is free.

WHAT: The club features six indoor tennis courts, a sauna, and men's and women's showers with locker rooms. Private and group tennis instruction is offered. There are five instructors. Courts should be reserved about a week in advance, because very little time is reserved for open court rental.

On Friday nights from 8:00 p.m. till midnight, and on Saturday nights from 7:30 to 11:30 p.m., tennis parties are hosted, featuring mixed doubles, men's doubles, and women's doubles tournaments. Light refreshments are served at these events.

WHEN: The winter season lasts from August 23 through May 15, and the summer season is from May 16 through August 22. Winter hours are 7:00 a.m. till 11:00 p.m., summer hours are 8:30 a.m. till 9:00 p.m.

HOW MUCH: Court rental is $45.00 an hour, private lessons, $29.00 per half hour, and group lessons, $392.00 per person to attend the class.

THE "NEW" JERSEY 34 TENNIS CLUB

WHERE: Route 34
Matawan, NJ
(908) 583-1011

WHAT: This tennis club focuses on tournaments and leagues. You can play in the women's singles, men's singles, women's doubles, men's doubles, or mixed doubles tournament. Prizes are awarded to the winners of each tournament. Then there's the Sunday evening mixer—a mixed doubles league that meets every Sunday from 7:00 to 9:00 p.m., September through May. This league gives everyone the opportunity to play different people during the course of each month.

WHO: Almost half of the members are single (about 40 percent), and there is an equal number of women and men. The age range is about 25 to 55.

WHEN: Leagues meet once or twice a week.

HOW MUCH: $30.00 will get you membership for one season. Contract rates for thirty-six-week segments go from $525.00 to $875.00, depending on when you play; cost of league participation (thirty-six weeks) is $44.00 a month during the day, $50.00 a month on evenings and weekends. For open time, members pay from $24.00 to $26.00 an hour, non-members from $28.00 to $30.00. Tournament participation costs $25.00 a person.

NORWALK RACQUET CLUB

WHERE: 490 Westport Avenue
Norwalk, CT
(203) 853-7727
It's best to drive there. Parking is free.

WHAT: This tennis club has six indoor courts and four instructors offering private and group lessons. Reserve courts about two days in advance, and bring your own equipment. The club sponsors singles and couples tennis parties from time to time.

WHEN: The club is open year round, every day from 7:00 a.m. till 11:00 p.m. Saturday night is the best time for singles to go.

HOW MUCH: You'll pay $60.00 an hour for private instruction; $330.00 for a fifteen-week class. An hour of court time will cost you between $35.00 and $45.00.

SETAUKET HEALTH & RACQUET CLUB

WHERE: 384 Mark Tree Road
East Setauket, NY
(516) 751-6100
The Long Island Railroad stops about two miles away, so try to get there by car. Parking is free.

WHAT: This is like a summer country club, with an outdoor swimming pool and lounge area, eighteen Har-Tru tennis courts (seven indoor and eleven outdoor), Nautilus and Universal exercise equipment, free weights, an indoor soccer area, and volleyball and basketball courts.

There are eight different classes offered—variations of aerobics, toning, and cardiovascular exercising. There's also an indoor and an outdoor snack bar, complete locker room facilities, and indoor and outdoor nursery facilities. This health and racquet club has hosted several corporate outings, conventions, singles parties, and private parties.

Reserve tennis courts about a week in advance; during the summer you'll have to wait about an hour if you don't have a reservation.

WHEN: The tournament season runs from May 11 to September 15, but the facilities are open year-round, from 6:30 a.m. till midnight. The club opens at 6:30 every weekday morning, and at 7:00 on weekends.

HOW MUCH: Pool and fitness membership costs $199.00 for individuals, $350.00 for couples, and $600.00 for a family of four. Tennis memberships are available at additional cost. The fee for open court time is $24.00 to $36.00 an hour. Membership costs $175.00 to $300.00 a year for the fitness membership; $1,080.00 a year for the tennis plus fitness program.

SOUND SHORE INDOOR TENNIS

WHERE: 303 Boston Post Road
Port Chester, NY
(914) 939-1300
Near the Port Chester and Rye train stations. You can park your car at no charge.

WHAT: Most of the time this tennis club is contracted out for the season, so there's very little open court time. There are twelve indoor tennis courts, and both individual and group lessons are offered. There are twenty-five instructors. You can rent equipment at the shop on location. You might also want to use the saunas and whirlpools.

Marion Smith Singles parties are held here every Friday and Saturday evening.

WHEN: The year is broken up into two seasons: September to May and May to September. The tennis club opens at 7:00 or 8:00 a.m., depending on what day it is, and it closes at either 7:00 p.m. or 11:00 p.m.

HOW MUCH: The fee for private tennis lessons is $68.00 an hour

WESTCHESTER INDOOR TENNIS

WHERE: 14 Sawmill River Road
Hawthorne, NY
(914) 592-3737
Take your car; park for free.

WHAT: This tennis club, which has six indoor courts, offers group and private instruction. There is no equipment rental. Saturday night parties are hosted here.

WHEN: The club is open year-round from 6:30 a.m. till 11:00 p.m. Your best bet is to play there on Saturdays and Sundays.

HOW MUCH: There's a charge of $60.00 an hour for private instruction, $42.00 an hour for the use of a tennis court.

YONKERS TENNIS CENTER, INC.

WHERE: 493 Sprain Road
Yonkers, NY 10710
(914) 968-6918
It's one and a half miles from the nearest train station, and three-quarters of a mile from the nearest bus stop, so you might want to drive. No charge for parking. Call and request directions—the tennis center has printed up a set of detailed directions on how to get there from both the North and South.

WHAT: There are six indoor tennis courts, saunas, and lockers. Special events include leagues, tournaments, and Friday night tennis parties. Courts should be reserved at least two weeks in advance.

Here's something worth noting for you singles. On Friday evenings, the Yonkers Tennis Center is rented out for the Set & Match singles parties—from 9:00 p.m. till 2:00 a.m. It's an evening of exercising and socializing—featuring tennis tournaments (round robin or club style) and cold buffet, snacks, beverages, and desserts. For those who don't play tennis, there's Pictionary, Backgammon, Trivial Pursuit, cards, and other activities.

The tennis club also rents out its facilities on Saturday nights from 8:00 p.m. till 1:00 a.m. for private parties, corporate outings, or fundraisers.

WHEN: The club is open every day of the week from September 15 through May 25. Hours of operation: 6:30 a.m. till 2:00 a.m.

HOW MUCH: Contract rates are $525.00 to $1,395.00 for thirty-three weeks of one-hour-a-week play. The hourly rate for use of a court is $21.00 to

$45.00. Private lessons are $65.00 an hour; group lessons are $275.00 for eleven weeks (four to a group, one hour a week). Racquet rental is free. Set & Match tournament participation costs $23.00 per person ($10.00 if you're attending the party without playing in the tournament). The cost of renting the tennis center for a Saturday night is $425.00.

SKATING RINKS

COMMACK ROLLER RINK

WHERE: 70 Veterans Memorial Highway
Commack, NY
(516) 499-4204

WHAT: This indoor roller skating rink is open all year; the schedule varies according to the season. Disco/dance music and Top 40 selections are played here, and there's a "nightclubby" feeling to it. The rink measures 80 feet by 180 feet, and there's also a snack bar and free parking facilities. The rink can be rented for private parties. Singles, take note: Tuesday evenings from 8:30 till 11:30 p.m. are reserved for adults only (18 and over). The rink gets very crowded on Friday and Saturday nights and on weekends during the day.

HOW MUCH: Sessions cost $6.00 a person; skate rental is $1.00

DARIEN ICE RINK

WHERE: Old Kings Highway North
Darien, CT
(203) 655-8251

WHAT: This indoor rink measures 85 feet by 200 feet. It's open to the public every Sunday from 1:00 to 3:00 p.m. and on holidays, but it can be contracted out for social parties and company parties at other times. A variety of music is played. Private and group lessons are offered at the rink. There's a snack bar (who doesn't get hungry skating?). You can park your car for free, or you can take the local bus.

HOW MUCH: The charge is $4.00 per session, $1.50 for skate rental.

HARVEY SCHOOL RINK

WHERE: Route 22
Katonah, NY 10536
(914) 237-3618

WHAT: This is a year-round indoor skating rink that measures 190 feet by 85 feet. There's no public skating, but you can take group lessons or private instruction. There is a snack bar on the premises. Parking is free, or you can take Metro North, if you don't drive.

HOW MUCH: A five-week series of group lessons costs $50.00

HOT SKATES

WHERE: 14 Merrick Road
Lynbrook, NY
(516) 593-1424
Accessible by train, bus, and, of course, car. Parking is free.

WHAT: You'll have to call for the schedule of sessions, because it varies—but the rink is open year-round. It measures 170 feet by 70 feet, and it's indoors. There's an adults-only session every Sunday night from 9:00 p.m. till midnight, and that would be the best time for singles to go—and there's an even mix of guys and gals. Music ranges from Top 40s to dance music, and the rink offers a state-of-the-art video and digital audio system. Visit the snack bar when your feet get tired.

Private parties can be booked at Hot Skates—promotional parties, fundraisers, or whatever. You can also take lessons there—private or group

HOW MUCH: A session costs $6.00, skate rental $1.00. Private lessons cost $14.00 for a half hour; or sign up for group lessons (you'll meet more people that way) at $39.00 for six half-hour sessions

---

ICE RINK AT ROCKEFELLER CENTER

WHERE: 600 Fifth Avenue
New York, NY
(212) 757-5730 or 5731

Take the F train to Forty-seventh/Fiftieth Street or to Fifth Avenue and Fifty-third Street

WHAT: If you haven't been to this outdoor ice skating rink, you've missed one of New York City's greatest attractions. The rink, which measures 66 feet by 120 feet, is sunk considerably below street level, so passers-by can stop and gaze down at the skaters. The view for skaters is of the surrounding skyscrapers and the gold statue that sits above the rink. There's a restaurant adjacent to the rink; those who dine there can look out and watch the skating.

The most spectacular time to go skating here is when the lighted Christmas tree is towering above the rink in all its glory. The season starts on October 20 and lasts through the end of April.

The rink plays a variety of music, and both group and private lessons are offered. It gets somewhat crowded on weekends during the day and on Friday evenings.

HOW MUCH: You'll pay $7.00 to $10.00 per session; $4.00 for skate rental; $19.00 for a half-hour private lesson. The cost of group lessons varies according to the size of the group.

SKATERS' WORLD ROLLER RINK

WHERE: Hambong Turnpike & Valley Road
(Ramapo Shopping Plaza)
Wayne, NJ 07470
(201) 694-9440

WHAT: This year-round indoor roller rink plays all kinds of music and has a snack bar with a full concession area. Skating instruction is offered to groups and to individuals. The rink is open for private parties on Monday, Tuesday, and Thursday mornings and Wednesday afternoons. Tuesday and Thursday nights are "Adult Night" from 9:00 p.m. till midnight; the Friday evening session is called "TGIF" and runs from 8:00 to 11:00 p.m.; Saturdays from 8:30 to 11:30 p.m. is "Saturday Night Fever"; Sunday is family night.

HOW MUCH: Admission prices vary according to the time you go, ranging from $4.50 to $6.00 a person. Group lessons cost $4.00 an hour, and private instruction costs $10.00 to $15.00 for a half hour.

SKY RINK

WHERE: 450 West 33rd Street
16th Floor Penthouse
New York, NY
(212) 695-6555
You'll be able to find parking nearby, and there's a parking lot within one block of the building, but if you're coming by subway, take the E train to Thirty-fourth Street and walk three blocks west.

WHAT: This Olympic-size rink, measuring 185 feet by 85 feet, is open year-round twenty-four hours a day! The rink was designed to accommodate a wide variety of skating interests: instructional and recreational figure skating, ice dancing, hockey, and parties and other social events. As with most skating rinks, you'll want to avoid the day sessions unless you enjoy being surrounded by little kids. Anyway, if you're going there to meet singles, you'll be going to the evening sessions (isn't it easier to flirt at night than during the day?).

If you want to schedule a private party, they can accommodate. According to the management, "No group is too small or party request too unusual for the party planners at Sky Rink."

Other amenities: coat check, lockers, pro shop, and snack bar.

Call the rink for announcements on session schedules and monthly skating specials.

HOW MUCH: The charge is $7.50 per session, $2.50 for skate rental. There are reduced admission rates for groups of ten or more. The cost for lessons varies.

WOLLMAN RINK

WHERE: 59th Street & 5th Avenue entrance to Central Park
New York, NY
(212) 517-4800
The rink is not situated right at the entrance, so you'll have to walk about ten minutes into the park.

WHAT: You can go ice skating at this outdoor rink from October through March or roller skating from April through September. During roller skating season, part of the rink turns into a mini-golf course. Whichever time you choose to go, you'll be surrounded by Manhattan's majestic skyscrapers, with a breathtaking view of both the Upper East Side and Upper West Side skyline. Lots of singles come here to skate under the stars around 8:00 or 9:00 p.m.

A variety of music is played here, and in addition to public sessions, there are group lessons and private instruction. The snack bar offers a good selection of foods, and there are tables inside plus benches outside. The rink measures 32,000 square feet.

There is no schedule of sessions because the sessions are continuous: Just show up at any time.

HOW MUCH: Admission costs $5.00 per adult, $2.50 per child. Skate rental costs $2.50. A thirteen-week series of group lessons costs $150.00, and private lessons cost $14.00 for fifteen minutes.

WORKSHOPS, SEMINARS, AND SUPPORT GROUPS

Many singles find that one of the best ways to meet interesting new people is through intellectual stimulation. New York offers a rich variety of workshops, seminars, lectures, and support groups that cater to a variety of intellectual and social needs.

You don't have to take a class specifically for the purpose of meeting someone; take one that interests you! Of course, it would be a nice little bonus if, in addition to your new knowledge and your "A" at the end of the semester, the person seated next to you—the one you had your eye on from day one—asked you to go out for a cup of coffee after class.

Support groups, too, can have tremendous social benefit—and don't underestimate their healing potential. Nothing can help you cope with a crisis more effectively than sharing your emotions and experiences with other people who are going through a similar crisis. You can find support groups through religious institutions or by contacting hospitals, therapy clinics, and community centers for referrals.

CENTER FOR LIVING AS A SINGLE PERSON (C.L.A.S.)

Sponsored by Peninsula Counseling Center

WHERE: 381 Sunrise Highway
Lynbrook, NY
(516) 599-1181

124 Franklin Place
Woodmere, NY

WHAT: The purpose of this organization is "to provide emotional support for individuals going through a divorce, separation, or death of a spouse." The program offers education and supportive discussion groups and workshops.

C.L.A.S. was established eight years ago. The majority of its members are over thirty years ago. To become a member, you would call for information and ask to be put on the mailing list.

The program director emphasizes that the goal of C.L.A.S. is to encourage a network of friendships, not necessarily to foster dating relationships.

Topics that are discussed at seminars and workshops include: Singles: How to Protect Yourself in Today's World"; "Decision Making for Singles"; "Open Discussion on Dating"; two-, three-, or four-session workshops on stress reduction and management, assertiveness, changing roles and transitions; eight-session support groups for the newly separated, divorced or widowed; and an eight-session post-support group for the separated and divorced dealing with such issues as forming new relationships, moving on, dating, constructive uses of anger, and constructive self-assertion.

At general meetings, guest speakers talk about legal issues, finances, single parenting, dating, travel, holidays, and planning for the future.

There is also a Drop-in Center available to C.L.A.S. members where they can discuss concerns and problems in a supportive environment with a professional social worker and a trained peer counselor.

DISCOVERY CENTER

WHERE: 200 West 72nd Street, Suite 68A
New York, NY
(800) 777-0338

WHAT: Discovery Center probably offers a course in just about everything you can think of: water sports, business/finance, wine tasting, publishing, screenplay writing, real estate, flying . . . you get the idea.

Here are some examples of workshops they offer especially for singles: "Travel for Singles," "Selective Coupling," "How and Where To Meet Friends & Lovers in New York," "How to Flirt, Date, & Meet Your Mate," "Dating Over 40," and "Love Relations: Knowing Quickly, Choosing Well." From the course names alone you should get a pretty good idea of the course content. Course fees range from $25.00 to $40.00.

Discovery Center also offers a three-hour social opportunity called "Party Meet," which has a format designed to help you socialize in a comfortable but structured way. First you exchange small talk with six to eight people in each group. Conversations are initiated by the leader of the group—a singles expert—who introduces new, provocative subjects for discussion as you rotate to the different groups. The cost of attending a Party Meet is $24.00.

EDUCATIONAL ALLIANCE WEST

WHERE: 21 East 13th Street
New York, NY
(212) 420-1150

51 East 10th Street
New York, NY

WHAT: Provides programs, events, and workshops that serve as a good meeting ground for singles. Educational Alliance West offers a wealth of singles services, ranging from weekly Sunday brunches (split up into two age groups: 25 to 40 and 35 to 55), to rap sessions designed to bring singles together in conversation. You can sign up for a workshop that analyzes singles classified ads, led by a CSW and psychodramatist. There are also workshops in "Sexual Re-Awakening," reading Tarot Cards, "Creative Visualization" (designed to help you make your dreams become reality), and the ancient healing art of Jin Shin Jyutsu. "Fun and Games" offers a comfortable group setting for Pictionary, Trivia Pursuit, Scruples, and other game-playing.

Equally valuable to singles are EAW's support groups, such as the Single Parent Support Group for both custodial and non-custodial parents; the Divorce Support Group for newly separated and divorced singles; the "Dating Again" support group for widowed and divorced singles who are apprehensive about opening their lives to romance, and a singles support group where concerns about relationships and single life are discussed. Each of these workshops is six sessions long and is led by a professional social worker.

A one-session workshop of interest to singles who would like to explore the behavioral psychology behind dating is "The Gender Gap: Overcoming Obstacles in Dating and Courtship."

On the last Thursday of every month, Jewish singles can meet at the 13th Street Cafe for coffee, conversation, and music. Or they can attend the Friday evening Chavurots—buffet-style dairy meals, traditional blessings, song and conversation.

Prices depend on the event. Sunday brunches cost $8.00 for members to attend; the gathering at the 13th Street Cafe costs $10.00 to attend; and support groups cost $50.00 for six sessions. Non-members can attend events and workshops at slightly higher fees.

KINDRED SPIRITS/SINGLE PARENTS GROUP

WHERE: 92nd Street Y
1395 Lexington Avenue
New York, NY
(212) 415-5618

WHAT: Kindred Spirits is primarily for divorced and widowed parents and their children. It sponsors leisure-time activities such as sporting events, cocktail parties, brunches, workshops, discussion groups, cultural activities, picnics and travel packages specially designed to meet the needs of single parents.

The majority of members are in their thirties and forties. To join, there is a $50.00 annual fee, which entitles members to price reductions at major events, as well as a yearly newsletter subscription and invitations to free members-only events. Members must pre-register for all events.

Specific activities that have been sponsored by Kindred Spirits in the past are: an excursion to Six Flags Great Adventure, Young Widows and Widowers meetings, Fire Island Summer Beachcomb, Club Getaway Mini-Week, Magical Mystery Tour, A Day at Sesame Place, a twenty-hour party cruise on the *Queen Elizabeth II*, a New York Philharmonic concert, and an evening at Stand Up New York Comedy Club.

The organization publishes a quarterly newsletter which contains a calendar of events, a question-and-answer column dealing with common issues of single parenthood, and brief articles written by psychologists and therapists.

THE LEARNING ANNEX

WHERE: 2330 Broadway
New York, NY
(212) 580-2828

WHAT: You've probably seen The Learning Annex's catalog at least once in your lifetime, or you may even be on their mailing list somehow. But in case you don't have their catalog, here's a rundown of some of the courses they offer that deal with issues of love and relationships.

"How To Flirt" explores "the many ways to transform meeting new people into instant adventure and self-discovery" and attempts to "increase your intuitive skills by recognizing nonverbal signals."

"How To Meet Someone Easily"—for men—covers techniques like how to use shyness to your advantage, how to read a woman's body language, how to keep her captivated with conversation, how to be sexy and exciting (okay, so it comes naturally to most of you, but it can't hurt to get a new perspective!), how to overcome your fear of rejection, and how to use five foolproof opening lines.

We won't describe them all, but you can get the general picture from the course names: "How To Drive Your Man/Woman Wild in Bed," "Making Friends Instantly," "How To Read a Woman/Man Like a Book," "The Art of Networking," "Letting Go and Moving On," and "How To Find a Lover."

The Learning Annex also offers two party concepts designed to help participants meet people in a relaxed atmosphere: "Progressive Dinner Parties"—where diners change seats after every course so everyone gets a chance to converse with everyone else—and "Getting To Know You" parties—which use a series of easy writing/communication exercises in small groups to explore attitudes and feelings about romance and relationships.

By the way, you can place a personal ad (or respond to one) in The Learning Annex catalog.

Of course, you can also choose from a wide variety of courses that don't focus on relationships but can nonetheless offer good opportunities to meet people with similar interests. To name just a few: wine tasting, screenplay writing, real estate, acting, image consulting, investment strategies, assertiveness training, weight control, body massage, etc.

NEW YORK AREA CENTER

(New York branch of the Landmark Education Corporation)

WHERE: (Mailing Address:)
P.O. Box 422789
San Francisco, CA 94142-2789
(New York Location:)
38th Street off Fifth Avenue
New York, NY

WHAT: Many of you have undoubtedly heard stories about EST, an intense approach to self-discovery and personal growth that was offered in the sixties and became a somewhat "cultish" experience. Well, since then, EST has branched out into a number of variations on that theme, and is no longer in existence as EST in its original form. Today you can register for a personal growth seminar called The Forum—an intensive, three-day event that has to be experienced to be understood. Basically you sit in a huge room with hundreds of other people for three consecutive days and exchange anecdotes about your life under the direction of a charismatic seminar leader. There is no formal objective; each participant derives unique experiences, insights, and breakthroughs from The Forum. It is an incredible opportunity to get in touch with your innermost feelings and to resolve life-long inner conflicts, as well as to bond with your fellow human beings. The cost is $500.00.

After experiencing The Forum, you can register for a number of other seminars on topics such as leadership, money, and relationships. Some of these seminars run for several weeks; others are one-day courses or weekend events.

One event that focuses on relationship issues is "Looking For Love In All the Wrong Places," described as "a day that will light your fire and keep it burning." Tuition is $100.00; find out when it will be offered in New York City.

Another one-day event centered on love and relationships is "Talk To Me," which deals with our inadequacies in communicating our emotions. Tuition is $100.00.

SUFFOLK COUNTY ADULT CHRISTIAN SINGLES

WHERE: Smithtown Gospel Tabernacle
Higbie Drive
Smithtown, NY 11787

WHAT: S.C.A.C.S. gathers "for the purpose of spiritual, emotional, and relational growth to provide the single adult with a loving, growing environment in which to learn about Christ and how to love those around us."

In its five years of operation, S.C.A.C.S. has developed a mailing list of 400 people, who are either single by choice or through divorce or widowhood. The majority are in the 41 to 50 age group. There is no formal membership procedure.

"Official" get-togethers are twice a month: a Bible discussion study group on the second Thursday of every month, and a "Singles Talk It Over" discussion group on the fourth Saturday of every month. At these discussion groups, topics of special interest to singles are brought into the forum, and small discussion groups are formed around each topic. Participants share their experiences, testimonies and questions. A staff of moderators provides leadership and ensures that discussions are presented with a Christian focus.

The Single Parent Ministry meets every Wednesday night; it's a thirteen-week program in which single parents focus on biblical single parenting techniques. Role playing and certain discussion formats are used to enhance parents' understanding of their roles. Youth programs and a nursery ministry are offered so that parents can bring their children with them to the church on those evenings.

Periodic Sunday brunches are sponsored by S.C.A.C.S., where participants enjoy food, fellowship, singing, and music. Each person contributes a dish to the meal.

Focus seminars for singles are offered, covering topics such as financial planning, self-esteem, and sexual issues for the single.

SUSAN RABIN SUPPORT GROUPS

WHERE: 52 West 88th Street
New York, NY
(212) 362-6520

WHAT: Workshops and support groups led by therapist Susan Rabin provide a relaxed and supportive environment for improving and practicing social skills. The maximum number of students in each class is thirty, and participants range in age from 18 to 70. There are generally more men than women attending.

Susan Rabin also provides group and individual counseling by appointment. She teaches a number of courses at the Discovery Center and at The Learning Annex, such as "How To Flirt, Date, and Meet Your Mate," "How To Read a Woman/Man Like a Book," and "Dating Over 40."

SINGLES' PUBLICATIONS, COMMUNITY NEWSPAPERS, AND PERSONALS

An increasing number of magazines have become aware of the ever-expanding singles market and have responded by adding sections especially for their single readership, including personal ads, nightlife directories, and calendars of events for singles. Other publications are geared solely to the singles market. These magazines, daily newspapers, and community papers contain a wealth of information for the active single.

Personals have become a very accepted way of hooking up with people—they were even the subject of a recent Broadway show—and they also make for entertaining reading material. If you've ever skimmed through the personals, you've probably seen a lot of clever ads, each trying to outdo the other.

For the people writing them it's a great opportunity to be creative and expressive. It's also a great opportunity for self-discovery; if you've never sat down and tried to write an ad about yourself, you'll see how difficult it is when you attempt it. You have a general sense of who you are—after all, you've spent every second of every day of your life with yourself!—but have you ever tried to describe yourself to someone else?

Try it now, just for fun. Start off with a list of adjectives that describe you, and then analyze your character. Which of your personality traits and physical features would be the most appealing to others? How honest can you be about your shortcomings?

Some people find this so hard to do that there are actually services you can hire to write these personal ads for you!

It is a challenge to convey who you are—the essence of your being—in thirty-five or forty words, or to read between the lines and figure out what someone is really like based on his or her personal ad.

For example, let's say a woman comes across a personal ad that says, "Wealthy, successful, silver-haired white male with baby-blue eyes"—what can she really tell about this man? He could be Paul Newman, for all she knows! The point is, the same description can be used to describe hundreds of different people; it doesn't capture the essence of a person. So the only way to really find out what someone is like is to take a chance and respond to the ad.

Singles who are thinking of placing a personal ad in a magazine—or responding to one—should exercise caution. The most intelligent way of avoiding a dangerous situation is to let your answering machine screen the response calls you get. Then, if you decide to call the person back to make a date, don't give out too much personal information during the initial conversation. And make sure you meet in a public place the first time around.

But you can probably tell from that one message on the answering machine, or from that one introductory letter, if someone is a little strange or unstable.

The new TV personals are a good concept; they work pretty much the same way as magazine or newspaper personals, except that your ad description is read out loud by a narrator. You can either opt to have your photo flashed on the TV screen during the spoken ad, or you can just let the network provide the backdrop—such as a beautiful nature scene.

Whether you buy the publications we've listed below because you want to place a personal ad, or just to check out the nightlife directories and other happenings around town, you'll find a lot of valuable, singles-oriented information.

CONNECTICUT MAGAZINE

WHERE: Communications International
789 Reservoir Avenue
Bridgeport, CT 06606
(203) 374-3388 (Classified Advertising Department)

WHAT: The main focus of this monthly magazine is on restaurants, travel, and real estate. There's a comprehensive "Dining Out" guide covering several counties in Connecticut and Westchester, categorized by cuisine. So if you're new to Connecticut, or if you're a New Yorker who likes to drive out for the occasional Sunday brunch—this listing will give you an excellent overview of your many options.

Of particular interest to singles is the "Private Affairs/Classified" section. There's a fifteen-word minimum to place an ad, and the rate is $2.45 per word. They need to receive your ad copy in advance: if you send it in by, say, June 20, then your ad will appear in the August issue. The cost of renting a Private Affairs box number is $10.00 per insertion.

A single issue is $2.50, or you can subscribe: Connecticut residents pay $17.00 for one year, $29.00 for two years, and $37.00 for three years. Out-of-staters pay an extra $5.00 per year.

DATE BOOK

WHERE: 70 Memorial Plaza
P.O. Box 473
Pleasantville, NY 10570
FAX: (914) 769-3660

WHAT: This is a free monthly activity guide for singles throughout the Westchester, Fairfield, and New Haven regions. The booklet offers about sixty pages of listings each month, detailing, in chronological order, a variety of events sponsored by singles organizations, social clubs, support groups, and religious groups. The publication is in its fifteenth year.

DATE BOOK also has a section called "Personal Dialogue," which contains classified ads hooked up to a 900-phone number. To hear an advertiser's message or to respond to an ad, you would call the service—which operates twenty-four hours a day—at a cost of $1.70 per minute. DATE BOOK also has traditional personal ads to which you can respond by letter or phone call.

A personal ad costs $20.00 to $55.00, depending on the number of words up to a hundred words, and 50¢ per additional word over a hundred.

JEWISH SINGLES NEWS

WHERE: P.O. Box 1053
New York, NY 10028
(212) 348-1755

WHAT: This monthly publication, serving upscale Jewish singles in the New York, New Jersey, and Connecticut area, lists information about a variety of activities and events for singles—including dinners, parties, lectures, sports and outdoor activities, trips, cruises, and overseas travel opportunities.

The personal ads section is called "Jewish Dialogue," and you can place a free personal ad (thirty-five words or less) by calling 212-888-1744 any time between 10:30 a.m. and 6:00 p.m., Monday through Friday. Or you can fax in your ad to 212-888-2350 at any time of day—or mail it to the address above. You have until the fifteenth of the month to call or send in your ad copy for the following month's issue.

To respond to an ad, call 900-226-1016, select "3" from the audio menu and then enter the four-digit extension number that appears at the end of the ad you're interested in. You'll be charged $1.79 per minute for your call.

Pick up a copy of *Jewish Singles News* at your local newsstand for $2.00, or subscribe for $24.00 a year (twelve issues).

QUEENS LEDGER NEWSPAPER GROUP

(incorporating *Long Island City Journal, Glendale Register,* and *Jackson Heights News*)

WHERE: P.O. Box 376
65-17 Grand Avenue
Maspeth, NY 11378
(718) 894-8585

WHAT: These freebie community newspapers can be picked up at various sites throughout Queens. In addition to local news items, editorials, and ads for community businesses and local events, all of them contain a "Personal Dialogue" section, filled with classified ads you can respond to by touch-tone phone. You can have your ad printed for free (up to thirty-five words); the rate for responding to ads is $1.70 per minute. Mail your ad to Personal Dialogue™, P.O. Box 8208, FDR Station, New York, NY 10150, and you'll be notified by mail when the ad will appear and how to retrieve the responses to your ad.

MANHATTAN SPIRIT

WHERE: 363 Seventh Avenue
New York, NY 10001
(212) 868-1417

WHAT: This is a freebie weekly paper that covers local news, movie listings, reviews of theater, music, literature, and TV shows, political commentaries, and classified ads.

The "Personal Dialogue" section contains classified ads, to which you can respond by touch-tone phone. You can have your ad printed for free (up to thirty-five words). The rate for responding to ads is $1.70 per minute. Mail your ad to Personal Dialogue™, P.O. Box 8208, FDR Station, New York, NY 10150, and you'll be notified by mail when the ad will appear and how to retrieve the responses.

MODERN SINGLES

WHERE: 448 Merrick Road
Suite 108
Oceanside, NY 11572

WHAT: Calls itself "The Free-Ad Free-Spirited Monthly." People who advertise in the classified section have made a written pledge that they will answer every response letter they receive within 20 days of placing the ad. You can place a personal ad for free, up to 40 words long.

The "Personal Dialogue" section contains classified ads you can respond to by touch-tone phone. You can have your ad printed for free (up to 35 words). The rate for responding to ads is $1.70 per minute. Mail your ad to Personal Dialogue™, P.O. Box 8208, FDR Station, New York, NY 10150.

There's also a "Chat Line" (900-226-2060) for adults only, which costs $9.95 for the first call; all calls within twenty-four hours of that first call are free.

Subscribe to *Modern Singles* for $15.00 a year (twelve issues), or look for a copy at your newsstand ($1.00).

NEW JERSEY MONTHLY

WHERE: MDR Publications
55 Park Place, P.O. Box 920
Morristown, NJ 07963-0920
(800) 669-1002

WHAT: Find out what's happening in Jersey every month by consulting this magazine's "Main Events" entertainment guide: it covers music, theater, comedy, dance, art, sports, tours, fairs and festivals, lectures and film, museums, and other special events—plus a section dedicated to singles events. Other regular departments include the "Dining Out" guide and the *New Jersey Classified.* In the "For Singles Only" section in the *New Jersey Classified,* you'll find several dating services and singles organizations listed in the "Social Services" section. The cost for placing a personal ad is $3.45 per word, with a twelve-word minimum. Add an extra $35.00 if you choose to rent a *New Jersey Monthly* mail box number. Submit your ad copy at least five weeks in advance of the issue date (for example, by July 20 for a September ad).

The magazine also publishes general-interest articles on a variety of topics.

Subscription rates are $24.95 a year (twelve issues); $38.00 for two years. Single copies are available for $2.95 plus $2.50 each for postage and handling. Or buy it on the newsstand for $2.95.

NEW YORK MAGAZINE

WHERE: 755 Second Avenue
New York, NY 10017-5906
(212) 643-6500

WHAT: Are there any New Yorkers—even tri-staters—who haven't picked up a copy of *New York Magazine* at least once in their lifetime? Doubtful.

This weekly magazine was a trendsetter for singles: it was because of *New York's* "Strictly Personals" classified ad section that the whole concept of personal ads became a rage. Aside from the obvious benefit of hooking up with people through these ads, they also make for entertaining reading material—with attention-grabbing headlines like "So I'm Not An Angel," "Go Ahead, Make My Decade!," "I'm Too Picky And A Little Immature," and "Built for Bikinis, Golf, and Kissing."

You can respond to the ads by letter or phone. Cost is $1.50 a minute to call on an ad. Cost of placing an ad is $33.00 per line, with a two-line minimum (approximately thirty-six characters per line). The magazine itself costs $2.50 per issue, or you can subscribe for $39.98 for fifty issues.

NEWSDAY

WHERE: Melville, NY 11747
and
2 Park Avenue
New York, NY 10016

WHAT: This is a daily newspaper covering local, national, and world news There's a New York City edition, a Queens edition, and a Long Island edition. Of particular interest to singles is Susan Dietz's weekly (Tuesday) column, "Single File," which covers varied topics of interest to singles, and "Single Scene," a section containing ads for dating services, dance parties, and other social events. There's also a classified ads section called "Getting Personal," which you can respond to by phone or letter

NIGHTLIFE

WHERE: M.J.C. Publishers Inc
5550 Merrick Road
Massapequa, NY 11758
(516) 797-0250

WHAT: In its twelfth year, this magazine has a variety of features and regular columns—interviews with celebrities; theater, movie, music, and art reviews; a nightlife directory; recommended restaurants; and travel tips—to name a few. There's a Long Island edition and a New York City edition of this monthly magazine.

Although it's not strictly for singles, the articles often cater to that segment. For example, one issue featured an article entitled, "In Search of Romance: Where To Meet Your Mate"

There's also a personal ads section, "Personal Connection," to which you can respond by phone. Get an issue of the magazine for $2.25, and you'll find a coupon in the personals section that entitles you to place a free personal phone ad (maximum twenty-five words). To respond to one of the personals, you just dial a 900-number and enter the box number you're responding to, then leave a message. The rate is $1.50 a minute

NY PERSPECTIVES

WHERE: 33 East 33rd Street
New York, NY 10016
(212) 447-0505

WHAT: This is a community newspaper serving Manhattan's East and West sides that focuses on movie, music, and arts reviews and contains several pages of directory listings for restaurants, art galleries, bars, and clubs. There's also an "Apartment Finders Network"—a free networking system featuring hundreds of apartments advertised for rent, share, or sublet (listed by tenants and building managers).

The "Personal Dialogue" section contains classified ads you can respond to by touch-tone phone. You can have your ad printed for free (up to thirty-five words). The rate for responding to ads is $1.70 per minute. Mail your ad to Personal Dialogue™, P.O. Box 8208, FDR Station, New York, NY 10150, and you'll be notified by mail when the ad will appear and how to retrieve the responses to your ad.

NY Perspectives is published every Tuesday and is available free of charge, limited to one copy per reader. Subscriptions are $42.00 for one year and must be prepaid.

QUEENS TRIBUNE

WHERE: 46-25 Kissena Boulevard
Flushing, NY 11355
(718) 359-7777

WHAT: A weekly community newspaper serving all of Queens that contains local news items, editorials, business and professional ads, and classified ads. It was founded in 1970 and is distributed to local businesses free of charge—so look for it in banks, stores, delis, and other public places.

The "Personal Dialogue" section contains classified ads you can respond to by touch-tone phone. You can have your ad printed for free (up to 35 words). The rate for responding to ads is $1.70 per minute. Mail your ad to Personal Dialogue™, P.O. Box 8208, FDR Station, New York, NY 10150, and you'll be notified by mail when the ad will appear and how to retrieve the responses to your ad.

THE SELLING POST SINGLES SCENE

WHERE: 45-38 Bell Boulevard
P.O. Box 604
Bayside, NY 11361

WHAT: Published weekly, this paper contains nothing but classified ads. It calls itself "New York's Original Free Ad Paper Since 1957" and features four pages of personal ads: "Dial & Date" and "To the Letter Personals." There's also a listing of singles clubs and activities.

To reply to ads by mail, write letters to those people whose ads interest you. Include information about yourself as well as your phone number or address. On the front of each envelope you send out, write the code number that appears in the ad, pay a forwarding fee of $2.00 per letter, and send the letters to The Selling Post Singles Scene, which will forward the letters to the respective advertisers.

To respond to "Dial & Date" ads, dial 900-456-8377 from a touch-tone phone, press the * key at any time during the recorded greeting, and then enter the five-digit ad number. Enter your assigned three-digit personal security code, and then press 1 to hear your first message. The procedures are outlined step by step in the "Dial & Date" section of *The Selling Post.*

SINGLE PARENT

WHERE: Parents Without Partners, Inc.
8807 Colesville Road
Silver Spring, MD 20910

WHAT: This bi-monthly magazine has been published for over thirty years by Parents Without Partners. It presents the latest information on raising children, personal growth for single parents, legislative news, and tips on dealing with financial and legal problems and general parenting problems.

PWP members receive the magazine as part of their membership benefits, but non-members can subscribe for $15.00 per year or $25.00 for two years.

PWP also has a Single Parent Clearinghouse through which you can order a variety of informational kits ("Raising Children Alone," "Non-Custodial Fathers/Mothers," "Family Law"), fact sheets, brochures ("Single Parenting and Community Service," "Single Parenting and Education," "Single Parenting and Legislation," "40 Tips for Better Single Parenting"), bibliographies ("Annotated Bibliography for Children and Teens on Divorce," "Never-Married Parents' Reading List," "Annotated Bibliography and Resource List for the Widowed"), and books.

SINGLE TIMES

WHERE: Box 1015
Valley Stream, NY 11582
(516) 565-9100

WHAT: This is a monthly newspaper exclusively for singles, with over eight hundred social activities listed in each issue—including dance parties, theater parties, rap groups, brunches, wine and cheese gatherings, hikes and trips, single-parent activities, workshops and lectures, and after-work socials.

The personal ads section, "Personal Touch," is divided into two sections: female advertisers and male advertisers. You can respond by letter and forward as many letters as you want to *Single Times*—which will, in turn, forward them to the appropriate advertisers. There is no fee for responding to the personal ads.

Single Times has been around for over eight years. Invest in a one-year subscription for $18.00, or try out an issue first—you can get one from your local newsstand for $1.50.

SINGLES ALMANAC

WHERE: Almanac Publications
725 Route 440
Jersey City, NJ 07304

WHAT: Founded back in 1968, this monthly publication offers a day-by-day calendar of social and cultural events for singles throughout the New York, Long Island, Westchester, New Jersey and Connecticut regions.

There's a free personals section called "Gettin' Personal. . ." Buy an issue of the *Singles Almanac* for $2.00, and fill out the coupon for a free personal ad (up to thirty words—extra words cost 25¢ each). Send it in, and you'll get a passcode to retrieve your "voice box mail." You can respond to an ad by calling 900-226-1030 and punching in the five-digit code of the ad that interests you. Rate: $2.00 for the first minute, and 95¢ per additional minute. You can also respond by mail, at a cost of $2.00 for one letter or $5.00 for three letters.

The subscription rate is $20.00 for twelve issues.

THE UPPER EAST SIDE RESIDENT / THE UPPER WEST SIDE RESIDENT

WHERE: 386 Park Avenue South, Suite 1108
New York, NY 10016
(212) 679-4822

WHAT: In addition to local news and general-interest items, this weekly Manhattan paper has a nightlife calendar, a cinema calendar, restaurant reviews, travel articles, a fashion section, health briefs, and a community bulletin board of classified ads.

You'll also find Thc "Personal Dialogue" section for singles here. You can have your ad printed for free (up to thirty-five words), and you can respond to ads by touch-tone phone; the rate is $1.70 per minute. Mail your ad to Personal Dialogue™, P.O. Box 8208, FDR Station, New York, NY 10150, and you'll be notified by mail when the ad will appear and how to retrieve the responses to your ad.

Roam Manhattan's streets for a while and you'll probably see a kiosk with a pile of "Resident" papers for the taking.

THE VILLAGE VOICE

WHERE: 36 Cooper Square
New York, NY 10003

(212) 475-3300
Classifieds: (212) 475-5555

WHAT: The *Village Voice* is a weekly newspaper with a liberal slant that covers Metropolitan and World news; in-depth exposés; sports; reviews of music, film, theater, television shows, dance, and restaurants; and a substantial directory of nightlife (clubs, concerts, bars, restaurants, etc.).

The *Village Voice* has a hefty classifieds section, "The Personals," that's chock full of personal ads that range from conservative to raunchy. If you have a fantasy you'd like to fulfill, consider advertising in "The Personals." Just about anything goes here. Here's an example of one of the more unconventional ads that appeared:

"Buxom Bi-WF needed by attractive monogamous 26-year-old white couple of 9 years to teach us the magic of menage-a-trois. Must be voluptuous and sexy, clean, discreet and disease free as we are the same."

The cost of placing a personal ad varies according to the type of response service you choose. There's no charge for printing the ad if you use the VOICE Response Line (900-230-VOICE); $25.00 if you want a mail box; and $10.00 per line to place an ad if you don't use the VOICE Response Line (plus $25.00 for the mailbox).

The NY Metro Rate (NY, NJ, and CT) for subscribing to the newspaper is $44.95 a year.

VILLAGE VOICE PERSON-TO-PERSON CLASSIFIEDS

WHERE: 36 Cooper Square
New York, NY 10003-7118

WHAT: Now you can place a free personal ad in a special supplement to the *Village Voice*. The weekly supplement contains over a thousand personal ads, all placed free of charge, and can be picked up in numerous kiosks throughout the city. To place an ad, call (212) 475-5555. To respond to an ad, call (900) 67-VOICE. In addition to the personal ads, there's a column called "Ask Isador," which offers advice on sex, dating, and relationships. The supplement also contains a restaurant guide and a "Situations Wanted" employment classified ad section.

VOLUNTEER ORGANIZATIONS, CHARITIES AND COMMUNITY SERVICES

Volunteering is a great way to get to know people and at the same time help those in need. The nineties are a more "we-oriented" generation than the past few decades have been, and many people are devoting their spare time to charity work. There are lots of different social events sponsored by volunteer organizations—the proceeds of which go toward research, medical care, and other aid for a particular cause. For example, bike-a-thons, dance-a-thons, walk-a-thons, charity balls, fashion shows, luncheons, and other benefits are frequently organized by the various charities.

Here are some organizations that will be happy to use your services and that will provide you with a sense of purpose and a new circle of friends.

AMERICAN DIABETES ASSOCIATION, LONG ISLAND CHAPTER

WHERE: 150 Motor Parkway, Level B
Hauppauge, NY 11788-5108
(516) 348-0400

WHAT: This organization, dedicated to finding a cure or preventative for diabetes, offers education to professionals, patients, and the general public in the form of literature and support groups. To become a volunteer, just fill out an application form and attend the Association's training sessions. You can be involved in a number of different aspects: leading support groups, general office work, or offering assistance at health fairs and fundraisers. Special events sponsored by the Association include golf outings, walk-a-thons, dinners, and raffle drawings.

The ADA sponsors an annual "Walktoberfest" in several cities through the United States. You can participate individually or as part of a team. Call the Walktoberfest hotline at (800) 281-4925 for details.

AMERICAN LUNG ASSOCIATION OF QUEENS

WHERE: 112-25 Queens Boulevard
Forest Hills, NY 11375
(718) 263-5656

WHAT: The Queens and Hudson Valley Chapters of this national organization, in conjunction with several corporate contributors, sponsored a major fundraising event in October 1992 called "The Hamptons Harvest Bike Trek." Participants were required to raise a minimum of $250.00 in sponsored pledges (or, if they entered with two or more fellow employees as a company team, $750.00 in pledges was required). Proceeds go toward the American Lung Association's programs, which advocate clean air and provide support and education for people with asthma, tuberculosis, and other lung diseases.

The Hamptons Harvest Bike Trek is a two-day 85-mile ride through eastern Long Island. Top fundraisers are eligible to win a variety of prizes, such as a weekend getaway for two at the Nevele, or round-trip airfare for two on AmericaWest Airlines.

Get on the mailing list so you'll be kept informed about upcoming events, or become a volunteer.

THE COMPASSIONATE FRIENDS

WHERE: 64 Edna Avenue
Levittown, NY 11756-4219
(516) 796-4141

WHAT: This is an international round-the-clock hotline to help bereaved parents and adult siblings to cope with the loss of a loved one. To volunteer, you *must* be a bereaved parent or sibling. Members get together for mutual support and counseling.

GAY MEN'S HEALTH CRISIS

WHERE: 129 West 20th Street
New York, NY 10011
(212) 337-3593

WHAT: This organization provides assistance, education, and support for people living with AIDS. There are over two thousand volunteers working here; to join the ranks, call for an application. There is a training program and a suggested time commitment for each volunteer program. You can provide office support, food preparation, or workshop instruction, or join the "Buddy Program" to offer one-on-one assistance. Or, you can be involved in accounting, communications efforts, legal services, or lobbying efforts.

Many special events are sponsored; among the biggest is the annual AIDS dance-a-thon fund-raiser, featuring a huge dance floor, DJ music, complimentary food and drinks, performances, and celebrity emcees—with a turnout of about six thousand people. The money raised by this event goes toward emergency financial assistance, a meal program, psychological counseling, legal services, and lobbying efforts.

LONG ISLAND BLOOD SERVICES

(A Division of the New York Blood Center)

WHERE: 155 Duryea Road
Melville, NY 11747
(516) 752-7300

WHAT: This volunteer service gets pledges from a variety of Long Island singles organizations to donate blood at the annual Singles Blood Drive. This year it was held at the Radisson Plaza Hotel in Melville, and activities at the event included entertainment, dancing, a fashion show, dining, refreshments, free raffles, prizes, and scuba diving demos

MARCH OF DIMES BIRTH DEFECTS FOUNDATION

(Long Island Chapter)

WHERE: 400 Crossways Park Drive
Woodbury, NY 11797
(516) 496-2100

WHAT: This is one of the largest charity organizations in the world, providing support services and sponsoring a variety of fundraisers to promote research to prevent birth defects and to assist victims of birth defects and their families

Among its various fundraising activities is the annual "Spotlight on Singles Expo," which was most recently held at the Radisson Plaza Hotel in Melville. Exhibitors such as matchmaking services, tour operators, publishers of singles-related publications, and vendors of jewelry, clothing, and cosmetics gather for this event and distribute informational materials about their organizations. On the other side of the room, across from the exhibit tables, participants can dance to live DJ music and take part in matchmaking games led by the emcee. Raffle drawings are held to award such prizes as free or discounted membership to the exhibitors' organizations, theater tickets, or free trips

NATIONAL MS SOCIETY

(New York City Chapter)

WHERE: 30 West 26th Street
New York, NY 10010-2094
(212) 463-7787

WHAT: Dedicated to fighting multiple sclerosis—the most common neurological disease affecting young adults today—this society provides research, medical care centers, counseling, equipment, crisis services, transportation, recreation programs, and physical therapy for the estimated ten thousand New Yorkers suffering from MS.

There is an annual MS Fall Bike Tour, which covers thirty-four traffic-free miles starting at Battery Park in lower Manhattan. The well-marked route takes bikers through Central Park, over the Queensborough Bridge, and through a variety of neighborhoods. Volunteers must raise a minimum of $55.00 in pledges in order to ride in the tour. Prizes are awarded to the volunteers who raise the most money in pledges: last year, it was two round-trip tickets to any Continental Airlines destination in the United States, Canada, or Mexico.

THE SHARING COMMUNITY

WHERE: 118 New Main Street
Yonkers, NY
(914) 963-2626, Ext. 22

WHAT: A shelter for the homeless that needs more volunteers to prepare and serve food and to assist with clerical work. Fundraisers and holiday get-togethers are sponsored.

SINGLES FOR CHARITIES, INC.

WHERE: 12 Split Rock Road
Syosset, NY 11791
(516) 496-7197

WHAT: This organization, which has over a thousand volunteers, coordinates a variety of volunteer projects such as fundraisers, toy and clothing drives, concerts, fairs, and sporting events. It provides services to various categories of disabled and disadvantaged individuals. Their motto: "Those who bring sunshine to the lives of others cannot keep it from themselves."

STANLEY ISAACS NEIGHBORHOOD CENTER

WHERE: 415 East 93rd Street
New York, NY 10128
(212) 360-7620

WHAT: This center provides tutoring for adults in reading, writing, and math. Childcare services are offered for those adults who need to bring their children along. There are currently about thirty volunteers; the organization has indicated that they need additional childcare volunteers and math tutors.

MUSEUMS, PARKS, AND OTHER GOOD MEETING PLACES

Imagine this scenario: You and your friend are enjoying a summer's-eve concert on Central Park's Great Lawn, and you notice two guys smiling over at you from their blanket. You smile back, and one of them makes his way over to invite you to share their wine and cheese. You and your friend are feeling adventurous—and you happen to think these guys are better-looking than Patrick Swayze!—so you decide to join them.

As the sun starts to cast its crimson glow across the darkening sky, the guys light a couple of candles and snuggle up closer to you and your friend.

Seduced by the beauty of the music, the spectacular sunset, and the nearness of these men, you start to think that maybe you can fall in love with a stranger.

Is that romantic enough for you?

How about this one:

You're wandering through the Metropolitan Museum on a hot summer's day, mainly to escape the intense August heat, and you just happen to wind up at one of your favorite exhibits: the Japanese Garden. You sit for a while, enjoying its simple serenity. Suddenly you realize someone has been asking you a question. You snap to and look up. Your eyes meet the most gorgeous pair of blue eyes you've ever seen. The woman repeats her question: "Do you know how to get to the Eighteenth-century furniture exhibit from here?"

Saying a silent thanks to your parents for dragging you to the museum all those years until you had the layout memorized, you offer to show her the way. As you walk through the grand exhibit halls, you get to know the basics about each other—what kind of work you do, where you live, and so on. It turns out you both love bike-riding, and you ask her if she wants to go rent bicycles in Central Park right after the museum. She says yes!

These scenarios are not so unlikely. Sometimes it's just a matter of being at the right place at the right time, and being open and receptive to conversations.

Take a look at the listings in this chapter on museums, parks, botanical gardens, lobbies and atriums, and other public areas. They're all potential meeting places for you. Many of the parks and public atriums sponsor concerts on a regular basis, and the museums offer tours, lectures, and courses. There is also a wide variety of walking tours being offered throughout the city, led by guides who expound on what you are seeing and the historical significance of various points of interest.

In addition to the places we've described in this chapter, we'd like to mention some general hangouts and events that have great potential as a meeting ground for singles:

- ☐ Art galleries
- ☐ Shopping Malls
- ☐ Flea Markets (Lots of singles sell their wares from these booths week after week, and lots of singles come to shop.)
- ☐ Bookstores and libraries (Suggested ice breaker: If someone is reading the inside flap of a book you've already read, say something like, "That was a fantastic book—I'd really recommend it." Or, "I hope you don't think I'm being nosy, but that's not one of that author's better works—let me recommend some others to you." The conversation could lead to nonliterary subjects if the attraction is mutual.)
- ☐ Laundromats (Experiment: Try going at different times of the day and different days of the week; you'll meet a greater variety of the people who go there.)
- ☐ Conventions and Trade Shows
- ☐ Writers' Retreats
- ☐ Washington Square Park (Bring a Frisbee or your roller skates, or stretch out in the sun with a book and a picnic lunch.)
- ☐ College Campuses (There are any number of events going on at various campuses every day of the week—lectures, films, concerts, etc.)
- ☐ Central Park, especially Sheep's Meadow on a Sunday afternoon (bring your Sunday *Times*)
- ☐ Columbus Avenue (Have Sunday brunch at one of the cafes.)
- ☐ The steps of the 42nd Street Public Library in Manhattan (Especially at lunchtime and after work. In the spring and summer, people flock there in greater numbers than the pigeons do!)
- ☐ Damrosch Park behind Lincoln Center (You can catch some great concerts and other performances there.)
- ☐ Rockefeller Center, Forty-seventh and Forty-eighth Streets on Fifth Avenue (There's a long row of benches surrounded by gorgeous flowers and greenery. Maybe you'll meet a nice single tourist and convince him or her to move to New York!)

MUSEUMS

ALICE AUSTEN HOUSE, MUSEUM & GARDEN

WHERE: 2 Hylan Boulevard
Rosebank
Staten Island, NY
(718) 816-4506

WHAT: From this restored seventeenth-century Dutch farmhouse you can get a great look at the New York Harbor and the Verrazano Bridge. This used to be Alice Austen's house. In case you don't know who she is, she was a pioneer in photography in the 1890s. Her photos numbered over eight thousand; they provide an interesting pictorial history of Staten Island and New York City.

There are changing photo exhibits, many of which are not the work of Alice Austen. But her photographs are the subject of a 20-minute videotape.

Special events at the Alice Austen House include antique fairs in the spring and fall, a Victorian tea in June, Photo Day in June, a Nautical Festival in August, a Christmas celebration, and various lectures and concerts.

HOW MUCH: The suggested contribution is $2.00.

AMERICAN MUSEUM OF NATURAL HISTORY

WHERE: Central Park West at 79th Street
New York, NY
(212) 769-5800

WHEN: Monday, Tuesday, Thursday, Sunday from 10:00 a.m. till 5:45 p.m., and Wednesday, Friday, Saturday from 10:00 a.m. till 9:00 p.m.

WHAT: If you haven't ventured into the Museum of Natural History since your third-grade field day trip, you should really go back for a long-overdue visit. Remember, as a kid, staring up at those gargantuan dinosaur skeletons? That was one of the most memorable exhibits, but there's so much else to see: a ninety-four-foot diving blue whale, an ancient Sequoia tree dating back thirteen centuries, and a roomful of dazzling gems and minerals—including a 563-carat Star of India sapphire.

And have you ever caught the laser light shows at the Nature-Max Theater? The screen is about forty feet high, and the surround-sound is intense. You can call 496-0900 for a schedule of events going on at the theater.

If you tend to get overwhelmed by museums of this size (forty exhibit halls containing about thirty-five million display pieces), you might want to take the "highlights tour" and just follow the guide. That's a lot easier than deciding which direction to walk and which exhibits to see. You can't fit them all in in a day. Highlight tours are given from 10:15 a.m. till 2:30 p.m. Monday through Sunday, and also at 6:30 p.m. on Wednesdays during the summer months. The starting point for the tour is at the Info Desk on the main floor.

Every week there are various lectures, workshops, and film festivals going on, so call the main number for a recording of events.

HOW MUCH: The suggested contribution is $4.00. Admission to the NatureMax Theater and Planetarium is also $4.00.

BROOKLYN HISTORICAL SOCIETY AND MUSEUM

WHERE: 128 Pierrepont Street (at Clinton Street)
Brooklyn, NY
(718) 624-0890

WHAT: One of the highlights of this museum is the Shellens Gallery of Brooklyn History, featuring exhibits of five landmarks: the Brooklyn Bridge, Coney Island, the Brooklyn Navy Yard, the Brooklyn Dodgers and Hall of Fame, and the "Honeymooners" stage set.

Special exhibits focus on various aspects of Brooklyn history, such as the Fulton ferryboat and Dutch homesteads.

There's also a mammoth wood-paneled library containing 125,000 books—mostly on the history of Brooklyn.

Call for a schedule of guided tours, films, and lectures.

HOW MUCH: Admission is $2.50 except on Tuesdays from noon till 5:00 p.m., when admission is free.

BROOKLYN MUSEUM

WHERE: Eastern Parkway at Washington Street
Brooklyn, NY
(718) 638-5000

WHAT: The Brooklyn Museum features five floors of art objects, including ceremonial objects, masks and dolls of the American Indian and African cultures; Oriental galleries; an Egyptian collection; American and European costumes; furniture dating back to the seventeenth century; and American and European painting and sculpture.

The museum also has library facilities, and classical music concerts are performed on Sundays from October through May.

HOW MUCH: The suggested contribution is $4.00.

THE CLOISTERS

WHERE: Fort Tryon Park
Upper Manhattan
(212) 923-3700
(Take the M4 bus all the way uptown.)

WHAT: This is actually part of the Metropolitan Museum of Art, but it bears no resemblance to the Met. Every exhibit at The Cloisters is dedicated to the art of the Middle Ages, and you'll hear medieval music in the background as you admire the famous Unicorn tapestries, Spanish frescoes, stained glass, goldwork, and flower and herb gardens. The actual structure of the museum is kind of a patchwork of various sections of European cloisters and other religious architectural pieces.

Go up to The Cloisters during the spring or summer so you can walk through the grounds and admire the view of the Hudson River. Garden tours are given at 1:00 p.m. every day except Monday in May, June, September, and October.

On Saturday afternoons the museum sponsors special programs such as gallery talks, lectures, films, and, occasionally, concerts.

HOW MUCH: The suggested contribution is $6.00.

THE COOPER HEWITT MUSEUM

WHERE: 2 East 91st Street (at Fifth Avenue)
New York, NY
(212) 860-6868

WHAT: The building used to be Andrew Carnegie's 64-room mansion, and it now contains more than 165,000 decorative art objects—furniture, ceramics, glass, woodwork, prints, embroidery, and textiles dating as far back as 3,000 years ago. This is the ultimate in luxury, with Scottish oak paneling, Art Deco chandeliers, and leaded-glass windows by Tiffany.

Don't miss the lush garden right next to the museum, where you can even catch a summer concert if you show up on the right Tuesday evening.

Courses and lectures are also offered by the Cooper-Hewitt, and walking tours of New York City originate here.

HOW MUCH: Admission is $3.00, except from 6:00 to 9:00 p.m. on Tuesdays—then it's free.

ELLIS ISLAND IMMIGRATION MUSEUM

WHERE: Departure point:
South Ferry, Battery Park
New York, NY
(212) 363-6304

WHAT: For eight years this building stood vacant and abandoned. But in 1990, it re-opened after $150 million was poured into its restoration. The significance of Ellis Island, for those of you who slept through history class, is that twelve million immigrants passed through the doors of what is now the museum during the first two decades of this century—hoping to start a new life in America. Many of us actually are descendants of the people who stepped off the boat onto Ellis Island, once called the Island of Tears.

The museum's exhibit rooms depict the history of immigration through maps, charts, political cartoons, advertising posters, papers and forms that had to be filled out by the immigrants, photos of immigrants and their families, piles of baggage, and displays of clothing that belonged to people of many different nationalities.

You can also see the rooms where immigrants' mental and medical well-being were tested. And there's a half-hour film consisting of a photo montage and live footage of the experiences of these early twentieth-century immigrants.

HOW MUCH: It doesn't cost anything to enter the museum, but the ferry costs $5.00. It runs every half-hour in the summer and every forty-five minutes in the winter.

THE FRICK COLLECTION

WHERE: 1 East 70th Street (at Fifth Avenue)
New York, NY
(212) 288-0700

WHAT: Frick was a coke and steel magnate from Pittsburgh and an avid art collector who settled in this Fifth Avenue European-style mansion. The most beautiful feature is the enclosed garden court with classical Roman-style atrium, complete with skylight, marble fountain, and splendid magnolia trees and flowers.

Summer concerts are performed in this garden on Sundays at 5:00 p.m. and Wednesday evenings at 5:30.

Frick's art collection included works by Rembrandt, Renoir, Vermeer, Constable, Turner, Whistler, and many of the other great masters.

HOW MUCH: Admission is $3.00.

METROPOLITAN MUSEUM OF ART

WHERE: Fifth Avenue at 82nd Street
New York, NY
(212) 535-7710 or (212) 879-5500

WHAT: Don't expect to cover all the exhibits at The Met in one day, or even in one week. There are over three million works of art here, drawn from a wide variety of civilizations, including ancient Egypt, Near East, Greece, and Rome; plus paintings, sculptures, musical instruments, costumes, and other items dating back to the Middle Ages.

If you don't know where to start, take the highlights tour—it's given at 10:15 a.m., 1:15 p.m., and 3:15 p.m. on Tuesdays through Fridays.

Chamber music concerts are held on Friday and Saturday nights in the Great Hall, a two-story atrium-like space at the main entrance of the museum that has skylit domes and a majestic arched balcony.

There's an information booth in the Great Hall where you can find out about the various tours, lectures, gallery talks, concerts, and special exhibits going on.

HOW MUCH: The suggested contribution is $6.00.

MUSEUM OF BROADCASTING

WHERE: 25 West 52nd Street
New York, NY
(212) 752-7684

WHAT: This is sort of like the "Nickelodeon" cable TV station of museums: it broadcasts old radio and TV programming on two-person consoles. Their radio collection is composed of about fifteen thousand programs, including such early broadcasts as an eyewitness account of the Hindenburg disaster. There are twenty-five thousand TV cassettes, featuring the best of such classics as Ed Sullivan, Alfred Hitchcock, M*A*S*H, and "Saturday Night Live." In addition to the two-person consoles, there's a theater that seats over fifty people, which offers daily screenings of a variety of TV shows from the old days.

Tours are given at 1:30 p.m. on Tuesdays. Ask at the information desk about lectures and seminars.

HOW MUCH: Admission is $4.50.

MUSEUM OF MODERN ART

WHERE: 11 West 53rd Street
New York, NY
(212) 708-9400

WHAT: A collection of over a hundred thousand art objects, including paintings, sculptures, drawings, prints, photographs, and design. You can stand and view the sculpture garden from a four-story, glass-enclosed Garden Hall.

MoMA also has a Department of Film, whose archives contain eight thousand films. There are two theaters on the lower level, seating about 200 and 450 people. Films are shown every day, and some evenings are devoted to the new works of independent and experimental filmmakers.

Consult the information desk for a schedule of upcoming films, lectures, and special exhibits.

HOW MUCH: Adult admission is $7.00, except from 5:00 to 9:00 p.m. on Thursdays—then you get to decide what you want to contribute.

MUSEUM OF THE CITY OF NEW YORK

WHERE: Fifth Avenue at 103rd Street
New York, NY
(212) 534-1672

WHAT: Everything in this museum is dedicated to the history of New York City. You'll see dioramas of historical city scenes; a reconstructed Dutch fort; antique furniture, toys and clothing; and reconstructions of old, noteworthy New York City homes. New York's history is also narrated in a multi-media slide show that runs about half an hour.

Special programs include jazz concerts, theater, mime, occasional Sunday afternoon concerts, and walking tours of the city.

HOW MUCH: The suggested contribution is $4.00.

POE COTTAGE MUSEUM

WHERE: Grand Concourse & E. Kingsbridge Road
Bronx, NY
(212) 881-8900

WHAT: This is the house that the classic mystery/horror short story writer Edgar Allan Poe lived in for the last three years of his life. The simple white colonial English/Dutch house, built in 1812, has a rather sad history. Poe's wife died of tuberculosis the first summer they lived in the house, even though they had moved there in the hopes that the country air might help her to recover. After his wife died, Poe and his mother-in-law lived in the house in poverty. He wrote parts of "Annabel Lee" and "The Bells" from this abode.

The caretaker of the grounds gives tours of the house by appointment, and upstairs you can see a twenty-minute audiovisual show recounting Poe's life in Manhattan and the Bronx.

Be sure to get a schedule of the free concerts held at the Poe Park Bandshell in the summer.

HOW MUCH: Admission is $1.00.

RICHMONDTOWN RESTORATION VILLAGE

WHERE: Richmond Road at Clarke Avenue & Arthur Kill Road
Greenbelt
Staten Island, NY
(718) 351-1611

WHAT: If you want to get an idea of what New York City was like during the colonial days, visit this ninety-six-acre restoration village. You can go into the old courthouse, America's oldest public school, a general store, and a doll museum.

The guides are dressed in colonial-style clothing, and they'll demonstrate the crafts of that period, including basket-weaving, pottery making, and harness making.

There are also many exhibits at the Transportation and Staten Island Historical Society Museums.

Special events include a county fair in the fall, Militia Day in the spring, an annual Christmas festival, candlelight tours in December, and free lectures, concerts, and other public performances.

HOW MUCH: Adult admission is $4.00.

SNUG HARBOR CULTURAL CENTER

WHERE: 1000 Richmond Terrace
Livingston
Staten Island, NY
(718) 448-2500

WHAT: The center is on eighty acres of beautifully landscaped grounds. Twenty-eight historical buildings of various architectural styles serve as museums, galleries, and performing arts centers.

The Staten Island Botanical Gardens, Staten Island Children's Museum, and the Veterans' Memorial Hall (a recital hall that seats two hundred) are all located at Snug Harbor Cultural Center.

Special events featured here are the jazz festival in February, outdoor summer concerts performed by the New York Philharmonic and Metropolitan Opera, an outdoor sculpture festival every summer, and various seminars and lectures.

HOW MUCH: It costs $2.00 to enter the Newhouse Center for Contemporary Art; otherwise, admission is free.

SOUTH STREET SEAPORT MUSEUM

WHERE: Fulton Street between Water & South Streets
New York, NY
(212) 669-9400/9424

WHAT: You could easily spend a whole day at the South Street Seaport, because there's a lot to do and see. The museum actually covers an eleven-block area that includes a replicated fish market, restored Federal row houses, and anchored sailing ships at the piers that you can board.

In the restored village, which is closed off to cars, there are plenty of restaurants, shops, and mini-museums to stop in on. In fact, at the glass-enclosed Pier 17, there are 120 shops, restaurants, and cafes.

The New Fulton Market is a replica of the 1882 New Fulton Market, where food was sold wholesale until the 1960s. Now there are four floors of restaurants and food stalls catering to every palate.

It's hard to be at the Seaport without being tempted into taking a cruise. The Seaport Line Harbor Cruise offers daytime and evening cruises, ranging in length from ninety minutes to three hours. Call 406-3434 for more information about that.

You'll also want to check out the "Summerpier" concerts on Saturday evenings in July and August.

HOW MUCH: It's free to walk around, but the various museums charge admission fees, and of course you have to pay for your meals and for the cruises. Call the seaport for specifics.

STATUE OF LIBERTY

WHERE: Liberty Island
New York City Harbor
(212) 732-1286
Ferry: (212) 269-5755

WHAT: Many of us have never taken a trip up to Ms. Liberty's crown—we leave that to the tourists—but we've admired her from afar. Well, it's definitely worth the ferry ride from Battery Park.

When you get up close, you'll see how massive the statue really is. She weighs 225 tons, her waistline measures 35 feet (you think *you* need to go on a diet!), and the torch she holds in her right hand is over 300 feet above sea level. To climb up to her crown for spectacular views of the harbor, you'd better be in fairly good shape. There's no elevator, and there are 171 stairs to climb.

At the base of the Statue of Liberty there's a sculpture garden with bronze statues.

HOW MUCH: The only thing you'll be charged for is the ferry ride: $6.00. It runs every forty-five minutes in the winter and every half-hour in the summer.

VAN CORTLANDT MANSION HOUSE

WHERE: Van Cortlandt Park, off Broadway & N. 242nd Street
Bronx, NY
(212) 543-3344

WHAT: Dating back to 1748, this landmark manor house was part of Frederick Van Cortlandt's wheat plantation. Part of its historical significance is tied to the Revolutionary War; General Washington and the French General Rochambeau planned their military strategy from this house and then went on to launch the victorious liberation march to Manhattan in 1783.

Nine of the mansion's rooms have been restored to the days of the American Revolution, with eighteenth-and nineteenth-century antique furniture and historical documents on display.

Every year at the beginning of May there's a Colonial Festival hosted here, where you can see craftsmen working at their trades. You can also attend frequent lectures and concerts; call for a schedule of events.

HOW MUCH: Admission is $2.00.

WHITNEY MUSEUM OF AMERICAN ART

WHERE: 945 Madison Avenue (at 75th Street)
New York, NY
(212) 570-3600/3676

WHAT: Dedicated to displaying contemporary American art, this museum has changing exhibitions as well as permanent collections of the works of Calder, de Kooning, Gorky, Hopper, Nevelson, and Noguchi. Special exhibits are often dedicated to film and video-tape.

Ask at the information desk about lectures, films, and summer concerts, as well as special upcoming exhibits.

HOW MUCH: Adults pay $5.00 admission, except on Tuesdays from 6:00 to 8:00 p.m.

PUBLIC ATRIUMS

CHEMCOURT

WHERE: 277 Park Avenue (at 47th & 48th Streets)
New York, NY
(212) 310-7366

WHAT: This three-story greenhouse, covering two Manhattan blocks, is filled with lush plants, white marble waterfalls, and tables and chairs. Concerts are performed at Christmastime, and there's a small art gallery in the lobby.

CITICORP CENTER

WHERE: 153 East 53rd Street
New York, NY 10017
(212) 559-2330

WHAT: The public atrium—referred to as The Market—occupies the first two levels of this architecturally distinctive forty-eight-story building (not counting the basement). Shops and restaurants surrounding the atrium serve a variety of ethnic cuisine (Italian, Greek, Swedish, American). Don't count on getting a seat at any of the tables if you go during standard lunchtime (noon till 2:00 p.m.), but you can carve out a seat for yourself on one of the granite ledges. Lots of people get approached when they hang out here; we've experienced and witnessed it many times.

Schedules are printed every month; pick one up in the lobby to see which concerts and special programs are coming up.

CRYSTAL PAVILION

WHERE: 805 Third Avenue (at 51st Street)
New York, NY 10017

WHAT: This multi-level atrium has many public seating areas, stores and restaurants in the lobby, and a small raised stage from which piano music is performed on Tuesdays and Thursdays from 12:30 to 2:30 p.m.

875 THIRD AVENUE

WHERE: The name is the address—it's on Fifty-second and Fifty-third Streets.

WHAT: This tri-level atrium has public seating on every level. The Market on the lower level has a good selection of take-out eateries, and you can sit at the tables in the center. Piano music is performed on Mondays and Wednesdays at 12:20 p.m.

GALLERIA ATRIUM

WHERE: 115 East 57th Street
New York, NY
(212) 751-9649

WHAT: The central atrium is surrounded by stores, glass-enclosed offices, and overhanging plants. There's some public seating and a restaurant. Lunchtime concerts are given year-round, on most Tuesdays and Fridays.

GRAND HYATT HOTEL

WHERE: 42nd Street at Lexington Avenue
New York, NY
(212) 883-1234

WHAT: The lobby occupies four floors, and it's worth a visit, with its spectacular multi-tiered Italian rose marble fountain, gold-chrome spiral staircase, and glass-enclosed bar. You do have to pay for your snacks or meals in the lobby bar (don't bother bringing your own), but you get entertainment included in the cost: piano music at breakfast and lunch and a trio in the evenings.

IBM GARDEN

(The Bamboo Court)

WHERE: Madison Avenue at 56th Street
New York, NY
(212) 407-3500

WHAT: A sixty-eight-foot-high glass-enclosed garden with a skylight, towering bamboo trees, and numerous potted plants and flowers. Tables and chairs are available for public seating, and there's no ban on bringing your own lunch into the atrium. Another point of interest: you'll find computer terminals in the atrium that you can access for a listing of cultural attractions.

Concerts are performed by the Juilliard School of Music on Wednesdays at 12:30 p.m.

NEW YORK MARRIOTT MARQUIS

WHERE: 1535 Broadway (at 45th & 46th Streets)
New York, NY
(212) 398-1900

WHAT: If you don't find the lobby right away when you walk in, that's because it's on the eighth floor—and it goes all the way up to the top of the fifty-story building. In the center there's a huge column, along which the glass-enclosed elevators run up and down. The lobby has black and white marble floors, lots of plants and artificial trees and flowers, tiny lights on the ivy-covered balconies, skylights, bars and restaurants, and public seating. Piano music is performed nightly from 5:15 till midnight.

OLYMPIC TOWER

WHERE: 645 Fifth Avenue (at 51st & 52nd Streets)
New York, NY
(212) 421-5980

WHAT: The public seating areas are surrounded by pink and gray granite walls, a cascading two-story waterfall, lots of greenery, and mirrors that make it look as if there's twice as much of everything. There are lots of boutiques to shop at in the arcade. A pianist performs from noon till 2:00 p.m. on Mondays, Wednesdays, and Fridays.

PARK AVENUE PLAZA

WHERE: 55 East 52nd Street (between Madison & Park Avenues)
New York, NY

WHAT: The atrium has dark-green marble columns, greenery, and a central waterfall—plus a cafe area with public seating. Live music is performed from noon to 3:00 p.m., Monday through Saturday.

WORLD FINANCIAL CENTER

WHERE: West Street, between Liberty & Vesey Streets
New York, NY
(212) 945-0505

WHAT: If you haven't been to Battery Park City lately, you might want to pay a visit. A lot has changed down there, and you'll be amazed at the distinctive architecture of this mammoth commercial and residential complex.

The 120-foot high glass and steel atrium, which looks out to the Hudson River, is adorned by 45-foot-high palm trees, a marble hourglass-shaped staircase, diamond-patterned marble floor, and benches. Adjacent to the Winter Garden is the Courtyard, with a gray and peach marble floor and glass roof. Stores and restaurants surround these two structures, and there's an exhibition space above the Courtyard on the second-floor balcony where you can see changing art exhibits ranging from cartoon art to paintings. The World Financial Center is also a great place to shop—there are dozens of boutiques selling everything from watches to glassware.

Then there's the Plaza, a three-and-a-half acre park on the waterfront with marble benches, two eighty-foot fountains, and greenery. The Plaza is connected to Battery Park by an esplanade.

You can enjoy a wide variety of entertainment at the World Financial Center: music, dance, theater, and poetry. Weekday performances are at 12:15 or 6:30 p.m., and on Sundays at 3:00 p.m.. Call the number above for a schedule of upcoming events.

WORLD TRADE CENTER

WHERE: Church, Liberty, Vesey, and West Streets
New York, NY
(212) 466-4170/4233

WHAT: Six buildings surround the five-acre concrete plaza area, which is decorated by sculpture, a central fountain, and a revolving bronze globe twenty-five feet high. Changing exhibits are presented on the mezzanines at One and Two World Trade Center, and there's "Noontime on the Plaza" entertainment from Monday through Friday between July and September.

Of course, there's the observation deck on the top floor of Two World Trade Center, which is the world's highest observation deck, even though the World Trade Center is no longer the world's tallest building. If you're afraid of the potentially lethal combination of wide open spaces and height, you might prefer the glass-enclosed observation deck on the 107th floor.

FESTIVALS AND CONCERTS

There are some general names and phone numbers you should know about—such as American Landmark Festivals, which sponsors free music performances (chamber music, symphony orchestras, opera, dance, etc.) at various locations throughout Manhattan. And if you don't already know about Bryant Park, behind the Forty-second Street Public Library between Fifth and Sixth Avenues, you can get half-price tickets there to same-day music and dance performances from Tuesday through Sunday, noon to 2:00 p.m. and 3:00 to 7:00 p.m.

And here are some other places you can go that offer a steady schedule of concerts.

CARNEGIE HALL

Seventh Avenue at 57th Street
New York, NY
(212) 903-9750

Top performers command high ticket prices, but there are also some free programs offered: the Youth Symphony Orchestra, the All-City High School Band, and the Senior Concert Orchestra of New York.

CATHEDRAL OF ST. JOHN THE DIVINE

1047 Amsterdam Avenue (at 112th St.)
New York, NY 10024
(212) 316-7400

Weekly "Peace" programs feature musical, dance, or drama performances from September through June; Bach's St. John's Passion every spring; Messiah performance at Christmas.

CENTRAL PARK

The Dairy, Sundays at 1:00 p.m., May through October. On the Great Lawn you can hear performances by the Metropolitan Opera in June and the New York Philharmonic in July and August.

CHURCH OF ST. ANN & THE HOLY TRINITY

Clinton and Montague Streets
Brooklyn, NY
(718) 875-6960

Over a hundred dance and music performances—classical, jazz, and opera—are performed under the series called "The Incomparable Arts at St. Ann's."

COLUMBIA UNIVERSITY

In St. Paul's Chapel, organ recitals and a Bach series are presented from February through April, May through June, and October through November. The "Post-Crypt" Coffeehouse features music performances on Fridays and Saturdays at 9:00 p.m. from October through December and February till May.

CORNELIA STREET CAFE

29 Cornelia Street
New York, NY
(212) 929-9869

Free evening entertainment (jazz, folk music, comedy, cabaret revues, and new play readings) takes place Sundays through Thursdays starting at 8:00 p.m.

CUPPING ROOM CAFE

359 West Broadway
New York, NY
(212) 925-2898

Jazz concerts (free) are given on Fridays and Saturdays from 9:00 p.m. to 1:00 a.m.; you don't have to order food to sit and listen to the music.

DONNELL LIBRARY CENTER

53rd Street between 5th and 6th Avenues
New York, NY
(212) 621-0642

Jazz concerts take place on Wednesdays at noon from September through June, and, from time to time, Sundays at 2:30 p.m.

FLUSHING COUNCIL ON CULTURE & THE ARTS

Flushing Town Hall
137-35 Northern Boulevard
Flushing, NY
(718) 463-7700

Rotating outdoor concerts take place during the summer months at Alley Pond Park, Astoria Park, Crocheron Park, Cunningham Park, Fresh Meadows, Flushing Meadows, the Forest Park Bandshell, and MacDonald Park in Forest Hills, Queens.

FOREST PARK

Forest Drive & Woodhaven Boulevard
Rego Park, NY

(718) 520-5933

The Seuffert Band performs concerts on Sunday afternoons at 3:00 p.m. at the Forest Park Bandshell; several other events are also hosted here on a regular basis, such as an annual country music festival, jazz concerts, and circus performances.

FORT TRYON PARK

Northern tip of Manhattan, South of Dyckman, West of Broadway, and East of Henry Hudson Parkway.

Classical music and dance performances are given on Tuesday evenings at 7:00 in July and August. There's also the Annual Medieval Festival in September.

GOLDMAN MEMORIAL CONCERT BAND

(212) 944-1501

This band rotates from one outdoor concert space to another: Manhattan's Central Park, Damrosch Park (at Lincoln Center), and South Street Seaport; Brooklyn's Prospect and Seaside Parks.

GRACE CHURCH

800 Broadway (at 10th Street)
New York, NY 10003
(212) 254-2000

Organ recitals take place on Wednesdays at lunchtime (12:30 p.m.) from September through May, and choral performances on some Fridays at 8:00 p.m. or some Sundays at 4:00 p.m.

JAZZMOBILE

(212) 866-4900

Catch one of their outdoor jazz and cabaret performances at various locations in the city during the summer months (July and August).

LA MAMA/LA GALLERIA

6 East 1st Street (Second Avenue)
New York, NY
(212) 505-2476

Their "Meet the Composer" series takes place one Saturday a month at 8:00 p.m. and one Sunday a month at 4:00 p.m. There are poetry, prose, and play readings on certain Fridays and Saturdays.

LINCOLN CENTER

Broadway at 66th Street
New York, NY
(212) 877-2011

In Alice Tully Hall, free concerts are offered by the Juilliard School of Music on some Tuesdays, Wednesdays, and Fridays. Avery Fisher Hall houses the Mostly Mozart concert series and open rehearsals of the New York Philharmonic. Damrosch Park hosts a variety of outdoor concerts and festivals (including the Jazz Festival, with free concerts all summer), The Metropolitan Opera performs throughout the city, and the New York Philharmonic performs rotating classical concerts.

MIDWOOD FIELD CONCERT SERIES

East 16th Street between Avenues K & L
Brooklyn, NY
(718) 469-1912

Big band, classical, and bebop concerts can be heard on summer Thursday evenings at 7:30 p.m.

PROSPECT PARK

Flatbush, Ocean, & Parkside Avenues at Prospect Park West
(718) 788-0055

Summer weekend performances at the Bandshell include jazz, Caribbean music, Latin music, classical, folk, and pop.

QUEENS COUNCIL ON THE ARTS

161-04 Jamaica Avenue
Jamaica, New York
(718) 291-1100

The council sponsors a variety of musical programs at the Queens Botanical Gardens and the Forest Park Bandshell.

QUEENS SYMPHONY, POPS IN THE PARK

(718) 275-5000

The Queens Symphony performs at various locations throughout the borough of Queens, including Astoria Park, Baisley Pond Park, Cunningham Park, Forest Park, and Belmont Race Track.

RIVERSIDE CHURCH

490 Riverside Drive (at 120th Street)
New York, NY
(212) 222-5900

Summer concerts are held on Tuesdays at 6:30 p.m. and on some Sunday afternoons; Carillon recitals take place on Saturdays at noon and Sundays at 3:00 p.m.

ST. BARTHOLOMEW'S CHURCH

Park Avenue at 51st Street

New York, NY
(212) 751-1616

"Great Music" concerts take place on some Sunday afternoons at 4:00 during the fall and spring months; there are noontime Messiah sing-alongs around Christmastime; and musicals and dramas are performed at St. Bart's Playhouse. Theatrical readings by well-known actors are sponsored by Free Theatrical Productions

---

ST. MARK'S IN THE BOWERY

Second Avenue at 10th Street
New York, NY
(212) 674-6377

Outdoor summer concerts are held on Thursdays in July at noon, performed in the courtyard by the 3rd Street Music School.

ST. PATRICK'S CATHEDRAL

Fifth Avenue at 50th Street
New York, NY
(212) 753-2261

Organ recitals are given on Sunday afternoons at 4:45. This organ has nine thousand pipes, the largest of which is thirty-two feet long

---

ST. PAUL'S CHAPEL

Broadway & Fulton Streets
New York, NY
(212) 602-0874

Classical "Noonday Concerts" are performed on Mondays and Thursdays at—you guessed it—noon.

ST. PETER'S CHURCH

619 Lexington Avenue (at 54th Street)
New York, NY
(212) 935-2200

You can hear Jazz Vespers on Sundays at 5:00 p.m., Jazz at Noon on Wednesdays, and Sunday concerts at 7:00 p.m.

ST. THOMAS CHURCH

Fifth Avenue at 53rd Street
New York, NY
(212) 757-7013

Occasional concerts are given at 7:30 p.m. There are organ recitals on Sundays at 5:00 p.m.; and a full choral offering of sung evening prayers on Tuesday, Thursday, and Sunday afternoons.

SNUG HARBOR CULTURAL CENTER

The outdoor summer concerts held at Veteran's Memorial Hall include performances by the New York Grand Opera, the Metropolitan Opera, and the New York Philharmonic.

STATEN ISLAND CHAMBER MUSIC PLAYERS

(718) 356-2094

This ensemble performs about sixty concerts a year at various parks, schools, and other public places.

SYMPHONY SPACE

2537 Broadway (at 95th Street)
New York, NY
(212) 864-1414

You can attend local and international performances in dance, music, drama, and film; concerts performed by the Mannes School Orchestra; and the "Wall-to-Wall" great composer series.

TEMPLE EMANUEL

Fifth Avenue at 65th Street
New York, NY
(212) 744-1400

Organ recitals are given on Fridays at 5:00 p.m. A lecture series takes place on three consecutive Sundays in March and November.

TRINITY CHURCH

74 Trinity Place (Broadway & Wall Streets)
New York, NY
(212) 602-0847

Chamber music, classical concerts, and vocal recitals can be heard at 12:45 p.m. on Tuesdays.

WASHINGTON SQUARE MUSIC FESTIVAL

Washington Square Park
New York, NY
(212) 431-1088

Outdoor classical music concerts take place on occasional Tuesday evenings at 8:00 in the summer months, as well as concerts performed by the Festival Orchestra.

WALKING & SIGHTSEEING TOURS

For those of you who like to take a more fitness-oriented approach to sightseeing by going on foot, here are some of the organizations that offer interesting city tours.

WALKING TOURS

ADVENTURES ON A SHOESTRING

300 West 53rd Street
New York, NY
(212) 265-2663

BRONX HERITAGE TRAIL

Bronx County Historical Society
(212) 881-8900

HERITAGE TRAIL

New York Convention & Visitors Bureau
2 Columbus Circle
New York, NY
(212) 397-8222

SIGHTSEEING TOURS

CITY HALL/GOVERNOR'S ROOM MUSEUM

Broadway & Murray Street
New York, NY
(212) 566-8681
Weekdays, between 10:00 a.m. and 3:00 p.m., by appointment.

COLUMBIA UNIVERSITY

114th - 120th Streets, from Broadway to Amsterdam Avenue
New York, NY

(212) 854-1754
Weekdays at 10:00 a.m., 2:00 or 3:00 p.m., depending on the time of year.

GRACIE MANSION

(The Mayor's official residence)
East End Avenue at 88th Street
New York, NY
(212) 570-4751
Wednesdays, by appointment only.

GRAND CENTRAL DISTRICT TOURS

Philip Morris Building
42nd Street & Park Avenue
New York, NY
(212) 986-9217
Fridays at 12:30 in good weather.

ROCKEFELLER CENTER

48th - 51st Streets, from 5th to 6th Avenue
New York, NY
(212) 6948-8676
One-hour tour of the NBC studios, RCA Observation Deck, and Radio City Music Hall.

SUPREME COURT OF NEW YORK

60 Centre Street at Foley Square
New York, NY
(212) 374-8524
Weekdays, 10:00 a.m., for group tours. Individual tours are arranged by appointment.

UNITED NATIONS

First Avenue at 42nd Street
New York, NY
(212) 963-1234
One-hour tour, given in twenty-five languages, starting every fifteen minutes between 9:15 a.m. and 4:45 p.m.

POETRY READINGS

Are you a closet poet? Maybe you've dabbled in some free verse or composed a few poems in your head while strolling through the park. Perhaps the sound of someone else reciting poetry is like music to your ears. In whatever way poetry touches you, the places listed below might interest you.

BACKFENCE

155 Bleecker Street (at Thompson St.)
New York, NY
(212) 475-9221

Free poetry readings are held on Sunday afternoons from August to January. There are also open readings, where you can share your own poetry with the audience. The Backfence is also a folk/rock music club.

DONNELL LIBRARY CENTER

20 West 53rd Street (between 5th and 6th Avenues)
New York, NY
(212) 621-0618

Poetry and prose readings take place on certain Mondays at 6:00 p.m. and some Tuesdays at 6:00 p.m. A book discussion series is held on designated Thursdays at 6:30 p.m.

LIFE CAFE

343 East 10th Street (at Avenue B)
New York, NY
(212) 477-8791

Every season except summer there are poetry readings on Tuesdays at 8:00 p.m. The Life Cafe also serves lunch and dinner, and a live band performs there one night a week. People at the bar are usually friendly and talkative.

PEN & BRUSH

16 East 10th Street
New York, NY
(212) 475-3669

Prose and poetry workshops are offered every month at this art and literary club, along with concerts, lectures on art or writing, and arts and crafts courses

POETRY PROJECT AT ST. MARK'S

10th Street & Second Avenue
New York, NY
(212) 674-0910

Every Monday at 8:00 p.m. you can attend poetry performances. Poetry readings take place on Wednesdays at 8:00 p.m. Sometimes, workshops on poetry and writing are given. Open readings are held on the first Monday of every month.

POETRY SOCIETY OF AMERICA

National Arts Club
15 Gramercy Park South
New York, NY
(212) 254-9628

Poetry readings are held on weekdays from October through May.

SPEAK EASY

107 MacDougal Street
New York, NY
(212) 5948-9670

Poetry readings are held at 7:30 p.m. on Mondays, and music performances every other Saturday from 4:00 to 7:00 p.m.

PARKS, ZOOS, BOTANICAL GARDENS AND BEACHES

The following listings should provide you with plenty of ideas about how to spend a pleasant day outdoors. What better way to lift your spirits up if you've been chained to the office all week long?

BARNEGAT LIGHTHOUSE STATE PARK

Long Beach Island, New Jersey

Two thousand acres along the Jersey shore consisting of a bathing beach, picnic area, and parking area—plus a lighthouse that's open to visitors. The view of the coastline from the top is worth the climb—217 steps.

BATTERY PARK

State Street & Battery Place, lower Manhattan

(212) 397-3101

This is where you can catch the ferries bound for Ellis Island and the Statue of Liberty, but you can also sit and enjoy a summer's day on the lawn or on one of the benches overlooking the Hudson River. There are often festivals and holiday programs going on.

BETHPAGE STATE PARK

Southern State Parkway and Bethpage Parkway, Farmingdale, Long Island

(516) 669-1000 (Long Island State Park Commission)

This is a golfer's paradise, with five eighteen-hole courses and a golf clubhouse. The 1,475-acre park also has bridle paths, ball fields, tennis courts, hiking trails, and picnic areas, plus a restaurant, cafeteria, and refreshment stands. An annual art exhibit is hosted here.

BRONX ZOO

Fordham Road at Bronx River Parkway, Bronx

(212) 367-1010

More than three thousand animals are housed in this 265-acre zoo. Highlights: Wild Asia, the African Plains, the Bengali Express Monorail, Jungleworld, World of Darkness, the Reptile House, House of Apes, World of Birds, and the South American rain forest.

BROOKLYN BOTANICAL GARDENS

1000 Washington Avenue, North of Prospect Park, Brooklyn
(718) 622-4433

You've probably only seen a small percentage of the twelve thousand varieties of plants that grow here. The gardens stretch over fifty-two acres, and there are lots of must-sees: the rose garden, with nine hundred varieties, the Japanese Hill & Pond Garden (consisting of a waterfall, an Oriental shrine, sculptured trees, a pond, and a pagoda), a replica of a fifteenth-century Buddhist temple with surrounding gardens, a glass-enclosed botanical museum (Steinhardt Conservatory), the Shakespearean herb garden, and a fragrance garden for the blind. If you visit in April or May, don't miss the opportunity to stroll down cherry blossom lane. Talk about romantic!

CENTRAL PARK

59th to 110th Streets, from Fifth Avenue to Central Park West, Manhattan
(212) 397-3156

Aside from the many, many picnic and suntanning spots you can carve out for yourself on Central Park's 840 acres of lawns, there are tons of recreational opportunities. You can rent boats and bicycles, take a ride on the carousel, visit the zoo (at the East Sixty-fourth Street entrance), take a guided tour of the park, go ice skating (in the winter, of course) at Wollman Rink or roller skating by Sheep Meadow, swim in Lasker Pool (106th Street), attend a concert, play, or puppet show, go horseback riding (you can rent a horse at Claremont Stable at 175 West Eighty-ninth Street), play tennis at the courts on Ninety-fifth Street (you need a permit), take a horse-and-buggy ride, organize a team and get a permit to play softball on one of the ball fields, or jog around the reservoir—or anywhere else in the park. If you hate to jog alone, look into the group runs that are organized by the N.Y. Road Runners Club; the groups meet at Engineer's Gate on Ninetieth Street and Fifth Avenue.

A little-known fact: you can volunteer to work in Central Park. Call the New York City Department of Parks and Recreation for details

CLAY PIT PONDS STATE PARK PRESERVE

83 Nielsen Avenue, Charleston, Staten Island
(718) 967-1976

This 250-acre state park sponsors historical field trips, lectures, workshops, films, and walking tours on weekends. Of special interest to hikers are Abraham's Pond and Ellis Swamp Foot Trails. There's horseback riding, too.

CONEY ISLAND

Ocean Parkway, Brooklyn

It's not what it once was, but it's a nice way to spend a day in the sun. The beach goes on for miles, and there's a two-and-a-half-mile boardwalk where you can hang out and ogle the passers-by—maybe even scope out someone you can get to know. Thrill-seekers can visit the amusement park; try Wonderwheel and Astroland. East of the amusement area is New York Aquarium, which is definitely worth a visit. You'll see three hundred different species of underwater creatures—including beluga whales, sharks, an electric eel that lights up, piranhas, octopi, gigantic turtles, seals, and penguins.

FLUSHING MEADOW PARK

Roosevelt Avenue, Long Island Expressway, and Grand Central Parkway, Queens

(718) 507-3000

Highlights of this 1,275-acre park are the lake, boathouse (where you can rent paddle boats and bicycles), zoo, ice skating rink, pitch-n-putt, the National Tennis Center, Theater-in-the-Park, Hall of Science, the carousel, and numerous ball fields. Throughout the summer the park hosts a variety of festivals: Queens Day, annual Columbian, Ecuadorian, and Korean festivals, and concerts.

FOREST PARK

Woodhaven Boulevard, Park Lane South, and Forest Park Drive, Queens

(718) 441-7213

The park is divided into three sections by main thoroughfares. At certain times, one of the sections is closed off to vehicular traffic. Forest Park has biking and horseback riding paths (the stables are at Trotting Course Lane), walking trails, tennis courts, paddleball/handball courts, ball fields, a golf course, and a newly renovated carousel with snack bar. The bandshell, a few yards past the carousel (north of the Woodhaven Boulevard entrance to the park) hosts a variety of concerts and festivals. Behind the bandshell is the golf course.

FORT TRYON PARK

South of Dyckman, West of Broadway, northern tip of Manhattan

(212) 923-3700

This is a sixty-two-acre park that offers spectacular views of the Hudson River and the Palisades. You can walk through the flower and herb gardens, visit The Cloisters museum, take a guided walking tour, attend the Annual Medieval Festival in September, and go to classical music concerts and dance performances on certain summer evenings.

JERSEY SHORE

New Jersey Transit Service: Call (800) 772-2222 or (201) 762-5100

The Jersey Shore encompasses numerous beaches and seaside resorts—Long Branch, Belmar, Spring Lake, Point Pleasant Beach, and Bay Head, just to name a few. New Jersey Transit will get you to ten seaside towns—from Long Branch to Bay Head—and the beach is always just a ten- to fifteen-minute walk from the train station.

JONES BEACH STATE PARK

Meadowbrook and Wantagh State Parkways, Wantagh, Long Island
(516) 669-1000 (Long Island State Park Commission)

There's a lot more to do here than get a tan and take a dip in the ocean: there's surfing, bay and pier fishing, pitch-n-putt golfing, softball fields, roller skating, and folk and square dancing. You won't go hungry if you spend the day at Jones Beach: there are a restaurant, cafeterias, and refreshment stands. Performances at the Marine Theater include musicals and concerts.

MYSTIC SEAPORT

Mystic, Connecticut
(203) 572-0711

Just a three-hour train ride (Amtrak) or drive from New York City, Mystic is a great one-day getaway that doesn't really require any advance planning. If you get an early start you should be able to cover all the highlights: Mystic Seaport Museum—a compound of commercial structures and ships restored to their nineteenth-century flavor (the era when Mystic was a major shipbuilding town); Olde Mistick Village—a model of an eighteenth-century small town; and Mystic Aquarium—don't miss the dolphin shows! Mystic offers a variety of lodging and restaurants, so you may want to extend your stay.

NEW YORK BOTANICAL GARDENS

Southern Boulevard, at 200th Street, Bronx
(212) 220-8777

You'll see roses, daffodils, azaleas, rhododendrons, magnolias, cherry trees, dogwoods, willows, beech trees, and bonsais. You'll also see a fern forest, a palm court, tropical and desert plants, and herb gardens. There's a romantic spot for picnicking by the brook.

PELHAM BAY PARK

Hutchinson Parkway, Pelham Bay Parkway, and City Island Road, Bronx
(212) 430-1890

The hiking trails seem to go on forever in this two-thousand-acre park, and there's a mile and a half of sandy beach divided into about ten sections—each of which seems to attract a different type of beachgoer. Apparently, section #8 is a good tanning spot for singles. There are plenty of things to do in Pelham Bay Park: golfing at two courses, biking, tennis, horseback riding, swimming, fishing, hiking, jogging, and bird watching.

PROSPECT PARK

Flatbush Avenue, Ocean Avenue, Parkside Avenue, and Prospect Park West and Southwest, Brooklyn
(718) 788-0055

Five hundred acres of meadows, wooded areas, lakes, walkways, and horseback riding paths. Special attractions include the boathouse (you can rent pedal boats), a restored carousel, a hundred-acre meadow with seven ball fields, tennis courts, an ice skating rink with the same name as the one in Central Park (Wollman Rink) located on East Drive between Lincoln Road and Parkside Avenue, a zoo and children's farm, and the bandshell—which offers a wide variety of entertainment during the summer. Guided tours of the park are sponsored by the Urban Park Rangers.

QUEENS BOTANICAL GARDENS

43-50 Main Street, at the entrance to Flushing Meadows Park, Queens
(718) 886-3800

Thirty acres of roses, chrysanthemums, crabapple and cherry trees, weeping willows, and much more. Lots of couples take their vows in the Wedding Garden here. Call for a schedule of exhibits, workshops, lectures, concerts, and films.

RAMAPO MOUNTAIN STATE FOREST

Oakland, Bergen County, New Jersey

About half of the acreage of this park has been dedicated as a natural preserve, in the middle of which sits Ramapo Lake. You can fish and hike in the forest; there are almost twenty miles of trails.

RIVERSIDE PARK

72nd Street to 145th Street, along the Hudson River, Manhattan

Visit Grant's Tomb at 110th Street or the boat marina at 79th Street. Get a schedule of the summer concerts and theatrical productions scheduled at the Riverside Park Rotunda.

ROCKAWAY BEACH/JACOB RIIS PARK

9th Street to 149th Street, Rockaway Peninsula, Queens
(718) 318-4000

This is a ten-mile beach with accompanying boardwalk, plus paddleball/handball courts, playgrounds, and picnic areas alongside the boardwalk. The entrance to Rockaway Playland is on Ninety-eighth Street; there's a good selection of rides and an amusement arcade. Go a little further past Rockaway Beach, and you'll get to Riis Park—with more beach, boardwalk, and handball courts, plus an Eighteen-hole pitch-n-putt.

STATEN ISLAND BOTANICAL GARDENS

1000 Richmond Terrace, Snug Harbor, Staten Island
(718) 273-8200

A variety of rose and other floral gardens, tree gardens, and herb gardens grace these premises. Check out the bonsai collection in the greenhouse, and the

Duck Pond. Every October the gardens host the Flower Show & Harvest.

STATEN ISLAND ZOO

614 Broadway, West Brighton
(718) 442-3100

This is home to a lot of the smaller species—like raccoons, otters, prairie dogs, reptiles, and birds. There's a new aquarium and a South American tropical forest.

SUNKEN MEADOW STATE PARK

Northern State and Sunken Meadow State Parkways, Kings Park, Long Island
(516) 669-1000 (Long Island State Park Commission)

Here you can sunbathe, swim in Long Island Sound, picnic, hike on the trails, play golf on one of three nine-hole golf courses, and play softball on one of the fields.

VAN CORTLANDT PARK

Broadway at 242nd Street, Bronx
(212) 430-1890

You can hike or jog through this thousand-plus acre park, have a picnic lunch by Van Cortlandt Lake, visit Van Cortlandt Mansion, play golf on either of the two public courses, go horseback riding, and—when there's snow—go cross-country skiing (bring your own skis).

VOORHEES STATE PARK

Hunterdon County, New Jersey

Campers and hikers can enjoy the many scenic trails that wind through this five-hundred-acre park. There's also an observatory, playgrounds, and picnic areas.

WASHINGTON SQUARE PARK

West 4th Street, MacDougal Street, Waverly Place, and University Place, Manhattan

On weekends there's always something going on at Washington Square—whether it's the annual art show (May and September), summer concerts, shows put on by street performers, or even Frisbee throwing and splashing around in the water fountain.

WILLOWBROOK PARK

Victory Boulevard near Richmond Avenue, Staten Island
(718) 698-2186

Go ice skating on the lake, rent a rowboat, or have lunch in one of the picnic areas.

WOLFE'S POND PARK & BEACH

Hylan Boulevard & Cornelia Avenue, Staten Island
(718) 698-2186

Twenty acres of this park are used by the public for bathing, rowboating, freshwater fishing, and picnicking.

QUESTIONNAIRE RESPONSES

One of the most enjoyable aspects of writing this book was talking to singles about their experiences and reading their comments on the questionnaires we distributed.

We heard from a good cross-section of singles—introverted and extroverted, established professionals and people just starting out in their careers, bar-hoppers and singles who don't go out much, divorced singles, single parents . . . .

The aim of our questionnaires and interviews was to find out how singles go about meeting other singles—where they go, what they talk about when they first meet someone, what they like in a partner, what kind of commitment they're looking for, and other issues related to single life.

We'd like to share with you—without mentioning any names, of course—the kinds of information we got.

When asked how they felt about meeting new people, most chose the response "It is comfortable and easy"; only a few said it makes them "a little uncomfortable."

The favorite way of meeting other singles was parties, but a few preferred the bar and club scene. Other ways of meeting people that they cited were through mutual friends, at work, at school, and company picnics. Only two of the respondents had used a dating service, but several had placed or responded to personal ads.

One of the questions we asked was, "Do you like being single?" "No" was the most common answer, but almost as many of the respondents said they liked being single "Sometimes." A very small percentage answered "Yes."

We asked people what they liked most and least about being single, and here are some of the responses.

PRO:

- Independence
- Freedom of doing things when I want to and being with somebody when I want to
- Not answering to someone
- I don't have to deal with just one person on a regular basis
- Freedom, variety, and opportunity to focus on myself
- Not having to call home if you were stoppin' for drinks

CON:

- ☐ Loneliness
- ☐ Being broke *all* of the time
- ☐ Loss of sexual interest, unless I am madly in love
- ☐ Always being alone, or not even dating
- ☐ Being alone on Sunday morning
- ☐ Not having that special someone to learn from one another and to just appreciate having someone there
- ☐ Long stretches of not being intimate with someone

What were these singles looking for in the way of commitment? Most were looking for "a steady, long-term commitment" and/or "marriage," but about a third of the respondents were looking for "someone to date casually."

We also asked respondents to describe what they thought the people they had dated were looking for. The overwhelming response was that the people they had dated "seemed to just be looking for a good time" and "seemed to be afraid of commitment." Only a few singles said they felt the people they'd dated "seemed to want a steady relationship."

Asked to list some of the important characteristics of a potential mate, responding singles wrote that they wanted someone who was:

- ☐ Compassionate
- ☐ Caring
- ☐ Sensitive
- ☐ Affectionate
- ☐ Somewhat intellectual
- ☐ Giving
- ☐ Committed
- ☐ Financially secure
- ☐ Attractive
- ☐ Sweet
- ☐ Single and sexy
- ☐ Honest
- ☐ Successful
- ☐ Generous
- ☐ Moderate
- ☐ Tall
- ☐ The right age for me
- ☐ An animal lover

Other attributes considered desirable were:

- ☐ A good sense of humor
- ☐ A good personality
- ☐ Money
- ☐ Spiritual awareness and a kind and gentle soul

- An appreciation of yoga or the ability to assume unusual physical positions *(What do you suppose he had in mind?)*
- A realization that money is totally useless except for one thing: its purchasing power
- Good lips
- A nice smile
- Attractive facial features

We next gave people an open-ended question that went like this: *When I'm attracted to a stranger, I show them I'm interested by* _________.

Here were some of the responses:

- Smiling
- Piercing eye contact, involving mouth at times
- Displaying my plumage and roaring *(Get the feeling some people didn't want to take this too seriously?)*
- Don't have the courage to even make eye contact
- Trying to make conversation or eye contact
- Just being friendly and waiting for them to show their interest first
- Smiling a lot and give out *my own* phone number
- Being inquisitive and getting to know the other person by questioning

Another open-ended question was, *I can tell someone is attracted to me by the way they* _________.

Responses:

- Undress
- Talk and act
- Smile, and their eyes keep meeting mine and sparkling
- Look at me
- How often they call
- How they treat me or try to get to know me better
- Respond with physical cues, body language, tactile stimulation

Here are some of the descriptions people gave us for their idea of the perfect mate:

- Someone who's humorous, good-looking, intelligent, and caring
- One like my Mom
- Someone who is intellectually stimulating, physically alluring, and emotionally mature
- Someone who is caring about me and others and responsible, but also fun to be with and not too serious
- Someone who's funny and speaks English
- Someone who's good looking, intelligent, funny, sincere, and interesting
- Someone who's honest, never-married, employed, has set goals in life, has a salary over $40K, loves animals, has a nice car or lives in Manhattan, stylish, polite, not self-centered, not a chauvinist, SEXY!

(Now here's a woman who really knows what she wants!)

- A guy who is committed, caring, affectionate, financially secure, attractive, witty, and *single*
- Someone who is caring, understanding, and financially secure
- A friendly, outgoing person

We asked our singles what they do and don't talk about when they first meet someone. Here are some of the Dos and Don'ts they came up with:

Do talk about:

- General topics
- Non-intrusive topics
- Anything and everything
- Our jobs, and we eventually start talking about our interests and what we enjoy or don't enjoy
- Money, sex, music, occupations, goals, astrology
- Sports, music, work, comedy, activities, hobbies

Don't talk about:

- Serious topics
- My difficult experiences
- Each others' past relationships. You want to get to know that individual for yourself—not how others saw him.
- Sex, relationships, family

Where do people like to go on first dates? Dinner or drinks seem to be the most popular first dates:

- A restaurant *(most common response)*
- Has to be a public place—a really nice place—their treat, of course!
- A concert
- Baseball game
- Out drinkin'
- Out for a drink or coffee somewhere so we can get to know each other

How bad would a first date have to be, or how much of a jerk would the person have to be, for you to not go out on a second date with someone? Here's what our singles told us: *I wouldn't go out with someone on a second date if* __________.

- I didn't have fun on the first date
- They won't allow me to handle them . . . in a gentle way, of course
- On the first date, they seemed to display a greater than average knowledge about thorazine and lithium *(Yeah, we got a kick out of that one, too.)*
- He's cheap
- He didn't call me back after the first date on the next day
- He's cheap, rude, and unattractive to me or we have nothing in common

- 1. They stand me up the first time, 2. Get fresh or rude, 3. Don't pay my way, 4. Are very boring, 5. Don't kiss well.
- They appear to have serious problems
- They are married, involved with someone else, or have children

We were curious about the best and worst dates people ever had, because their experiences could give other singles some suggestions or words of warning. These were some of the better descriptions:

BEST DATES:

- I was taken to a gallery reception at Soho, dinner in Little Italy, dancing at a club, and then we went on a horse & buggy ride through Central Park in the moonlight. *(Wow, let's get that guy's phone number and spread it around!)*
- Going to a nice restaurant and then slow-dancing the rest of the night
- I can't think of the best one . . . I had a few! . . . but a lot of times the first date is the best one because the person is new—and besides, my curiosity disappears by the second date.
- We had ice cream sundaes at an old-fashioned ice cream parlor and then went to a small park in the neighborhood where we kissed all evening.

WORST DATES:

- I went out with a man and he and his friends were doing drugs in the bathroom.
- My friend fixed me up on a blind date. It was an absolute nightmare—the guy was old, obnoxious, and very stupid. I hated every minute of it!
- An absolutely unattractive blind date
- I went to the theater with a guy I'd admired from afar for a long time. During intermission, we had absolutely nothing to say to each other, and after the play, I suggested going for drinks hoping we could finally get some conversation going, but he wanted to go see a movie. Then, on the train ride home, we rode back in silence.

And finally, we asked our singles to describe their overall impression of the dating scene in New York. As you'll see, there are some jaded singles out there, but there's still a lot of hope that something better will come their way.

- Opportunities exist, but it takes a little more effort to seek them out.
- Hot . . . steamy . . . but stuffy, too.
- There isn't enough social interaction.
- What I like about dating is spending time with someone new, but my main gripe about the current dating scene is the bar scene.
- People are liars. They are all unhappy in their situations.
- It's the PITS!!

- ☐ Don't trust anybody, and before you get "serious," get an investigator to check them out.
- ☐ It's okay.
- ☐ In general, I guess it's all right. I mean, it's part of the process of growing up. It's very frustrating when you reach a certain age, because you want to feel some kind of being settled. I'm not saying married, but just having someone there, someone who understands you. Being alone is not that much fun. I mean, you're not really alone—you have your work, friends, family—but it's not quite the same. But the dating scene is okay, you get to meet interesting people, and you get to learn things about people.

You might get a good feeling from knowing that, a couple of months after this thirty-year-old woman turned in her questionnaire, she met a great guy at Rascal's on East Twenty-first Street in Manhattan, and they've been seriously involved for almost a year now, and they're saving up for their wedding.

It could happen to you, too. Never, *never* give up hope!

INDEX